Amo, Amas, Amat and More

Amo, Amas, Amat and More

How to Use Latin to Your Own Advantage and to the Astonishment of Others

EUGENE EHRLICH

Introduction by
WILLIAM F. BUCKLEY, JR.

A Hudson Group Book

Fitzhenry & Whiteside
Toronto, Ottawa, Halifax
Winnipeg, Edmonton
Vancouver

A hardcover edition of this book is published by Harper & Row, Publishers, Inc.

AMO, AMAS, AMAT AND MORE

© 1985 by Eugene Ehrlich. Introduction © 1985 by William F. Buckley, Jr.

Fitzhenry & Whiteside Limited
195 Allstate Parkway
Markham, Ontario L3R 4T8

Canadian Cataloguing in Publication Data

Ehrlich, Eugene.
  Amo, amas, amat and more

Includes index.
ISBN 0-88902-947-4

1. Latin language—Terms and phrases.
I. Title.

PA2389.E38   1987   473.1   C87-095064-6

To Norma

Contents

Acknowledgments

I wish particularly to thank Christopher Dadian, of the Department of Classics, The Johns Hopkins University, who gave thoughtful attention to the pronunciation scheme employed in this book as well as to the translations provided. If any errors are still to be found in the work, they are my own responsibility. All that can be said at this time is *errare humanum est*, and while I would appreciate hearing from readers who find these errors, I would also hope to be forgiven.

My associates at The Hudson Group gave me support all through the joy of compiling this book. My longtime collaborator Gorton Carruth put up with my divided attention to other responsibilities. Hayden Carruth taught me the rudiments of the IBM Personal Computer so that an ancient language could be treated, perhaps for the first time ever, within the confines of a cathode ray tube. Only once did his ministrations fail to rescue me from the effects of my computer illiteracy: At one time I lost an entire section of the book somewhere within the computer memory, and for all I know, it is lurking there to this day. Raymond Hand, Jr., helped free me for work on this book and assisted with the free renderings of certain Latin proverbs.

Carol Cohen, Harper & Row's Editorial Director of Trade Reference Books, showed enthusiasm for this book right from the start and supported me with encouragement and guidance all the way to completion. Her ideas for developing the project helped immeasurably.

The above-mentioned personal computer obviates acknowledgment of a typist's help, but a final word must be added for the help in indexing supplied by Felice Levy, who has participated with me on many editorial projects.

Preface

The idea for this book came quickly, as do most of my ideas for books. The execution was not as fast. Years of collecting expressions suitable for inclusion, followed by months of translation and writing, have finally yielded a volume I hope will prove entertaining as well as instructive for readers.

A word must be said about the choice of expressions. Utility was the principal criterion. There is no doubt that readers are plagued by writers and speakers who blithely drop Latin phrases into their English sentences with no hint of translation. Without questioning the motives of the Latin-droppers, one can safely say that most modern audiences require some assistance. Word-for-word translations provided in some English dictionaries do not always suffice, so the attempt is made in many entries of this book to supply more enlightening free translations as well as literal translations. Besides helping readers and listeners to cope with Latin used by others, it is hoped that *Amo*, *Amas*, *Amat* . . . will spare its readers the ignominy of an infelicitous choice when they venture into Latin. The most common misuse I encounter is the confusion of *e.g.* with *i.e.*, but there are many others. Once *e.g.* and *i.e.* were accepted for inclusion in this book, it became necessary to treat in the list of entries all but the most arcane scholarly abbreviations and expressions.

Medical and pharmacological Latin were never serious candidates for inclusion: Prescriptions are filled a million or more times a day without the Latin once required to say "take twice a day" and the like. But Latin still is seen in everyday writing about matters of law, and the law is a serious matter. The problem was to limit the number of entries of this type to those most frequently encountered—consider *in re* and *corpus delicti* and a multitude of others. Fortunately, engineers, computer scientists, electronics experts, and other modern wizards hit their stride long after Latin had disappeared from most school curricula, so they make no contribution to this volume despite the fact that modern Latin words are continually being devised to enable the Vatican to deal knowledgeably with modern science and technology, just as modern Hebrew must face this requirement. Of course, it is not only ancient languages that must cope with this problem. Modern English, in fact, brings new words into use every day, sometimes inventing them—often from Latin and Greek sources—and sometimes adding meanings to existing English words. Indeed, where appropriate, English accomplishes its purpose by borrowing existing words from modern foreign languages.

While the majority of the entries in this book date back to classical times, there is some treatment of phrases that came into use during the Middle Ages. As will be seen, some of the Latin included in the entry list is used—should one say was used?—in church services.

Once the list of candidate entries had grown to reflect these many sources and areas of learning, a much more difficult task had to be accomplished, that of selecting, among a vast number of available maxims and proverbs, those that would be most interesting and useful for the modern reader. One principle of selection was the inherent wisdom reflected in the thought. Another was the insight into a civilization implicit in a thought. As I worked through the entry list again and again, I was struck by the universality of people's problems throughout the ages, and the satisfying solutions afforded, despite the often contradictory nature of these solutions. It is hoped that the reader will share the pleasure of this recognition.

So *Amo*, *Amas*, *Amat* . . . took form, sometimes growing recklessly and demanding to be pruned, at other times crying out for fuller treatment of a particular topic.

Now a word must be said about the pronunciations supplied in this book. No one knows just how Latin was pronounced by the Romans. I was taught by my instructors at Townsend Harris High School and the City College of New York to pronounce the name *Caesar* as though the first letter were a *k*. Others may pronounce that first letter as though it were *ch*, as in *chew*. This dispute, along with several other questions of pronunciation, is moot. Let me assure the reader, however, that using the pronunciations offered in this book will make it possible to pronounce Latin without incurring the scorn of most people who have studied the language in American public schools.

EUGENE EHRLICH

Pronunciation Notes

This volume uses a respelling scheme to represent the sounds of Latin. Stresses are indicated by typographic means.

Stress. Stressed syllables are shown in capital letters, and unstressed syllables as well as words of a single syllable are shown in lower case. Thus, *Deo* (to God) is pronounced DAY-oh, *familia* (family) is pronounced fah-MIH-lee-ah, and *ars* (art) is pronounced ahrs.

Vowels. Like English vowels, certain Latin vowels have various qualities. The samples given here help in sounding out the Latin words in the pages that follow.

Pronunciation		English	Latin Word	Latin Pronunciation
AH *or* ah	*as in*	far	*fabula*	FAH-buu-lah
AY *or* ay	*as in*	fake	*fecere*	FAY-keh-reh
AW *or* aw	*as in*	tall	*hominem*	HAW-mih-nem
E *or* e	*as in*	pet	*et*	et
EH *or* eh	*as in*	pet	*petere*	PEH-teh-reh
EE *or* ee	*as in*	sweet	*vita*	WEE-tah
IH *or* ih	*as in*	dig	*signum*	SIH-gnuum
OH *or* oh	*as in*	both	*dolor*	DOH-lawr
OO *or* oo	*as in*	moon	*unum*	OO-nuum
UU *or* uu	*as in*	put	*unum*	OO-nuum

After the letter *q*, and sometimes after *g* and *s*, the Latin *u* has the sound made by the English *w*. This is no surprise for speakers of English. Consider the words *quick*, *guava*, and *suave*. Thus, *quandoque* (sometimes) is pronounced kwahn-DOH-kweh.

Diphthongs. Like English, in which, for example, the diphthong *oi* is given a single sound (as in *point*) and *ou* is given a single sound (as in *loud*), Latin has its share of diphthongs.

Diphthong	Pronunciation	English		Latin Word	Latin Pronunciation
ae	Ī	*as in*	my	*Caesar*	KĪ-sahr
ae	ī	*as in*	my	*lacrimae*	LAH-krih-mī
au	OW or ow	*as in*	now	*Augustus*	ow-GUU-stuus
ei	AY or ay	*as in*	faint	*deinde*	DAYN-deh
eu	HEHOO	*(no equivalent)*		*eheu*	eh-HEHOO*
oe	OY or oy	*as in*	boy	*proelium*	PROY-lee-uum
ui	OOEE or ooee	*as in*	phooey	*huius*	HOOEE-uus

*Pronounce as a single sound: HEHOO as a blend of HEH and OO, not pronouncing the second H.

Consonants. Latin consonants are pronounced in the same way as their English equivalents, with the following exceptions.

1. The Latin *c* is pronounced as though it were a *k*. Thus, *Cicero* is pronounced KIH-keh-roh.
2. The Latin *g* is always pronounced like the *g* in the English word *give*. Thus, *geometria* (geometry) is pronounced gay-oh-MEH-tree-ah, and *dignus* (worthy) is pronounced DIH-gnuus.
3. The Latin *s* is always pronounced like the *s* in the English word *set* or *pest* or *pets*. Thus, *semper paratus* (always ready) is pronounced SEM-pehr pah-RAH-tuus.
4. A *j* is often seen before a vowel in some Latin texts where one would expect to see an *i*. Whichever letter is used, the sound is taken as an initial *y*, as in the English word *young*. This means that the *i* (as well as the *j*) functions as a consonant. Thus, the Latin word for *law*, whether spelled *ius* or *jus*, is pronounced yoos, but when *i* appears before

a consonant, *i* is pronounced as a vowel. As speakers of a modern language, we are not dismayed by such apparent anomalies. Consider the pronunciation of the English word *union* (initial syllable YOON) and that of the English word *unable* (initial syllable un).

5. The Latin *v* is always pronounced as though it were a *w*. Thus, *veni*, *vidi*, *vici* is pronounced WAY-nee, WEE-dee, WEE-kee; and *ave atque vale* is pronounced AH-weh AHT-kweh WAH-lay.

English pronunciation. In many entries in this volume, Latin phrases are given English pronunciations as well as Latin pronunciations. This is done for Latin phrases that have been taken into the English language and given distinctive pronunciations. Such words are respelled for the reader in readily recognizable letter combinations to show the English pronunciations.

In the case of one sound, respelling is not sufficient, so an additional symbol is needed to approximate English pronunciation. The symbol ə is used to indicate the indistinct vowel sound represented by the first syllable of the English word *ago* (ə-GOH) and the second syllable of the English word *ever* (EV-ər). Thus, while the Latin pronunciation of *sui generis* is given as SOO-ee GEH-neh-rihs, the English pronunciation appears as SOO-ee JEN-ə-rəs.

amo I love
amas you love
amat he, she, or it loves

. . .

—the beginning of the paradigm of
a first conjugation Latin verb
in the present indicative

Amo, Amas, Amat and More

Introduction

by William F. Buckley, Jr.

It is not plain to me why I was asked to write the introduction to this book. (There are true Latinists around. Not in abundance, but for instance one thinks of Garry Wills, or Ernest Van den Haag, just to mention two noisy, and brilliant, writers.) Nor is it obvious why I accepted the invitation (the little stipend is being forwarded to charity).

I suppose I am asked because the few Latin phrases I am comfortable with I tend to use without apology. For instance, for some reason I find it handier even in idiomatic exchanges to say "per impossibile" over against, say, "assuming that the impossible were actually to take place." Nor is the usefulness of *per impossibile* sui generis—if you see the kind of situation one is capable of falling into. And, of course, there are those Latin phrases that have a utilitarian function, as for instance the lawyers' "nolle prosequi," which has become so thoroughly transliterated as to have acquired English conjugational life: thus, "The case against Dr. Arbuthnot was nol-prossed"—the lawyer's vernacular for "The prosecutor decided not to prosecute the case against Dr. Arbuthnot."

So, there are those Latin phrases—and, really, there are not so many of them—that cling to life because they seem to perform useful duties without any challenger rising up to take their place in English. Sometimes these special exemptions from vernacularization in the mother tongue derive from the distinctive inflection that flows in from the Latin. There is no English substitute, really, for "He faced the problem *ad hoc*," which is much easier than the cumbersome alternative in English ("He faced the problem with exclusive concern given to the circumstances that particularly surrounded it"). Other Latin phrases, the kind against which Fowler inveighed, have the sense of being dragged in, and the reader, when he comes across them, will judge on the basis of circumstances whether he is on to a felicitous intonation communicated by the Latin and not by the English. The scholarly Mr. Ehrlich, for instance, includes in this collection "Ab asino lanam," giving as the English meaning (which is different from the English translation), "blood from a stone." And further elucidating, "Anyone who tries to achieve the impossible is doomed to failure. Thus, an attempt to get *ab asino lanam*, literally, 'wool from an ass,' will inevitably fail." The above is for the scholar, not the practitioner of idiom.

But then why not? Mr. Ehrlich, in his introduction, touches on the difficulty of assembling a list meagerly. Inevitably some readers would be dissatisfied. For all one knows, there is someone about who day in and day out denounces efforts to reason with the Soviets as ventures *ab asino lanam*, and it would ruin their life if a collection of Latin sayings were published that left out that expression. Better, then, to include "ab asino lanam," and the kitchen sink; which Mr. Ehrlich does, and I am very glad that he decided to do so.

Probably the principal Latin-killer this side of the Huns was Vatican II. The other day, sitting alongside a Jesuit college president, I mentioned, by way of indicating the distinctive training of English Jesuits, that my schoolmasters at Beaumont College, when engaged in faculty discussions, addressed each other in Latin. He replied matter-of-factly that so it had been with him and his classmates. "But now, after fifteen years, I would have a problem with relatively simple Latin."

No doubt about it, the generations of Catholic priests trained in Latin, and the seepage of Latin to parishioners, students, altar boys, will diminish, drying up the spring which for so many centuries watered the general knowledge of Latin, and held out almost exclusively, after the virtual desertion of Latin from curricula in which it held, in e.g. English public schools, an absolutely patriarchal position. But it is not likely that the remaining bits and pieces will all be extirpated by the vernacular juggernaut. And even if that were so, it would happen generations down the line. Meanwhile I know of no book to contend in usefulness with that of Mr. Ehrlich, who has given us this resourceful, voluminous, and appetizing smorgasbord.

Dramatis Personae

Caesar. *Gaius Iulius Caesar*. 100–44 B.C. Born at Rome. Soldier, statesman. *Bellum Gallicum (The Gallic War)*, *Bellum civile (The Civil War)*.

Cato. *Marcus Porcius Cato*. 234–149 B.C. Born in Tusculum, in central Italy. Roman statesman. *De agricultura (On Agriculture)*.

Catullus. *Gaius Valerius Catullus*. 84?–54? B.C. Born at Verona, in Cisalpine Gaul. Best known for his tempestuous love affair with a Roman gentlewoman (probably the notorious Clodia), whom he immortalized in his poems under the pseudonym Lesbia. *Carmina (Poems)*.

Cicero. *Marcus Tullius Cicero*. 106–43 B.C. Born at Arpinum in central Italy. Jurist, statesman, writer, philosopher. *Orationes (Orations)*, *Rhetorica (Writings on Rhetoric)*, *Philosophica (Political and Philosophical Writings)*, *Epistulae (Letters)*.

Claudian. *Claudius Claudianus*. A.D. 4th cent.–c. 404. From Alexandria. A speaker of Greek. Came to Italy and mastered Latin, which was the language of his writings. Court poet under the emperor Honorius; his poetry eulogized his patrons. *De consulatu Honorii (On the Consulship of Honorius)*, *De consulatu Stilichonis (On the Consulship of Stilicho)*.

Epicurus.   341–270 B.C. Born at Samos, a Greek island in the Aegean. Moral and natural philosopher. Our knowledge of his system derives to a great extent from the Roman poet Lucretius. *Epistulae* (*Letters*), Κύριαι Δοξαι (*Kyriai Doxai, Principal Doctrines*).

Horace.   *Quintus Horatius Flaccus*. 65–8 B.C. Born at Venusia, in southern Italy. Member of the literary circle brought together by Maecenas under the patronage of the emperor Augustus. *Carmina* (*Odes*), *Epodi* (*Epodes*), *Satirae* (*Satires*), *Epistulae* (*Verse Letters*), *Ars Poetica* (*The Poetic Art*).

Juvenal.   *Decimus Iunius Iuvenalis*. A.D. 1st–2nd cent. Born at Aquinum, Italy. Author of verse satires attacking corruption of Roman society. *Satirae* (*Satires*).

Livy.   *Titus Livius*. 59 B.C.–A.D. 17 or 64 B.C.–A.D. 12. Born at Padua, in northeastern Italy. Historian. *Ab urbe condita* ([History of Rome] *from the Founding of the City*).

Lucan.   *Marcus Annaeus Lucanus*. A.D. 39–65. Born at Cordoba, in Spain. Courtier in the reign of Nero. Fell from grace and eventually was forced to commit suicide after becoming implicated in the Pisonian conspiracy. *Pharsalia*.

Lucretius.   *Titus Lucretius Carus*. Prob. 94–55 B.C. Probably member of an aristocratic Roman family, the Lucretii. Poet and philosopher. *De rerum natura* (*On the Nature of the Universe*).

Manilius.   *Marcus Manilius*. 1st cent. B.C.–A.D. 1st cent. Facts of his life unknown. *Astronomica* (a didactic poem on astrology).

Marcus Aurelius.   *Marcus Aurelius Antoninus*. A.D. 161–180. Roman emperor. *Meditationes* (*Meditations*).

Martial.   *Marcus Valerius Martialus*. c. A.D. 40–c. 104. Born at Bilbilis, in Spain. Depicted Roman society in epigrammatic verse. *Epigrammata* (*Epigrams*).

Ovid.   *Publius Ovidius Naso*. 43 B.C.–A.D. 17. Born at Sulmo, in central Italy. Intended by his father for a legal career, but gave it up to devote himself to poetry. Member of the literary circle of Messalla. Exiled to an island in the Black Sea by Augustus, who was offended by Ovid's *Ars Amatoria*, though there may have been other offenses as well. *Amores* (*Love Poems*), *Ars Amatoria* (*The Amatory Art*), *Metamorphoses*.

Persius. *Aulus Persius Flaccus*. A.D. 34–62. Born at Volaterrae, in northern Italy. Stoic satirist. *Satirae* (*Satires*).

Petronius. *Petronius Arbiter*. A.D. 1st cent. Probably the courtier referred to by Tacitus as Nero's *arbiter elegantiae*. *Satyricon*.

Phaedrus. c. 15 B.C.–c. A.D. 50. A Thracian, born a slave. Eventually became freedman in the household of the emperor Augustus. *Fabulae* (*Fables*).

Plautus. *Titus Maccius Plautus*. 3rd–2nd cent. B.C. Born at Sarsina, in central Italy. Author of comic dramas based on Greek originals.

Pliny the Elder. *Gaius Plinius*. A.D. 23/4–79. Born at Comum, now Como, in north central Italy. Military commander in Germany, provincial administrator, counselor to emperors Vespasian and Titus. *Naturalis historia* (*Natural History*).

Pliny the Younger. *Gaius Plinius Caecilius Secundus*. c. A.D. 66–c. 112. Nephew and adopted son of Pliny the Elder. Senatorial career; lawyer, civil administrator. *Epistulae* (*Letters*).

Plutarch. *L*. (?) *Mestrius Plutarchus*. Before A.D. 50–after 120. Born and lived most of his life in Chaeronea, in northeastern Greece. Prolific (over 200 titles attributed to him) and influential. *Moralia*, *Vitae* (*Lives*).

Publilius Syrus. 1st cent. B.C. Came to Rome as a slave, perhaps from Antioch. Author of mimes. *Sententiae* (*Maxims*).

Quintilian. *Marcus Fabius Quintilianus*. c. A.D. 30–before 100. Born at Calagurris, in Spain. Teacher of rhetoric; among his pupils was Pliny the Younger. *Institutio oratoria* (*The Teaching of Oratory*).

Seneca the Elder. *Lucius Annaeus Seneca*. c. 55 B.C.–

between A.D. 37 and 41. Born at Cordoba, in Spain. Student of and writer on rhetoric. *Controversiae, Suasoriae*.

Seneca the Younger. *Lucius Annaeus Seneca*. Between 4 and 1 B.C.–A.D. 65. Born at Cordoba, in Spain. Son of Seneca the Elder, counsellor to Nero, philosopher, poet. *Dialogi (Dialogues), Naturales quaestiones (Natural Questions*, inquiries in physical science), *Apocolocyntosis (The Pumpkinification* [of the emperor Claudius]), *Tragedies, Epigrams*.

Suetonius. *Gaius Suetonius Tranquillus*. c. A.D. 69–? Practiced law briefly, held various posts in the imperial service, secretary to the emperor Hadrian. *De vita Caesarum (Lives of the Caesars* [from Julius to Domitian]).

Tacitus. *Cornelius Tacitus*. c. 56 A.D.–after 115. Probably from northern Italy or Gaul. Historian, held several official posts. *Annales (Annals), Historiae (Histories), Agricola* ([biography of his father-in-law, Cnaius Iulius] *Agricola), Germania*.

Terence. *Publius Terentius Afer*. c. 190–159 B.C. Born in North Africa, brought to Rome as a slave. Author of comic dramas adapted from Greek models by Apollodorus of Carystus and Menander. *Andria (The Girl from Andros), Hecyra (The Mother-in-Law), Heauton timorumenos (The Self-Punisher), Eunuchus (The Eunuch), Phormio, Adelphi (The Brothers)*.

Tertullian. *Quintus Septimius Florens Tertullianus*. c. A.D. 160–c. 240. Born at Carthage, in North Africa. Trained as a lawyer. Converted to Christianity at age 35, wrote in defense of his new faith, and on moral, ethical, religious problems.

Varro. *Marcus Terentius Varro*. 116–27 B.C. Born at Reate, in central Italy. Wrote on language, education, history, biography, philosophy, music, medicine, architecture, literary history and philology. *De lingua latina (On the Latin Language)*.

Vegetius. *Flavius Vegetius Renatus*. A.D. 4th–5th cent. Bureaucrat in the imperial service. *Epitome rei militaris (Manual of Military Affairs)*.

Virgil. *Publius Vergilius Maro*. 70–19 B.C. Born near Man-
tua, in northeastern Italy. Early in his career deeply in-
fluenced by Catullus, member of the literary circle of
Asinius Pollio. Later, through Maecenas, came under the
patronage of the emperor Augustus. *Aeneid*, *Georgics*,
Eclogues.

ab absurdo
ahb ahb-SUUR-doh
from the absurd

One who argues *ab absurdo* seeks to establish the validity of his position by pointing out the absurdity of his opponent's position. While an argument *ab absurdo* may have the effect of demolishing one's opponent's position in debate, it usually does not of itself prove the validity of one's own position.

ab aeterno
ahb ī-TEHR-noh
since the beginning of time

Anything that has existed *ab aeterno*, literally "from eternity," has no assignable date of origin. This phrase can be used to describe almost any human folly: "Wars have been fought *ab aeterno*."

ab asino lanam
ahb AH-sih-noh LAH-nahm
blood from a stone

Anyone who tries to achieve the impossible is doomed to failure. Thus, an attempt to get *ab asino lanam*, literally "wool from an ass," will inevitably fail.

11

ab extra
ahb EHK-strah
from the outside

This phrase, the opposite of AB INTRA, finds use in such thoughts as "We are mistaken in believing that peace will come to the Middle East through the efforts *ab extra* of world powers."

ab imo pectore
ahb EE-moh PEH-ktaw-reh
from the heart

When we speak from the heart, we speak sincerely, but the Romans spoke *ab imo pectore*, literally "from the bottom of the breast (or chest)."

ab incunabulis
ahb ihn-koo-NAH-buu-lees
from infancy

The Latin word **incunabula** may be translated as "cradle, swaddling clothes, infancy, or origin." The English "incunabula" refers to the earliest stage or beginning of anything, but most often to copies of books that date back to the period before A.D. 1500, when the use of movable type in printing was in its formative stage. The Latin *ab incunabulis* has nothing to do with books.

ab initio
ahb ih-NIH-tee-oh
from the beginning

The Latin equivalent of "from the start" or "from inception." "Lack of adequate capital doomed the company to failure *ab initio*." (See AB ORIGINE and AB OVO.)

ab intra

ahb IHN-trah

from within

The insider's role is played out *ab intra*. "The only hope for reform of an institution is through effort expended *ab intra*."

ab irato

ahb ih-RAH-toh

unfair, unprovoked

This phrase may be taken literally as "from an angry man." Thus, any action taken *ab irato* is to be understood as arising from anger rather than reason, and responses to such actions will be weighed carefully by reasonable people. "Orders to fire subordinates were given *ab irato*, and therefore were not carried out until the President had a chance to reconsider."

ab origine

ahb aw-RIH-gih-neh

from the first

Ab origine may be translated as "from the very beginning, source, or origin." The English word "aborigine"—the preferred form is "aboriginal"—comes directly from this phrase and means "original or earliest known inhabitant of a place." "Scholars who are interested in gaining full understanding of an institution, for example, find it valuable to pursue *ab origine* studies in the hope that knowledge of the beginnings of an institution under study will shed light on its present status." (See AB INITIO and AB OVO.)

ab ovo

ahb OH-woh

from the very beginning

The literal meaning of *ab ovo* is "from the egg," so a thorough search is a search *ab ovo*, a thorough analysis is an analysis *ab ovo*, and a complete presentation is one made *ab ovo*. It is interesting to note, however, that *ab ovo* may imply a tedious thoroughness: "Once again we were subjected to a sententious *ab ovo* account that lasted more than an hour and lulled most of us to sleep." (See AB INITIO and AB ORIGINE.)

ab ovo usque ad mala
ahb OH-woh UUS-kweh ahd MAH-lah
from start to finish

A colorful Roman phrase reminiscent of our own "from soup to nuts," since it is literally translated as "from the egg to the apples," but with a meaning that is quite different. "From soup to nuts" refers to completeness, for example, of a multicourse dinner or a Sears Roebuck catalogue. *Ab ovo usque ad mala*, by contrast, means "from start to finish." The expression derives from the fact that Roman dinners often began with eggs and ended with fruit. "Your plan was inadequate *ab ovo usque ad mala* and had no chance for success."

absit invidia
AHB-siht ihn-WIH-dee-ah
no offense intended

When we say *absit invidia*, literally "let ill will be absent," our words reflect the power that Romans attributed to animosity, whether or not openly expressed. They believed, as do many people today, that ill feelings toward someone could cause that person great harm, so they absolved themselves of the intention to harm someone by saying *absit invidia*—the English expressions "no offense" and "no offense intended," by comparison, are mere social gestures intended to prevent ill feelings. *Absit invidia* may also be extended: **absit invidia verbo** (WEHR-boh) means "may it be said without giving offense." (See ABSIT OMEN.)

absit omen
AHB-siht OH-men
may this not be an omen

The rough equivalent of "Protect me, O Lord," *absit omen*, literally "may the omen be absent," was used to invoke divine protection against evil when something foreboding occurred. The Romans, strong believers in divination, employed soothsayers to interpret omens as a means of foretelling the future. Soothsayers were so popular that the Romans had many words for these practitioners, among them **auspex** (OW-speks) and **haruspex** (HAH-ruu-speks). An **auspex** relied on observation of the behavior of birds to foretell the future, and we are indebted to this highly specialized word for our own words "auspices" and "auspicious." A *haruspex* found special value in examining the entrails of sacrificial animals to foretell the future, but also made interpretations based on less gory activities, such as observation of lightning and other natural phenomena. While we do not pay as much attention to omens today, there are those who may say *absit omen* or its equivalent—"knock on wood"?— when a black cat crosses in front of them.

absolvo
ahb-SAWL-woh
I acquit

A judge acquitting a person after a trial may say, "*Absolvo!*" The term may also be used ironically by persons other than judges. For example, a domestic contretemps may end with one of the parties to the dispute using *absolvo* to close the discussion. On the other hand, this use of *absolvo* may protract the conflict.

ab uno disce omnes
ahb OO-noh DIS-keh AWM-nays
from one example learn about all

This maxim, literally "from one learn all," found in Virgil's *Aeneid*, applies to situations in which the import of a single observation is universally applicable. It is careless application of *ab uno disce omnes* that may trap us in faulty generalizations.

ab urbe condita
ahb UUR-beh KAWN-dih-tah
since the founding of the city

Abbreviated **A.U.C.** The city referred to is ancient Rome, the Big Apple of its day. Romans dated years from the founding of their city, in 753 B.C. Tradition has it that in that year Romulus and his twin brother, Remus, built Rome. In infancy the twins were thrown into the Tiber, the river still running through modern Rome, but were saved by a shepherd and suckled by a wolf. Romulus became the first king of Rome upon its founding. Remus was put to death because he mocked his brother's city. *Ab urbe condita* is also given as **anno urbis conditae** (AHN-noh UUR-bis KAWN-dih-tī), "in the year of the founding of the city," also abbreviated **A.U.C.**

abusus non tollit usum
ahb-OO-suus nohn TAWL-lit OO-suum
misuse does not nullify proper use

Broadly applied, this maxim teaches that the value of a procedure, an object, etc., is not destroyed by improper use. The helicopter, for example, was thought of by its principal inventor as a lifesaving machine. If *abusus non tollit usum* is correct, the machine's use in war does not mean the helicopter itself is evil. The value of television as an instructional medium, to take another example, is not destroyed by those who watch the tube all day long. In yet another sense, the maxim may be applied by prescriptive linguists to what they construe as corruptions in usage. *Abusus non tollit usum* for them means that improper use of a word does not destroy its proper use, and those who deal imprecisely with the language are not given carte blanche to work their destructive ways. Recognizing the Latin maxim, Eric Partridge entitled one of his works on language *Usage and*

Abusage. There is another form of *abusus non tollit usum*, which is recognized by jurists as conveying that same thought: **ab abusu ad usum non valet consequentia** (ahb ahb-OO-soo ahd OO-suum nohn WAH-let KAWN-seh-KWEN-tee-ah), "the consequences of abuse do not apply to general use," suggesting that a right should not be withheld because some people abuse it.

abyssus abyssum invocat
ah-BIHS-suus ah-BIHS-suum IHN-waw-kaht
one misstep leads to another

A warning, literally "hell calls hell," in the Psalms of David and a typically Roman maxim as well. In *The Screwtape Letters*, C. S. Lewis said: "The safest road to Hell is the gradual one— the gentle slope, soft underfoot, without sudden turnings, without milestones, without signposts." We can easily see that the first cigarette, the first drink of whiskey, the first step down any inviting path, is difficult to prevent, yet we must always be on guard: *Abyssus abyssum invocat*.

a capite ad calcem
ah KAH-pih-teh ahd KAHL-kehm
thoroughly

Literally "from head to heel," *a capite ad calcem* may be thought of as the Latin equivalent of "from top to bottom" or "from stem to stern." "The candidate, claiming that the entire municipal government was rotten, promised a reorganization *a capite ad calcem*."

accessit
ahk-KEH-siht
honorable mention

This word literally means "he (or she) came near," but in academic settings, particularly in European universities, an *accessit* (pronounced ak-SES-it in English) is the recognition awarded the runner-up in a competition for a medal or other honor. Academic terminology still relies to a great extent on Latin. This is not surprising, since the earliest universities were concerned primarily with, and conducted their official business in, classical languages. *Accessit* has a certain cachet: "I had hoped to win first prize, but I knew I would be content with an *accessit*" is far more comforting than "close but no cigar" or even "honorable mention."

Acheruntis pabulum
AH-keh-RUUN-tihs PAH-boo-luum
food for the gallows

Acheruntis pabulum should not be applied willy-nilly to all the poor wretches who sit on death row, but only to those who may be thought of as deserving to die. Acheron—the Romans called it **Acheruns** (AH-keh-ruuns)—was one of seven rivers said to flow around Hell. Thus, any person adjudged sufficiently evil may be said to be *Acheruntis pabulum*, literally "food of Acheron."

a cruce salus
ah KROO-keh SAH-luus
salvation (comes) from the cross

The cross is, of course, the symbol of the death of Christ, and Christ's death meant redemption for his followers. Thus, *a cruce salus* is the teaching that salvation comes from belief in Christianity.

acta est fabula
AHK-tah ehst FAH-buu-lah
it's all over

In the classical theater, with no curtain to draw across the stage, the words *acta est fabula*, literally "the drama has been acted out," signified the end of a performance. In another context, Emperor Augustus is said to have uttered *"Acta est fabula"* just before he died, establishing a pattern followed by Rabelais, whose last words are said to have been *"La farce est jouée,"* "the farce is ended." *Acta est fabula* may be spoken appropriately whenever a life or an unfolding event comes to an unhappy end, or one could say, "It's curtains."

acta sanctorum
AHK-tah sahn-KTOH-ruum
deeds of the saints

Accounts of the lives of the Christian martyrs and saints are used in teaching the faith. The most famous collection is the monumental *Acta Sanctorum*, initiated by the Bollandists, a group named for Jean Bolland, the seventeenth-century Flemish Jesuit, and in English usually called *Lives of the Saints*. This great work, still the responsibility of the Bollandists, is arranged according to the dates of the ecclesiastical calendar. It is approaching seventy volumes in length and still growing.

ad absurdum
ahd ahb-SUUR-duum
to absurdity

See REDUCTIO AD ABSURDUM.

ad arbitrium
ahd ahr-BIH-tree-uum
at pleasure

Anything done of one's own will is performed *ad arbitrium*. "In this life, how many actions are really taken *ad arbitrium*?" Another expression for the same thought is **arbitrio suo** (ahr-BIH-tree-oh SOO-oh), "on his (or her) own authority."

ad astra per aspera
ahd AH-strah per AH-speh-rah
to the stars through difficulties

The motto of Kansas, teaching us that we achieve great things only by encountering and overcoming adversity.

ad augusta per angusta
ahd ow-GUU-stah per ahn-GUU-stah
to honors through difficulties

Augusta refers to holy places, *angusta* to narrow spaces. This maxim tells us, therefore, that we cannot achieve great results without suffering, the suffering being represented here by squeezing through narrow spaces. A fit motto for dieters.

ad calendas graecas
ahd kah-LEN-dahs GRĪ-kahs
never

The literal translation of this Roman version of "when hell freezes over" is "at the Greek calends." The rub is that the calends, the first day of the month, was a feature of the Roman calendar, and the Greeks had no calends. It was on the calends that interest on borrowed money was to be paid, so for Roman debtors they were **tristes calendae** (TRIH-stays kah-LEN-dī), "the unhappy calends."

ad captandum vulgus
ahd kah-PTAHN-duum WUUL-guus
in order to win over the masses

Actions taken *ad captandum vulgus* are intended to please the common people. The implication is that such actions may not be in the best interest of society, but are intended only to achieve popularity. Politicians campaigning for office, for example, are wont to promise reforms *ad captandum vulgus* and never give a thought to accomplishing them.

ad clerum
ahd KLEH-ruum
to the clergy

A statement made by a church leader and intended only for the ears of the clergy is made *ad clerum*, as opposed to a statement **ad populum** (ahd PAW-puu-luum), "to the people."

a Deo et Rege
ah DEH-oh et REH-geh
from God and the King

Divine monarchs saw themselves as representatives of God on earth, so documents issued by them were often signed *a Deo et Rege*.

Adeste Fideles
ahd-EH-steh fih-DAY-lays
O come, all ye faithful

A Christmas hymn written in Latin, date and author uncertain.

ad eundem gradum
ahd eh-UUN-dem GRAH-duum
to the same degree

Often abbreviated **ad eundem**, this phrase can be used to apportion blame or praise justly among parties to a deed. "The judge held both litigants accountable *ad eundem*." *Ad eundem gradum* has a special use when applied to academic life. Construing *gradum* as an academic rank, under special circumstances a student holding a Master of Arts degree from one university may be awarded the same degree by another university without examination, such degree being termed "M.A. *ad eundem gradum*."

ad gloriam
ahd GLAW-ree-ahm
for glory

>See AD MAIOREM DEI GLORIAM.

ad gustum
ahd GUU-stuum
to one's taste

>A cookbook expression. "Add salt *ad gustum*."

ad hoc
ahd hawk
for this (purpose)

An *ad hoc* (pronounced ad HOK in English) committee is a temporary committee established to accomplish a particular task. Once an *ad hoc* committee has completed the job for which it was established, it is disbanded.

ad hominem
ahd HAW-mih-nem
against the man

>See AD REM and ARGUMENTUM AD HOMINEM.

adhuc sub iudice (or judice) lis est
AHD-huuk suub YOO-dih-keh lees est
the case is still before the court

Members of the legal profession are enjoined from public discussion of any matters that are under adjudication (*sub iudice*). People under indictment and public officials accused of misconduct in office may invoke *adhuc sub iudice lis est* as a means of avoiding public discussion of their problems.

ad infinitum
ahd ihn-fee-NEE-tuum
without limit

Abbreviated **ad inf.** and **ad infin.**, this phrase is the Latin equivalent of "forever, to infinity, endlessly," and in English is pronounced ad in-fə-NIT-əm. "Her husband went on *ad infinitum* on the question of equal division of household chores." (See AD NAUSEAM.)

ad interim
ahd IHN-teh-rim
in the meantime

This phrase, which has an English counterpart, "in the interim," is often abbreviated **ad int.**

ad kalendas graecas
ahd kah-LEN-dahs GRĪ-kahs
never

Alternative spelling for AD CALENDAS GRAECAS.

ad libitum
ahd LIH-bih-tuum
extemporaneously

Literally meaning "at pleasure" and abbreviated **ad lib.** in Latin, this expression is popularly used as a noun phrase or modifier in English in the form "ad lib" to express absence of planning. "His worst jokes were carefully planned ad libs."

ad limina apostolorum
ahd LEE-mih-nah ah-PAW-staw-LOH-ruum
to the highest authority

This expression, literally "to the thresholds of the Apostles," is applied to matters appropriate for papal consideration and disposition before the tombs of St. Peter and St. Paul. Often abbreviated **ad limina**, the expression finds its widest use in more mundane applications: "The chairman of the Romance Languages Department suggested that the committee was beyond its authority and that the matter be taken *ad limina*." In such a case, the question would surely be settled by higher campus authority.

ad litem
ahd LEE-tem
for the suit or action

Among lawyers, an *ad litem* decision is taken as valid only for the lis (lees), the controversy under adjudication. Thus, a guardian *ad litem* is appointed by a court to act for a minor only in regard to the problem of the minor before the court, not to serve as a substitute father.

ad litteram (also literam)
ahd LIHT-teh-rahm
to the last jot

Littera has as one of its meanings "letter of the alphabet." *Ad litteram*, literally "to the letter," means "precisely." "We must live up to our agreement *ad litteram*."

ad locum
ahd LOH-kuum
at or to the place

Abbreviated **ad loc.**

ad maiorem Dei gloriam
ahd mah-YAW-rem DEH-ee GLAW-ree-ahm
for the greater glory of God

Motto of the Society of Jesuits. The abbreviation **A.M.D.G.**
appears as an epigraph in books produced by the Jesuit order.
The full expression is sometimes cited as the rationale for actions taken by any Christians.

ad nauseam
ahd NOW-seh-ahm
to the point of (causing) nausea

Anything unpleasurable that appears to go on endlessly may
be said to be proceeding *ad nauseam*, literally "to seasickness."
The clear meaning of this phrase, in English pronounced ad
NAW-zee-əm, is that such activity has reached the point at
which it is almost more than a body can bear. Nothing that gives
pleasure can properly be described in this way. "The lecturer
went on *ad nauseam*, apparently determined to read to us
every last word in his notes."

ad patres
ahd PAH-trays
dead

The literal translation of *ad patres* is "to the fathers" or "to
the ancestors." To go *ad patres* is to die; to send someone *ad
patres* is to kill that person.

ad perpetuam rei memoriam
ahd per-PET-oo-ahm REH-ee me-MAW-ree-ahm
for the perpetual remembrance of the thing

Words traditionally used to open papal bulls.

ad populum
ahd PAW-puu-luum

to the people

Populus means "the entire people." An *ad populum* state-ment is one intended for the ears of the masses.

ad praesens ova cras pullis sunt meliora
ahd PRĪ-sens OH-wah krahs PUU-lees suunt
me-lee-OH-rah

a bird in the hand is worth two in the bush

This conservative maxim translates literally as "eggs today are better than chickens tomorrow." The advice is appropriate for all who take risks, e.g., stockbrokers' clients and crapshoot-ers: It is usually more prudent to hold on to what one has than to risk everything in speculation.

ad quem
ahd kwem

for (or to) which (or whom)

ad quod damnum
ahd kwawd DAHM-nuum

to what damage

A legal writ used for assessing damages relating to land taken for public use.

ad referendum
ahd reh-feh-REHN-duum

for further consideration

Ad referendum, which translates literally as "for referring," is a diplomats' term. Diplomats who accept a proposal for their governments *ad referendum* indicate by their actions that final acceptance is dependent on the approval of the diplomats' governments. *Referendum* has come over directly into English with the meaning of "a vote by all qualified voters on a matter of public concern."

ad rem
ahd rem
to the matter at hand

Ad rem, literally "to the thing," can be rendered in various ways. With the meaning "pertinent" or "relevant": "The attorney was admonished to make only *ad rem* comments or be silent." "In a straightforward manner": "Because of the limitation on debate, it is vital to speak *ad rem* if we are to conclude our considerations within the allotted time." Above all, it must be noted that *ad rem* is the phrase that contrasts with AD HOMINEM. Debaters who argue *ad rem* address the matter at hand to score points in the debate; debaters who argue *ad hominem* attack their opponents to score points.

adsum
AHD-suum
present!

A formal answer to a roll call, literally "I am here."

ad unguem
ahd UUN-gwem
perfectly

This phrase, literally "to a fingernail," is used to convey the thought of accomplishing something well or precisely. A sculptor in ancient times would test the smoothness of a finished surface by running a fingernail over it.

ad unum omnes
ahd OO-nuum AWM-nays
unanimously

Literally "all to one." "The delegates accepted the resolution *ad unum omnes*."

ad usum Delphini
ahd OO-suum del-FEE-nee
expurgated

A modern Latin phrase, translated literally as "for the Dauphin's use." An edition of classic works prepared for the Dauphin, heir to the throne of Louis XIV of France, carried the title *Ad usum Delphini*. The works, as might be expected, were expurgated to avoid offending the royal young man, so any expurgated work today may be termed *ad usum Delphini*.

ad utrumque paratus
ahd oo-TRUUM-kweh pah-RAH-tuus
prepared for the worst

A mature person is ready to cope with any eventuality, including the final one. The Romans described such a person as *ad utrumque paratus*, literally "ready for either (eventuality)." (See SEMPER PARATUS.)

ad valorem
ahd wah-LOH-rem
in proportion to value

Abbreviated **ad val.** An import duty fixed *ad valorem* is one established on the basis of the commercial value of the imported item. Like death and taxes, *ad valorem* has been with us so long that it now is part of the English language and pronounced ad və-LOH-rəm.

ad verbum
ahd WEHR-buum
verbatim

The phrase *ad verbum*, literally "to the word," is the Roman equivalent of the English "verbatim," which is a direct borrowing from medieval Latin. (See VERBATIM ET LITTERATIM.) The Romans had several other expressions for "word-for-word": **e verbo, de verbo,** and **pro verbo**. Perhaps this tells us something about the difficulty of making accurate copies before printing was invented.

adversa
ahd-WEHR-sah
things noted

A scholarly expression referring to observations one has made.

adversaria
ahd-wehr-SAH-ree-ah
a journal

Adversaria, literally "that which has been turned to," is a plural noun referring to notes or brief written comments. "Her *adversaria* were fascinating in their perceptions." It also refers to annotations or commentaries written on a facing page of a book. As a singular noun, an *adversaria* (English pronunciation ad-vər-SA-ree-ə) is a journal or commonplace book, a book used for recording one's observations as well as for collecting poems, brief essays, and any other material one finds worth keeping.

adversus solem ne loquitor
ahd-WEHR-suus SOH-lem nay LOH-kwih-tawr
don't waste your time arguing the obvious

This maxim advises one literally, "don't speak against the sun." When confronted by an all-important, irrefutable fact, there is no point in disputing further. The smoking gun, the telltale blond hair, the lipstick smudge, all signal the end of the discussion for any reasonable culprit: it is time for plea bargaining. (See IN FLAGRANTE DELICTO.)

ad vitam
ahd WEE-tahm
for life

A legal term sometimes found in wills, with the meaning of "for use during a person's life only." (See AD VITAM AUT CULPAM.)

ad vitam aeternam
ahd WEE-tahm ī-TEHR-nahm
forever

Ad vitam aeternam, literally "for eternal life," conveys the idea of "for all time." "Here is the money, but know that this is payment *ad vitam aeternam*."

ad vitam aut culpam
ahd WEE-tahm owt KUUL-pahm
for life or until a misdeed

The origin of *ad vitam aut culpam* rests in the feudal practice of conveying property or privilege that would not revert to the grantor until the death or misbehavior of the person receiving the benefit. One can see that such a grant might impose discipline on the recipient to behave properly or risk loss of the beneficence. Today, any gift given with strings attached, such as an automobile to one's son on condition that he drive it safely, might be said to be made *ad vitam aut culpam*.

advocatus diaboli
ahd-waw-KAH-tuus dee-AH-baw-lee
devil's advocate

The Roman Catholic Church uses the term **promotor fidei** (proh-MOH-tawr fih-DEH-ee), "promoter of the faith," or *advocatus diaboli*, to designate the church official appointed to argue against a proposed canonization or beatification. It is this official's responsibility to find the flaws in the evidence presented by those who support the proposed designation of the **beatus** (beh-AH-tuus), "the blessed person." In this trial of opposing forces, it is expected that the truth will emerge to support or deny canonization. A person playing devil's advocate today is too often a person fond of taking the unpopular side of any issue under discussion, and primarily for the sake of argument.

aeger
Ī-gehr
sick

In Latin, *aeger* as a noun means "an invalid"; as an adjective it means "sick." In British universities, *aeger* (Ī-jər) is the traditional term used on students' medical excuses for failing to appear for an examination, and a medical excuse itself may also be called an *aeger*. (See AEGROTAT.)

aegrescit medendo
ī-GREH-skit meh-DEN-doh
the remedy is worse than the disease

Aegrescit medendo, Virgil's phrase, literally means "the disease worsens with the treatment." Those who question the efficacy of some medical treatment may use this phrase appropriately as their battle cry.

aegri somnia
Ī-gree SAW-mnee-ah
a sick man's dreams

An *aegri somnia*, Horace's phrase, may be translated more freely as "a hallucination." "They tend to treat everything I say as an *aegri somnia*." The Romans appear to have been acutely aware of the role of the emotions in causing symptoms of illness. Virgil spoke of **aegra amans** (Ī-grah AH-mahns), "lover's disease," and Livy spoke of **aeger amore** (Ī-ger ah-MOH-reh) to describe the same condition, in apt recognition of the pathology of romance.

aegrotat
ī-GROH-taht
a note from the doctor

Aegrotat literally means "he (or she) is sick." Thus, in British universities, an *aegrotat* (Ī-groh-tat) is an official medical excuse. (See AEGER.) But the meaning extends beyond that. An *aegrotat* is also an unclassified degree that may be granted by a British university to a student who completes all academic requirements save final examinations, if the student is too sick to sit for the examinations.

aequam servare mentem
Ī-kwahm ser-WAH-reh MEN-tem
to keep one's cool

Aequam servare mentem, which translates literally as "to keep an unruffled mind," recognizes the value of maintaining a clear head while conducting the business of life, especially when making important decisions. Horace, in his *Odes*, suggested **aequam memento rebus in arduis** (meh-MEN-toh REH-buus ihn AHR-duu-ees) **servare mentem**, adjuring us to remember to maintain a clear head when attempting difficult tasks.

aequo animo
Ī-kwoh AH-nih-moh
calmly

Aequo animo, literally "with a calm mind," refers to evenness of mental attitude. Anyone who has composure or equanimity usually behaves *aequo animo*.

aere perennius
Ī-re peh-REN-nee-uus
everlasting

The Romans, who knew the characteristics of certain metals, used the word **aes** (īs) for copper and its alloys, brass and bronze. When, therefore, they wished to respond to someone who had done a favor, they might use *aere perennius*, literally "more durable than bronze," to suggest that the friendship shown would last forever. Certainly a more felicitous response than "I owe you one."

aetatis suae
ī-TAH-tihs SOO-ī
of his (or her) age

Aetatis alone means "of the age," while *aetatis suae* means "in a particular year of one's life." Tombstones once carried such inscriptions as "Died *aetatis suae* 37," or "**A.S.** 37." *Aetatis suae* is also given as **anno** (AH-noh) **aetatis suae**, meaning "in the year of his (or her) age."

aeternum vale
ī-TEHR-nuum WAH-lay
farewell forever

A suitable inscription for a tombstone, perhaps also a suitable phrase to use when ending a love affair.

a fortiori
ah fawr-tee-OH-ree
with stronger reason

A fortiori may be interpreted as meaning "even more certain" or "all the more." Thus we can say: "If you refuse to trust
him with the petty cash box, *a fortiori* you must not let him
handle our bank deposits."

a fronte praecipitium a tergo lupi
ah FRAWN-teh prī-kih-PIH-tee-uum ah TEHR-goh
LOO-pee
between a rock and a hard place

A fronte praecipitium a tergo lupi is literally "a precipice in
front, wolves behind." What to do when caught between
equally hazardous or difficult alternatives or, as we once said,
"between the devil and the deep blue sea"?

age quod agis
AH-geh kwawd AH-gihs
pay attention to what you are doing

Age quod agis, literally "do what you are doing," is excellent
advice for those who become careless in their work as well as
for those who fail to do what they are supposed to do.

Agnus Dei
AH-gnuus DEH-ee
Lamb of God

Agnus Dei, the epithet applied to Christ by John the Baptist,
is represented in the figure of a lamb supporting a cross or a
banner with a cross emblazoned on it. The lamb, often shown
with a halo about its head, represents Christ. A medallion
stamped with this figure and blessed by the Pope is also an
Agnus Dei. The words *Agnus Dei*, translated as "O Lamb of

God," are heard in the office for burial of the dead in the Catholic mass, and the music for this part of the service is called an *Agnus Dei*.

a latere
ah LAH-tehr-eh
from the side

Cardinals in the particular confidence of a pope—having the ear of the pope—are said to be *a latere* cardinals. A papal emissary enjoying such confidence is called **legatus** (leh-GAH-tuus) **a latere**. In a broader sense, any person who is a close adviser to an important official can be given the informal appellation *a latere*, implying power for the adviser and status for the official. In government, a plenipotentiary may be thought of as a *legatus a latere*. *A latere* is also used in law, with the meaning "collateral," in describing succession to property.

albae gallinae filius
AHL-bī gahl-LEE-nī FEE-lee-uus
a lucky devil

Albae gallinae filius, literally "a son of a white hen," found its meaning in a Roman folk tale. An eagle was said to have dropped a white hen into the lap of Livia, the wife of Emperor Augustus. This remarkable incident was interpreted by soothsayers as a favorable omen, since white hens were believed to bring good fortune. We refer to a particular type of lucky fellow as someone "born with a silver spoon in his mouth," and the phrase *albae gallinae filius* may be used in this sense as well.

albo lapillo notare diem
AHL-boh lah-PIHL-loh noh-TAH-reh DEE-em
to mark a day with a white stone

Colors have symbolic meanings in all cultures. For the Romans, white was the symbol of happiness, black of misfortune.

Thus, in a trial a vote for acquittal was cast with a white stone, for condemnation, a black one; and a happy day was marked with a white stone, an unhappy day with a black one. The latter procedure was this: At the end of each day, a Roman—according to Pliny the Younger, this superstitious practice dated back to the Thracians—would judge whether the day had been happy or unhappy. Once decided, the Roman would drop a pebble of the appropriate color into an urn, so at the end of a month he could empty the urn and be able to look back over the month past. (See NIGRO NOTANDA LAPILLO.) We still speak of red-letter days, so why not an *albo lapillo*, a white-stone day?

alea iacta est
AH-lay-ah YAH-ktah est
the die is cast

Julius Caesar, preparing in 49 B.C. to enter Rome from Gaul, where he was governor, came to the Rubicon, the river that marked the boundary between Cisalpine Gaul and Italy. Caesar knew that once he crossed the Rubicon he would be in great danger, since he would be seen as defying his government. Suetonius reported that Caesar, anxious over the possible effects of the move he was considering, on the night before making his decision saw an apparition that impelled him to take the warlike step. (Plutarch gave a different account. According to Plutarch, on the night before the crossing, Caesar was so troubled by the gravity of his contemplated action against the mother country that he dreamed he had sexual intercourse with his own mother.) Both sources do agree, however, that when Caesar finally made up his mind to move boldly, he said, "*Iacta alea est*," a common phrase of the time. Even today, "The die is cast" means that a bold and irretrievable decision has been made. Caesar's decision eventually resulted in triumph. Those who know only the English translation of *alea iacta* (or *iacta alea*) *est* may think erroneously that *alea* refers to another kind of "die," rather than the singular form of "dice." It is also worth pointing out that in English, "to cross the Rubicon" is to commit oneself to a hazardous enterprise by taking a decisive action that cannot be undone.

alere flammam
AH-leh-reh FLAH-mahm
to feed the flame

Ovid spoke of **alere flammas**, "to feed the flames," in a figurative sense, which is the intention today whenever we say *alere flammam* or *alere flammas*. "Further discussion on this matter will only serve *alere flammam*." One may also use these phrases when speaking of rekindling feelings of love, ambition, and the like. Old flames never die?

alias dictus
AH-lee-ahs DIH-ktuus
otherwise called

The full ancestor of the English word "alias," with the meaning "an assumed name." As a Latin word, *alias* can be translated as "at another time." While our own use of *alias* usually limits its application to circumstances less than honorable—in contrast with "pen name" and "stage name"—the Romans did not intend this. They used *alias dictus* in referring to someone's nickname, employed without any interest in deception. In modern law, the expression may be used in much the same way as "also known as" (abbreviated **a.k.a.**) is employed. "Schmidt *alias dictus* Smith owned the business for only two months."

alieni generis
ah-lee-AY-nee GEH-neh-rihs
of a different kind

alieni iuris (or juris)
ah-lee-AY-nee YUU-rihs
subject to another's authority

Alieni iuris, a term in law, literally means "of another's law." When, for example, a court places an infant (someone below the legal age of maturity) or a mentally incompetent person under control of a guardian, the infant or incompetent person is said to be *alieni iuris*. Those who are *alieni iuris* cannot exercise control of their ordinary legal rights, but must submit to the authority of appointed guardians.

aliquando bonus dormitat Homerus
ah-lih-KWAHN-doh BOH-nuus DAWR-mih-taht
hoh-MAY-ruus
you can't win 'em all

A modification, literally "sometimes even good Homer dozes," of Horace's line concerning Homer (see QUANDOQUE BONUS DORMITAT HOMERUS). The intention is that even the best of writers do not always knock us out, or more broadly, even the greatest in any field are not always up to form. This is said to excuse one's own less than perfect efforts or to criticize gently the work of another that is not up to usual quality.

alis volat propriis
AH-lees WAW-laht PROH-pree-ees
she (he) flies on her (his) own wings

Motto of Oregon. The intention is clear: Oregonians are proud of their ability to get along on their own. Anyone who has the same independent spirit can also adopt this motto. In line with today's enlightened parenthood, a parent watching proudly as a child manages independently can say *alis volat propriis*. The Latin gives no indication of gender, so the statement can be made of any newly independent offspring. The translation "she flies on her own wings" reflects the customs of a less enlightened day, when gender was applied to ships of state as well as to other ships. (For the crossword puzzle fan, it is worth mentioning that **ala** (AH-lah) means "wing.")

alma mater
AHL-mah MAH-tehr
nourishing mother

Alma mater is the epithet applied by Romans to Ceres, goddess of growing vegetation; to Cybele, a nature goddess; and to other bounteous goddesses. Roman poets referred to the country of their birth as *alma mater*. Today, the expression is used to refer to one's college or university, and more narrowly, to the official song, statue, or other symbol of the institution. Columbia University, just one of many, has a large statue of Alma Mater (in English AL-mə MAH-tər) standing in front of its administration building, and this statue is a favorite background for snapshots taken by proud parents of entering freshmen. The symbolism is clear: The university is the bounteous, fostering mother of all its graduates. (See ALUMNUS.)

alter ego
AHL-tehr EH-goh
bosom pal

Literally translated as "another I" or "another self," an *alter ego* is an inseparable friend. The intention is that an alter ego (English pronunciation, awl-tər EE-goh) may be considered as speaking or acting for the other person. Another way of conveying the same thought is given in the next phrase, ALTER IDEM, which is far less common.

alter idem
AHL-tehr EE-dem
another self

Cicero used the expression **tamquam** (TAHM-kwahm) **alter idem**, "as if a second self," to describe a completely trustworthy friend, an ALTER EGO. *Idem* means "the same," while *ego* means "I," but both phrases convey the same meaning. Anyone who is your *alter idem* or *alter ego* is your inseparable friend.

altissima quaeque flumina minimo sono labi
ahl-TIH-sih-ɪnah KWĪ-kweh FLOO-mih-nah
MIH-nih-moh SOH-noh LAH-bee
still waters run deep

Literally "the deepest rivers flow with the least sound," this Roman proverb suggests that we not sell short those who eschew self-promotion, at the same time cautioning us to watch out for people given to blowing their own horns.

alumnus
ah-LUU-mnuus
nursling, foster child

We all know the English word "alumnus" as a graduate or former student of an academic institution, and even of an institution not commonly thought of as academic, so it is interesting to understand the Latin *alumnus*, with the meanings given above. When we understand *alumnus* in its Roman intention, we can better understand the idea of ALMA MATER as "nourishing mother." It is also worthwhile to discuss other forms of the word *alumnus*. The plural of *alumnus* is **alumni** (ah-LUU-mnee; in English, ə-LUM-nī). The feminine of *alumnus* is **alumna** (ah-LUU-mnah; in English, ə-LUM-nə). The feminine plural is **alumnae** (ah-LUU-mnī; in English, ə-LUM-nee or ə-LUM-nī). Clear?

amantes sunt amentes
ah-MAHN-tays suunt ah-MEHN-tays
lovers are lunatics

The foolish things that lovers do are considered justification for this maxim. In *A Midsummer Night's Dream*, Shakespeare's Theseus puts it thus:

> The lunatic, the lover, and the poet
> Are of imagination all compact.

Those of us who still have our wits will take this into account when we are smitten. After all, Publilius Syrus advised us that **amare et sapere vix deo conceditur** (ah-MAH-reh et SAH-peh-reh weeks DAY-oh kawn-KAY-dih-tuur), "even a god finds it hard to love and be wise at the same time."

amantium irae amoris integratio est
ah-MAHN-tee-uum IH-rī ah-MOH-rihs
ihn-teh-GRAH-tee-oh est
lovers' quarrels are the renewal of love

How much truth there is in this old Roman proverb is anyone's guess, but Terence is the source for this insight, and others have picked it up. Robert Frost said in one poem that he would choose as an epitaph: "I had a lover's quarrel with the world." What better way to express one's love affair with life? (See QUI BENE AMAT BENE CASTIGAT for further wisdom.)

a maximis ad minima
ah MAH-ksih-mees ahd MIH-nih-mah
from the greatest to the least

This expression refers to objects or abstractions, not people. "She concerned herself with all of society's problems, *a maximis ad minima*."

a mensa et toro
ah MEN-sah et TAW-roh
a legal separation

A mensa et toro, with the literal meaning of "from table and bed," is found in the legal phrase "divorce *a mensa et toro*," referring to a decree forbidding husband and wife to share living quarters. *Mensa* is translated in this construction as "a table for dining," but it also means "altar" or "sacrificial table" in other uses, as well as "a table used by moneychangers" for doing their business. Those with a cynical attitude toward marriage and divorce thus might well read cruel humor into a divorce *a mensa et toro*. Even more ironic is the meaning of **torus** (TAW-ruus), from which we have the form *toro*. *Torus* has many meanings, one of which is "bed" and another, "marriage couch," but in other contexts it carries the meaning of "bier."

amicus curiae
ah-MEE-kuus KOO-ree-ī
an impartial spokesman in a court of law

An *amicus curiae*, literally "friend of the court," is a person not party to a litigation who volunteers or is invited by the court to give advice on a matter pending before it. Currently, several organizations, in particular the American Civil Liberties Union, appear regularly as **amici** (ah-MEE-kee) **curiae** (plural of *amicus curiae*) in cases that interest them.

amicus humani generis
ah-MEE-kuus hoo-MAH-nee GEH-neh-rihs
a philanthropist

Literally "a friend of the human race."

amicus usque ad aras
ah-MEE-kuus UU-skweh ahd AH-rahs
a friend to the end

Literally "a friend as far as to the altars," this expression can be taken as "a friend unto death," but it is also interpreted as "a friend up to the point where friendship conflicts with religious or ethical beliefs." Pericles of Athens is said to have responded in this latter sense when refusing to swear falsely for a friend.

amor
AH-mawr
love

The word used to express fondness or passion. (See the next four entries.)

amor nummi
AH-mawr NUUM-mee
cupidity

Literally "love of money." (See RADIX OMNIUM MALORUM EST CUPIDITAS.)

amor patriae
AH-mawr PAH-tree-ī
patriotism

Literally "love of country."

amor proximi
AH-mawr PRAW-ksih-mee
love of one's neighbor

Leviticus adjures "love thy neighbor as thyself." At the same time, we must be careful not to covet our neighbor's wife.

amor vincit omnia
AH-mawr WIHN-kiht AWM-nee-ah
love conquers all

This famous line of Virgil's (also given, to the despair of beginning Latin students, unaccustomed to the flexibility of Latin word order, as **amor omnia vincit** or as **omnia vincit amor**) is quoted by Chaucer in the "Prologue" to *The Canterbury Tales*.

Incidentally, Virgil goes on to say, **et nos cedamus amori** (et nohs keh-DAHM-uus ah-MAWR-ee), "and let us yield to it [love]."

anguis in herba
AHN-gwihs ihn HEHR-bah
a hidden danger

Literally "a snake in the grass." Virgil, in his *Eclogues*, used the expression **latet** (LAH-tet) **anguis in herba**, "a snake lies concealed in the grass," to call attention to a hidden danger. The danger may be of any type, even though the English "snake in the grass" is usually a person who has turned against his friend, particularly an adulterer who has taken up with the friend's wife.

animal bipes implume
AHN-ih-mahl BIH-pays ihm-PLOO-may
a human being

Literally "a two-legged animal without feathers," *animal bipes implume* is the Latin translation of Plato's definition of man, and thus a contemptuous designation for **Homo sapiens** (literally "wise man," itself a world-class self-serving expression). Two other uses of *animal* are worthy of note here. **Animal disputans** (DIH-spuu-tahns) is "an argumentative person," and **animal rationale** (rah-tee-oh-NAH-leh) is "a reasoning person," and like *animal bipes implume*, both may be translated as "a human being."

animis opibusque parati
AH-nih-mees OH-pih-BUUS-kweh pah-RAH-tee
ready for anything

Literally meaning "prepared in minds and resources," this upbeat saying is one of two mottoes of South Carolina. The other is DUM SPIRO SPERO, "where there's life there's hope."

Any prudent person is always *animis opibusque parati*, but this saying has special application for those who embark on a new adventure, and it may also serve those who anticipate the unpredictable final adventure of all mortals, as any life insurance salesman will tell you. Thus, South Carolina pictures itself as prudent in the one motto and tenacious in the other. No wonder nothing could be finer than to be in Carolina.

anno aetatis suae . . .
AHN-noh ī-TAH-tihs SOO-ī
in the year of his (or her) age . . .

This is the full expression often given as AETATIS SUAE. It is seen on tombstones as well as in old texts and family Bibles, often abbreviated **A.A.S.** "Died A.A.S. 64."

anno Domini
AHN-noh DAW-mih-nee
in the year of our Lord

The full version of the abbreviation **A.D.** Modern Western calendars reckon passage of time from the birth of Christ, the commencement of the Christian era, but there is disagreement over the precise year of Christ's birth. (See the next four entries.)

anno hegirae
AHN-noh HEH-gih-rī
in the year of the hegira

The year A.D. 622 is the year in which Muhammad fled from Mecca to Medina, and the month is generally given as September, so it is A.D. 622 that is taken as the beginning of the Muslim era, the precise date for the first day of the Muslim era corresponding to July 16, 622. The Arabic word for "flight" is *hijirah*, from which came the Latin word **hegira** (HEH-gih-rah) and

then the English word "hegira" (hi-JĪ-rə). To commemorate
Muhammad's flight, Muslims make the same journey as a pil-
grimage. *Anno hegirae* is abbreviated **A.H.** in giving dates in
the Muslim calendar. The curious may be gratified to learn that
1421 A.H. will commence early in A.D. 2000.

anno mundi
AHN-noh MUUN-dee
in the year of the world

Yet another term for reckoning passage of time from a fixed
event. *Anno mundi*, abbreviated **A.M.**, marks the number of
years that have passed since the world began. In the Hebrew
tradition, the year of creation corresponds to 3761 B.C. The Irish
theologian Ussher in the mid-seventeenth century computed
the date of creation as 4004 B.C. Thus, the year A.D. 2000 will
correspond to 5761 A.M. or 6004 A.M., depending on whose date
of creation is preferred.

anno regni
AHN-noh REHG-nee
in the year of the reign

Abbreviated **A.R.**, *anno regni* is used to mark the passage of
years in the reign of a monarch.

anno urbis conditae
AHN-noh UUR-bis KAWN-dih-tī
in the year since Rome was founded

For Romans, "the city," **urbs** (uurbs), was none other than
Rome, so *anno urbis conditae*, literally "in the year of the
founded city," refers to the number of years that have passed
since 753 B.C., the traditional date of the founding of Rome. (See
AB URBE CONDITA.)

annuit coeptis
AHN-noo-it koh-AYP-tees
He (God) has favored our undertaking

This saying, from Virgil's *Aeneid*, appears on the reverse of the great seal of the United States, which can be seen by all but the most impecunious on the reverse of the United States one-dollar bill. By employing *annuit coeptis* in this way, we join many other countries in suggesting that God takes a special interest in particular societies. (See E PLURIBUS UNUM and NOVUS ORDO SECLORUM.)

annus mirabilis
AHN-nuus mee-RAH-bih-lihs
a remarkable year

Any year in which great events occur may be called an *annus mirabilis*, for example, A.D. 1666, when a great fire raged in London for almost a week and virtually destroyed that city. The phrase is also used to designate a year in which figures of great importance were born, particularly when that year produced important people in great numbers. Thus, the year 1809 is considered an *annus mirabilis*. Consider first Charles Darwin and Abraham Lincoln, who were born in that year, and then go on to Alfred, Lord Tennyson and to Nikolai Gogol, Oliver Wendell Holmes, Edgar Allan Poe, and Felix Mendelssohn, as well as Louis Braille, Edward FitzGerald, William Gladstone, Fanny Kemble, Cyrus McCormick, and even Kit Carson—they don't hardly make years like that one no more.

ante bellum
AHN-teh BEL-luum
before the war

The period before any war may be characterized as *ante bellum*, but in the United States the phrase generally is applied to the period before the Civil War. In English, "antebellum" (ant-i-BEL-əm) is used as an adjective with the meaning "prewar": "The antebellum South is looked back upon with great nostalgia by some Americans."

ante Christum
AHN-teh KREE-stuum
before Christ

Abbreviated **A.C.** (See ANNO DOMINI.)

ante meridiem
AHN-teh meh-REE-dee-em
before noon

Meridies (meh-REE-dee-ays) means "noon" or "midday." A.M., the English abbreviation for *ante meridiem*, refers to time prior to noon and after midnight. (See POST MERIDIEM.)

ante mortem
AHN-teh MAWR-tem
before death

Ante mortem, abbreviated **A.M.** but not to be confused with ANNO MUNDI or with ANTE MERIDIEM, which have the same abbreviation, is an easily understood phrase that refers to the period in which death is imminent. The phrase has fathered an English adjective, "antemortem" (ant-i-MAWRT-əm): An antemortem statement is a deathbed statement and therefore is given great weight in a court of law, since a person who knows death is near is presumed to have no reason to tell anything but the truth.

ante partum
AHN-teh PAHR-tuum
before childbirth

The period before childbirth may be described as *ante partum*. (See POST PARTUM.)

apage Satanas
AHP-ah-geh SAH-tah-nahs
away with thee, Satan

The concept of Satan as the archfiend is part of the Judeo-Christian tradition. The meaning of the noun *satan* (SAW-tawn) in Hebrew, from which we work through Greek to find our way to *Satanas* in Latin, is "adversary," and we still contend with Satan today. Matthew says: "Get thee behind me, Satan." Today, with a little Latin, anyone confronted by temptation may say, "*Apage Satanas*."

apologia pro vita sua
ah-paw-LAW-gee-ah proh WEE-tah SOO-ah
a defense of his life

An *apologia* (English pronunciation, ap-ə-LOH-jə) is especially a written justification for one's opinions or actions. John Henry Newman, the celebrated Anglican theologian who converted to Catholicism in 1845, wrote *Apologia Pro Vita Sua* (1864), his religious autobiography, in which he defends the things he did in his life by way of explaining the basis for his faith. He was made a cardinal in 1879 and is known usually as Cardinal Newman. Anyone can write an *apologia pro vita sua*, but it is clear that any such attempt will be looked upon as effrontery in light of Cardinal Newman's accomplishment, which is considered a literary masterpiece.

a posteriori
ah PAW-steh-ree-OH-ree
from effect to cause

Reasoning *a posteriori*, literally "from what comes after," is a logical process in which propositions are derived from the observation of facts, or in which principles are established from generalizations based on facts. Thus, *a posteriori* reasoning, also called "inductive reasoning," is based initially on experience. (See A PRIORI.)

apparatus criticus
ah-pah-RAH-tuus KRIH-tih-kuus
critical matter

This modern Latin expression, sometimes written **criticus apparatus**, is used to designate supplementary scholarly information, such as variant readings or notes, intended to assist the serious reader of a text. Often abbreviated **apparatus**, explanatory information of this type can have such great bulk that the original text is dwarfed by it, to the delight of the editor and the dismay of the less than devoted reader. "The Yale Edition of Samuel Johnson's works is noted for the completeness of its *apparatus criticus*."

a priori
ah pree-OH-ree
from what is already known

Reasoning *a priori*, literally "from what comes before," is a logical process in which consequences are deduced from principles that are assumed. Thus, *a priori* reasoning, also called "deductive reasoning," is based initially on assumptions that derive from prior knowledge. (See A POSTERIORI.)

aqua et igni interdictus
AH-kwah et IH-gnee in-tehr-DIK-tuus
banished

This expression may be translated as "forbidden water and fire." Caesar and Cicero used **interdicere alicui** (in-tehr-DIH-keh-reh AH-lih-kwee, "to deny to someone") **aqua et igni**, as an expression meaning "to banish." A banished person is denied society; that is, no member of the community may provide him with life's necessities.

aqua pura
AH-kwah POO-rah
distilled water

Literally "pure water."

aqua vitae
AH-kwah WEE-tī
whiskey

Literally "water of life," *aqua vitae*, originally an alchemist's term, appears to be the most amusing euphemism ever invented for hard liquor. Yet no one would deny that *aqua vitae* at times is literally just what its name promises. Physicians are said to carry spirits in their bags, ready for use as restoratives, and formidable amounts of strong drink have been used in Hollywood movies to anesthetize patients about to undergo emergency surgery. The Scandinavians, perhaps because of their long, hard winters, may have been even more justified than the Romans in calling spirits *aqua vitae*. They came up with *akvavit*, a gin-like liquor flavored with caraway seeds, and the alternative spelling of *akvavit* is *aquavit*. But an additional word must be said of the origin of the word *whiskey*: It derives ultimately from the Irish and Scottish Gaelic *uisage beatha*, and what does this phrase mean? "Water of life."

a quo
ah kwoh
from which

arbiter bibendi
AHR-bih-tehr bih-BEN-dee
a toastmaster

Literally "the judge of the drinking," an *arbiter bibendi* in Roman times was much more than a mere toastmaster, as we know the latter term today. Whereas the principal duty of a toastmaster is to preside at a banquet, introducing after-dinner speakers and those who propose toasts, the *arbiter bibendi* kept an eye on the amount of wine drunk at feasts, giving special attention to the proportion of water added to the wine to bring it down to a reasonable strength. In classical times, only the dissolute drank wine at full strength.

arbiter elegantiae
AHR-bih-tehr eh-leh-GAHN-tee-ī
an authority in matters of taste

Anyone established as *arbiter elegantiae* or **arbiter elegantiarum** (eh-leh-GAHN-tee-AH-ruum) is considered the last word in matters of elegance or style.

Arcades ambo
AHR-kah-days AHM-boh
two of a kind

Virgil, in his *Eclogues*, wrote of *Arcades ambo*, literally "Arcadians both," two men of exceptional skill in pastoral poetry and music. Ancient Arcadia, in the Peloponnesus, was perceived as a region of rustic simplicity and contentment, where poetry and music flourished. Thus, in one sense, *Arcades ambo* may be taken as "two persons having like tastes, characteristics, or professions." But the expression has another interpretation: In *Don Juan*, Lord Byron used the phrase ironically: "*Arcades ambo, id est* [ihd est]—blackguards both." Byron's intention has overtaken Virgil's, so *Arcades ambo* today more often is used pejoratively.

arcanum arcanorum
ahr-KAH-nuum ahr-kah-NOH-ruum
secret of secrets

The ultimate secret, the secret of nature that supposedly underlies the work of the alchemist, astrologer, and magician.

argumentum
ahr-goo-MEN-tuum
an argument or proof or appeal

Rhetoric was important to the Romans, so they had many phrases in which *argumentum* was combined with other terms, as can be seen by reading on below. It must be made clear here that *argumentum* is not a disagreement, but a proof, especially one adduced to illuminate or clarify.

argumentum ab auctoritate
ahr-goo-MEN-tuum ahb ow-ktoh-rih-TAH-teh
a proof derived from authority

argumentum ab inconvenienti
ahr-goo-MEN-tuum ahb in-kawn-WEH-nee-EN-tee
an appeal based on the hardship or inconvenience involved

argumentum ad absurdum
ahr-goo-MEN-tuum ahd ahb-SUUR-duum
an appeal pointing out the absurdity of one's opponent's point of view, rather than establishing the merits of one's own position

See REDUCTIO AD ABSURDUM.

argumentum ad captandum
ahr-goo-MEN-tuum ahd kah-PTAHN-duum
an appeal based primarily on arousing popular passions

See AD CAPTANDUM VULGUS.

argumentum ad crumenam
ahr-goo-MEN-tuum ahd kroo-MAY-nahm
an appeal based on money or the promise of profit

A **crumena** (kroo-MAY-nah), a leather pouch that held money, was secured by a strap around a Roman's neck. Thus the meaning of *argumentum ad crumenam* as an appeal to the pocketbook—and what is more convincing?

argumentum ad hominem
ahr-goo-MEN-tuum ahd HAW-mih-nem
an argument against the man

Argumentum ad hominem is an effective rhetorical tactic, appealing to feelings rather than intellect, or directed against an opponent's character rather than the subject under discussion. *Argumentum ad hominem* is considered a logical fallacy, in that such an argument fails to prove a point by failing to address it. There is no doubt, however, that in practical politics and in many a court of law, *argumentum ad hominem* is persuasive. (See AD REM and ARGUMENTUM AD REM.)

argumentum ad invidiam
ahr-goo-MEN-tuum ahd ihn-WIH-dee-ahm
an appeal to envy or other undesirable human traits

A powerful tool for the demagogue.

argumentum ad rem
ahr-goo-MEN-tuum ahd rem
a relevant argument

See AD REM.

argumentum baculinum

ahr-goo-MEN-tuum bah-koo-LEE-nuum

an appeal to force

Argumentum baculinum has long been a popular and effective form of persuasion. In *Argumentum baculinum*, the force is suggested by wielding a walking stick (**baculum**), but a *baculum* was also the scepter that symbolized magisterial authority, so the force implied may also be that of governmental authority or legal compulsion.

arma virumque cano

AHR-mah wih-RUUM-kweh KAH-noh

arms and the man I sing

The opening words of Virgil's great epic poem, the *Aeneid*. In an epic, a hero has many demanding adventures, which the poet describes in elevated style. The *Aeneid* traces the experiences of Aeneas, defender of Troy, after the destruction of Troy, in the legendary war precipitated by Helen's abduction by Paris in about 1200 B.C.

arrectis auribus

ah-REH-ktees OW-rih-buus

on the alert

Literally "with ears pricked up." While the phrase describes the characteristic appearance of an animal intent on finding or fighting its prey, it can be used in giving advice to our friends: "In the city, ever *arrectis auribus*."

ars amandi

ahrs ah-MAHN-dee

art of love

Literally "the art of loving."

Ars Amatoria
ahrs ah-mah-TOH-ree-ah
The Art of Love

The title of Ovid's work on the amatory art, with full accounts of how to find and keep a lover. This how-to book of ancient Rome—it was published about 2 B.C.—is still worth reading. Within a few years after *Ars Amatoria* appeared, Ovid was banished from Rome by Emperor Augustus, and he died an exile in A.D. 17. Ovid, in his autobiographical work *Tristia*, gives two reasons for his exile: *carmen*, "song," and *error*, an unspecified "indiscretion." From his extended justifications in *Tristia* and other late works, it is clear that Ovid believed *Ars Amatoria* had offended the prudish Augustus.

ars artium
ahrs AHR-tee-uum
logic

Literally "the art of arts."

ars est celare artem
ahrs est keh-LAH-reh AHR-tem
true art conceals the means by which it is achieved

Ovid's maxim in *Ars Amatoria*, literally "it is art to conceal art," has it that in the best works of art the audience is not distracted by the artist's technique, but responds instead to the power of the work, as the artist intended. True art must appear artless. *Ars est celare artem* as a critical evaluation of a work of art, thus, is a high compliment.

ars gratia artis
ahrs GRAH-tee-ah AHR-tis
art for art's sake

The motto of the true artist, now preempted by Hollywood: Metro-Goldwyn-Mayer, the motion picture producers, use it as part of the M-G-M trademark.

ars longa, vita brevis
ahrs LAWN-gah WEE-tah BREH-wihs
art is long, but life is short

The Greek physician Hippocrates coined this aphorism, here given in its Latin translation, telling us that the art of healing has a life much longer than that of its practitioner (and patient, we might add), but *ars longa, vita brevis* is generally extended to all the arts today. The principal intent, no matter how *ars* is interpreted, is to point out that we are mortal and must anticipate death. Longfellow, in his "Psalm of Life," put it this way for all of us:

> Art is long, and Time is fleeting,
> And our hearts, though stout and brave,
> Still, like muffled drums, are beating
> Funeral marches to the grave.

A sobering thought.

ars moriendi
ahrs maw-ree-EN-dee
the art of dying

The Romans put much store in dying nobly. (See PAETE, NON DOLET.)

ars poetica
ahrs paw-AY-tih-kah
the art of poetry

Also the title, *Ars Poetica*, of an epistolary poem of Horace, written about 20 B.C., expounding his literary theory.

arte perire sua
AHR-teh peh-REE-reh SOO-ah
to trip oneself up

Here—recall the English adjective "artful," as in the Artful Dodger in *Oliver Twist*—ars takes on a meaning akin to wiles or cunning or machinations, so a literal translation of *arte perire sua* is "to perish by one's own machinations." The expression is not unlike our own "hoist with his own petard," literally "blown up by his own bomb," but understood as "trapped by his own machinations."

artes perditae
AHR-tays PEHR-dih-tī
lost arts

Any skills forgotten by a culture are *artes perditae*. "Addition and multiplication, as a trip to any supermarket will demonstrate, are *artes perditae*."

artes, scientia, veritas
AHR-tays skee-EN-tee-ah WEH-rih-tahs
arts, science, truth

Motto of the University of Michigan.

Artium Baccalaureus
AHR-tee-uum bah-kah-LOW-ray-uus
Bachelor of Arts

Abbreviated **A.B.** or **B.A.** This, of course, is the undergraduate degree awarded by colleges and universities. The derivation of the term is not clear. It has been suggested that the medieval Latin term *baccalaureus*, "bachelor," was adapted from **baccalarius** (bah-kah-LOW-ree-uus), meaning "laborer" or "tenant." This discussion is intended solely to suggest the possibly humble origin of the bachelor of arts degree, awarded formally after four years' hard labor or, too often, after four years' tenancy in a college dormitory.

Artium Magister
AHR-tee-uum mah-GIS-tehr
Master of Arts

Abbreviated **A.M.** or **M.A.** Another university degree.

asinus asinum fricat
AH-sih-nuus AH-sih-nuum FRIH-kaht
one fool rubs the other's back

Two people who lavish excessive praise on one another—perhaps no one else sees anything praiseworthy in either of them—exemplify *asinus asinum fricat*, literally "the ass rubs the ass." No group has a corner on the market for *asinus asinum fricat*. Wherever people of small talent gather, someone sooner or later will establish a chapter of the Mutual Admiration Society.

a tergo
ah TEHR-goh
from behind

This expression is applied most often today to a position in sexual intercourse in which the male lies behind the female.

auctor ignotus
OW-ktawr ih-GNOH-tuus
an unknown author

Not a putdown. An *auctor ignotus* is an author whose work has not gained the recognition it merits.

audaces fortuna iuvat (or juvat)
ow-DAH-kays fawr-TOO-nah YOO-waht
fortune favors the bold

Also given as **audentes** (ow-DEN-tays, "the daring") **fortuna iuvat**. This motto for the bold and successful and for those who aspire to success was cited by many Roman writers. The English proverb "Nothing ventured, nothing gained" captures the spirit of this common Roman saying.

audemus iura (or jura) nostra defendere
ow-DAY-muus YOO-rah NAW-strah deh-FEN-deh-reh
we dare defend our rights

The motto of Alabama, perhaps calling attention to that state's dedication to protecting its rights against infringement by the federal government.

audi alteram partem
OW-dee AHL-teh-rahm PAHR-tem
there are two sides to every question

Literally "hear the other side." A plea for reason and fairness in discussion.

aura popularis
OW-rah paw-puu-LAH-rihs
temporary celebrity

Cicero's expression for the public's favorite at a particular time, who is said to be enjoying *aura popularis*, literally "the popular breeze." But breezes subside.

aurea mediocritas
OW-ray-ah meh-dee-AW-krih-tahs
moderation in all things

Those of us who are satisfied with lives of security and contentment seek *aurea mediocritas*, literally "the golden mean." We are willing to live out our days without taking great risks, without indulging in excesses. *Aurea mediocritas* is an expression used by Horace, in his *Odes*; he intended it in the meaning just described: "Who loves the golden mean is safe from the poverty of a hovel and free from the envy of a palace."

aureo hamo piscari
OW-ray-oh HAH-moh pih-SKAH-ree
money talks

Literally "to fish with a golden hook," *aureo hamo piscari* recognizes the marvelous persuasiveness of cash on the barrelhead. This in not unlike **auro quaeque ianua panditur** (OW-roh KWĪ-kweh YAH-noo-ah PAHN-dih-tuur), which we know as "a golden key opens any door," but which translates literally as "any door is opened by means of gold."

auri sacra fames
OW-ree SAH-krah FAH-mays
money-mad

Those who live only to acquire wealth are characterized by Virgil as having *auri sacra fames*, literally "the cursed hunger for gold."

Aurora
ow-ROH-rah
goddess of the morning

In Roman mythology, Aurora was responsible for such duties as extinguishing stars at the end of night. But there was more to her: She had a weakness for mortal men, her favorite being Tithonus, son of the king of Troy. After stealing him away, she inveigled Jupiter into giving Tithonus immortality, but neglected to arrange for eternal youth for the poor fellow. In time, he grew old and unappealing, so Aurora locked him in his room. All that was heard from Tithonus from then on was a feeble cry from time to time. As a final act of mercy, Aurora turned him into a grasshopper. We know Aurora today mostly in the terms *aurora australis* and *aurora borealis*, the southern lights and northern lights, which delight and mystify us, pronounced in English ə-ROH-rə aw-STRAY-ləs and boh-ree-AL-əs.

auspicium melioris aevi
ow-SPIH-kee-uum meh-lee-OH-ris Ī-wee
an omen of a better time

Yet another expression revealing the Romans' deep concern with auguries. Finding a white stone, a flower growing in a rock, or any other sign of good things to come—*auspicium melioris aevi*—was taken quite seriously.

Austriae est imperare orbi universo
OW-stree-ī est im-peh-RAH-reh AWR-bee
OO-nih-WEHR-soh
it is Austria's destiny to rule the world

The motto of Emperor Frederick III, one of the Hapsburgs. The fact that the Hapsburgs no longer dictate to anybody, not even the Austrians, is a commentary on the impermanence of power. The abbreviation of Frederick's motto, whether rendered in German or in Latin, is itself worthy of mention: **A.E.I.O.U.** is the abbreviation of the German *Alles Erdreich ist Oesterreich unterthan*, "the whole world subjected to Austria," retaining for moderns the irony as well as the initial letters of the Latin phrase.

aut bibat aut abeat
owt BIH-baht owt AHB-ay-aht
you're either for us or against us

This saying, a borrowing from the Greek, in the literal sense is taken as "let him either drink or depart." In an extended meaning, *aut bibat aut abeat* can be used to force participation on an unwilling member of a plan or conspiracy. Either the hesitating fellow goes along with the others, or he is no longer welcome.

aut Caesar aut nihil
owt KĪ-sahr owt NIH-hil
all or nothing

Literally "either Caesar (that is, emperor of Rome) or nothing," associated with Julius Caesar, who said he would sooner be number one man in a village than number two in Rome, and a motto of Cesare Borgia (1476–1507). The favorite son of Pope Alexander VI, Borgia was known for his crimes and violence, even against members of his own family. One of his lovable practices, according to legend, was that of poisoning the wine of rivals before joining them in toasting mutual friendship. Borgia's failure to achieve his ambition to seize total power reflects badly on the efficacy of his underhanded methods. *Aut Caesar aut nihil* is also given as **aut Caesar aut nullus** (NUU-luus, "nobody"), with the same meaning.

aut disce aut discede
OWT DIH-skeh owt dih-SKAY-deh
either learn or leave

A suitable motto for a school sufficiently principled, not to mention well endowed, to be able to insist on excellent academic standards.

aut viam inveniam aut faciam
owt WEE-ahm in-WEH-nee-ahm owt FAH-kee-ahm
where there's a will there's a way

Literally "I'll either find a way or make one," *aut viam inveniam aut faciam* is the credo of the person who plugs along, unwilling ever to admit defeat. Such a person is determined, not obstinate.

aut vincere aut mori
owt WIN-keh-reh owt MAW-ree
victory or death

A Roman motto, literally "either to conquer or to die," intended to inspire soldiers preparing for battle, also found (in French) in a stanza of the *Marseillaise*. Gilbert and Sullivan mock this spirit in their *Pirates of Penzance*. The fair young maidens exhort the departing constabulary to fight bravely against the threatening pirates: "Go, ye heroes, go and die." Anyone who has ever prepared for battle will understand the effectiveness of such encouragement.

ave atque vale
AH-weh AHT-kweh WAH-lay
hail and farewell

Ave, "hail," was the Roman equivalent of "hello," and *vale* the equivalent of "goodbye," as well as the Roman farewell to the dead. Catullus used this expression in closing a poem on the death of his brother: "**Atque in perpetuum, frater** (in per-PEH-too-uum FRAH-ter), **ave atque vale.**" "And forever, brother, hail and farewell!"

ave Caesar, morituri te salutant
AH-weh KĪ-sahr MAW-rih-TOO-ree tay sah-LOO-tahnt
hail, Caesar, those who are about to die salute you

A line suitable for the clever schoolboy making his appearance before a board of examiners. The words are those of Roman gladiators entering the arena to launch into mortal combat. Suetonius tells us in his *Lives of the Caesars* that Emperor Claudius (A.D. 41–54) so enjoyed these spectacles, he ordered that even those who fell accidentally be put to death. He wanted to watch their faces as they died. No wonder the gladiators referred to themselves as "those who are about to die." The full expression is also given as **ave, Caesar, morituri te salutamus** (sah-loo-TAH-mus), "hail, Caesar, we who are about to die salute you."

ave Maria
AH-weh mah-REE-ah
hail Mary

The angels' salutation to the Virgin, from Luke, in English pronounced AH-vay mah-REE-ə.

a verbis ad verbera
ah WEHR-bees ahd WEHR-beh-rah
from words to blows

An expression useful in describing a discussion that is heating up.

Ave Regina Caelorum
AH-weh ray-GEE-nah kī-LOH-ruum
Hail, Queen of Heaven

Title of a hymn in honor of the Virgin, the Queen of Heaven.

a vinculo matrimonii
ah WIN-kuu-loh mah-trih-MOH-nee-ee
an absolute divorce

A divorce *a vinculo matrimonii*, literally "from the bond of marriage," and also called a divorce *a vinculo*, is one that releases husband and wife from all legal commitments of marriage. It is interesting to note that *vinculum* (WIN-kuu-luum, "bond") also means "noose" and "chain."

beatae memoriae
bay-AH-tī meh-MAW-ree-ī
of blessed memory

Used on tombstones and memorial plaques.

Beata Maria
bay-AH-tah mah-REE-ah
Blessed Mary

Maria, of course, is the Virgin Mary. Other Latin expressions are also used in referring to Mary, including **Beata Virgo** (WEER-goh, Blessed Virgin) and **Beata Virgo Maria** (Blessed Virgin Mary). The abbreviations **B.M.** and **B.V.** for *Beata Maria* and *Beata Virgo* are sometimes seen.

beati pacifici
bay-AH-tee pah-KIH-fih-kee
blessed are the peacemakers

In Matthew, the opening words of the eighth beatitude of the Sermon on the Mount, concluding "for they shall be called sons of God."

beati pauperes spiritu
beh-AH-tee POW-peh-rehs SPIH-rih-too
blessed are the poor in spirit

In Matthew, the opening words of the Sermon on the Mount, concluding "for theirs is the kingdom of heaven." The irrepressible Alexander Pope wrote a beatitude of his own: "Blessed is the man who expects nothing, for he shall never be disappointed."

beati possidentes
beh-AH-tee PAW-sih-DEN-tays
possession is nine points of the law

Literally "blessed are those who possess" (for they shall receive). This expression finds its principal meaning in conveying the idea that one may claim property most easily before the law when one has physical possession of it—consider the longtime squatter on land deeded to another person. In a cynical vein, *beati possidentes*, translated literally, may be taken as a commentary on the uncanny knack of the haves to acquire ever more, while the have-nots acquire ever less.

beatus
beh-AH-tuus
the blessed person

See ADVOCATUS DIABOLI.

bellum
BEHL-luum
war

An important word in the expansionist Roman world, but not always looked upon with favor: Horace wrote of **bella detesta matribus** (BEHL-lah day-TEH-stah MAH-trih-buus), "wars, the horror of mothers," and Virgil wrote of **bella horrida bella** (BEL-lah HAWR-rih-dah BEL-lah), "wars, horrid wars."

bene
BEH-neh
well

A noteworthy observation incorporating this adverb is **bene qui latuit** (kwee LAH-too-iht) **bene vixit** (WEE-ksiht), literally "he who has lived in obscurity has lived well." The line is from

Tristia, Ovid's extended lament about his enforced exile from Rome, and its meaning is not to be taken as a panegyric for the simple life. Rather, Ovid is expressing bitterness over the way things have turned out for him, telling us that the powerful— Emperor Augustus *et al.*—are envious of brilliance and attractiveness in others, so *bene qui latuit bene vixit*, "keep a low profile if you wish to survive." Whistle-blowers, beware.

beneficium accipere libertatem est vendere
beh-neh-FIH-kee-uum ahk-KIHP-eh-reh
lee-behr-TAH-tem est WEHN-deh-reh
to accept a favor is to sell one's freedom

In *Hamlet*, Polonius advises his son:

> Neither a borrower, nor a lender be;
> For loan oft loses both itself and friend,
> And borrowing dulls the edge of husbandry.

So much for Shakespeare's wisdom on extending kindness as well as receiving it. Let's turn to a Roman playwright. *Beneficium accipere libertatem est vendere*, a maxim attributed to Publilius Syrus, recognizes only the problems of those on the receiving end. And the New Testament? The Acts of the Apostles: "It is more blessed to give than to receive." So traditional sources of wisdom appear to agree that acts of kindness may lead to misery rather than to improvement in the quality of our lives, and we are left confused and uncertain. Perhaps everything depends on the spirit in which we give and the terms under which we borrow.

bis dat qui cito dat
bihs daht kwee KIH-toh daht
he gives twice who quickly gives

This Latin proverb, quoted by Cervantes in *Don Quixote*, may serve as a fitting motto for professional fund-raisers, who so often have to badger self-professed donors into delivering on their pledges. There is little joy in such gifts, nor is there satisfaction in any act of charity or kindness given reluctantly and only after repeated appeals.

bis repetita placent
bihs reh-peh-TEE-tah PLAH-kent
a little originality, please

A derogatory comment, literally "the things that please are those that are asked for again and again," appropriate for a derivative work. Horace was telling us in *bis repetita placent* that certain works of art please once, but others, tried and true, are imitated widely and always please. Thus, when we see a work obviously patterned after a previous, successful work, we may say *bis repetita placent* or merely *bis repetita*, telling the creator of the imitative work that he is catering to the public's taste rather than attempting something original.

bis vivit qui bene vivit
bihs WEE-wiht kwee BEH-neh WEE-wiht
he lives twice who lives well

Milton, in *Paradise Lost*, couched the same wisdom in these words:

> Nor love thy life, nor hate; but what thou liv'st
> Live well; how long or short permit to Heaven.

So we are being told that quality of life is much more important than longevity. But *bis vivit qui bene vivit*, besides counseling us to lead productive lives, offers a consoling thought to recall when a friend dies young.

bona fide
BAW-nah FIH-deh
in good faith

This phrase can also be translated as "honestly," "sincerely," or any other word or expression denoting "without deception."

Bona fide has been used as an adjective phrase in our own
language so often that we all know it by its English pronunciation, BOH-nə-fīd. To produce *bona fides* (English pronunciation
BOH-nə FĪ-deez) means to show good intentions in dealing
with others, show credentials, prove one's identity or ability,
etc. No fraud or deceit is intended or shown. (See MALA FIDE.)

bonis avibus
BAW-nees AH-wih-buus
under favorable signs

Literally "under good birds," a phrase indicating that the
omens are favorable for a contemplated action. The Romans
relied so heavily on birds, **aves** (AH-ways), as tools in divination
that the noun **avis** (AH-wihs) is translated as "sign" or "omen" as
well as "bird," and **avi mala** (MAH-lah) and **avi sinistra** (sih-NIH-
strah) mean "bad omens." But the Romans were not the only
ones who found magic in birds. Consider, for example, the persis-
tent use of the dove as a symbol of peace, innocence, and love.

bonum vinum laetificat cor hominis
BAW-nuum WEE-nuum lī-TIH-fih-kaht kawr
HAW-mih-nihs
good wine gladdens a person's heart

The Psalms speak of "wine that maketh glad the heart of
man," referring to the bountiful favors provided by God. In the
modern world, *bonum vinum laetificat* may find wider application as a slogan for promoting consumption of wine and spirits.

brutum fulmen
BROO-tuum FUUL-men
an empty threat

Brutum fulmen, literally "an insensible thunderbolt," reminds us of Pliny's phrase **bruta fulmina et vana** (BROO-tah
FUUL-mih-nah et WAH-nah), "thunderbolts that strike blindly

and in vain." Those who argue bombastically or who threaten idly without the inclination or ability to follow up on their threats are said to offer only *brutum fulmen*. One can also apply the phrase to governments that continually threaten their adversaries but never make good on the threats—to the relief of the rest of us, whose sons would be the ones sent to fulfill the threats.

c or ca.

See CIRCA.

cacoëthes carpendi
kah-koh-AY-thehs kahr-PEN-dee
a mania for finding fault

Cacoëthes, derived from *kakoethes*, a Greek word that combines *kakos*, "bad," with *ethos*, "habit," describes any compulsion or uncontrollable urge. *Cacoëthes* can be used alone to mean "mania" or "passion," even "disease." With *carpendi*, a form of *carpere* (KAHR-peh-reh), meaning "to pluck," as fruit from a tree, the phrase becomes highly useful in describing the uncontrollable urge of an inveterate nitpicker.

cacoëthes loquendi
kah-koh-AY-thehs loh-KWEN-dee
compulsive talking

Anyone who goes on talking and talking and talking and talking may be said to exhibit *cacoëthes loquendi*. (See CACOËTHES CARPENDI.)

cacoëthes scribendi
kah-koh-AY-thehs skree-BEN-dee
an incurable itch to write

Another form of *cacoëthes*. In the fuller phrase **insanabile** (in-sah-NAH-bih-lay, "incurable") **cacoëthes scribendi**, Juvenal in his *Satires* harshly described the compulsion to write—that is, to become a published writer—still prevalent today. We see the phrase used now as an uncharitable appraisal of a writer deemed untalented, implicitly advising said person to abandon writing and pursue some more suitable vocation. Juvenal's full statement is worthy of translation: "An inveterate and incurable itch for writing besets many and grows old in their sick hearts." No laughing matter is this incurable itch.

cadit quaestio
KAH-dit KWĪ-stee-oh
the argument collapses

Cadit quaestio, literally translated as "the question falls," is said when the central idea of an argument or a legal case collapses: "*Cadit quaestio*, there is nothing further to be said; let us move on to other matters."

caeca invidia est
KĪ-kah in-WIH-dee-ah est
envy is blind

We are accustomed to thinking of love as blind, but Livy's aphorism *caeca invidia est* tells us that envy also is blind: Those possessed by envy overlook facts that would alleviate or eliminate the debilitating condition.

caeli enarrant gloriam Dei
KĪ-lee eh-NAHR-rahnt GLOH-ree-ahm DEH-ee
the heavens bespeak the glory of God

Often abbreviated *caeli enarrant*, this quotation from the Psalms cites the stars and the planets as brilliant evidence of the wisdom and power of God. *Caeli enarrant* is a fitting expression on seeing the full moon or a particularly spectacular celestial display. *Caeli enarrant* is also a fitting comment—a star is born

—on the brilliant debut of a musical prodigy, an outstanding new writer or actor, or any young person coming to the favorable attention of the public for the first time.

caelum non animum . . .

See COELUM NON ANIMUM . . .

caetera desunt
KĪ-tay-rah DAY-suunt
the rest are missing

See CETERA DESUNT.

caeteris paribus
KĪ-teh-rees PAH-rih-buus
other things being equal

Also given as **ceteris** (KAY-teh-rees) **paribus**. "The President said that *caeteris paribus* he would appoint a woman to the post."

Campus Martius
KAHM-puus MAHR-tee-uus
the field of Mars

In the early republic, Romans used the term *Campus Martius* to designate a field on the eastern bank of the Tiber that they used as an encampment when the army was mobilized—Mars, of course, was the Roman god of war. The *Campus Martius* was also used for athletic contests, in themselves a kind of warfare, and for meetings of the **comitia** (koh-MEE-tee-ah), the assembly of the Roman people for the election of consuls, magistrates, and other officials, as well as to decide on mobilization of the army.

caput mortuum
KAH-puut MOR-too-uum
worthless residue

The literal meaning of *caput mortuum* is "death's head," a skull. The term was used by the alchemists to designate the residue in a flask after distillation was complete. *Caput mortuum* now can be taken as any worthless residue, even a useless person.

caput mundi
KAH-puut MUUN-dee
the Big Apple

The Romans thought of Rome as *caput mundi*, literally "the head—the capital—of the world," and perhaps justifiably so. After all, Poe spoke of "the glory that was Greece and the grandeur that was Rome." And did not all roads lead to Rome? Those who boost their own hometowns may use *caput mundi* in the same way the Romans did.

caritas
KAH-rih-tahs
love, charity

Forgetting that charity designates "love of humanity," we tend to think of it exclusively as "giving to the poor." By *caritas* the Romans meant "dearness" or "high price." (**Carus** [KAH-ruus], meaning "dear," is an etymological ancestor of the word "whore.") Thus, when Cicero wrote of a year in which the cost of living was high, he used the phrase **annonae** (AHN-noh-nī, "crops") **caritas**. Eventually *caritas* designated another kind of dearness, the highest love or fellowship—charity as we now know it in the sense conveyed in Corinthians: "And now abideth faith, hope, charity, these three; but the greatest of these is charity."

carpe diem
KAHR-peh DEE-em
enjoy, enjoy

This famous advice, literally "seize the day," is from Horace's *Odes*. The full thought is **carpe diem, quam minimum credula postero** (kwahm MIH-nih-muum KRAY-duu-lah PAW-ster-oh), which may be translated as "enjoy today, trusting little in tomorrow." Thus, *carpe diem* from ancient times until the present has been advice often and variously expressed: Enjoy yourself while you have the chance; eat, drink, and be merry, for tomorrow we die; make hay while the sun shines; enjoy yourself, it's later than you think. In another century *carpe diem* was also an exhortation to maidens to give up their virginity and enjoy all the pleasures of life.

Robert Herrick (1591–1674):

> Gather ye rosebuds while ye may,
> Old Time is still a-flying,
> And this same flower that smiles today
> Tomorrow will be dying.

castigat ridendo mores
KAH-stih-gaht ree-DEN-doh MOH-rays
laughter succeeds where lecturing won't

The literal translation of *castigat ridendo mores* is "it (or he or she) corrects customs (or manners) by laughing at them." This phrase, therefore, gives us the essence of satire, whose target is the folly of mankind, and whose technique is ridicule.

casus belli
KAH-suus BEL-lee
justification for making war

Casus literally means a "fall" or "falling," but the word was used by the Romans in many ways, signifying an occasion, opportunity, misfortune, mishap, destruction, downfall, etc. Thus, Virgil refers to **casus urbis Troianae** (UUR-bis troy-AH-nī), "the fall of the city of Troy." *Belli* is the genitive of **bellum** (BEL-luum, "war"), and Cicero refers to **bellum domesticum** (doh-MEH-stih-kuum), "familial strife," telling us that, alas, marital problems and family disputes are not a recent invention. Historians seek to establish the *casus belli* for each of the many wars that have befallen mankind. Diplomats, we expect, are concerned with avoiding a *casus belli* when relations between nations are strained. But those intent on making war are sure to find a *casus belli* or invent one.

casus foederis
KAH-suus FOY-deh-ris
a situation triggering action under a treaty

Casus in its many meanings is discussed under CASUS BELLI. *Foederis* is the genitive of **foedus** (FOY-duus), which literally is "a league" or "an alliance between two states," but came to mean the document creating the alliance. Those of us who have studied the events leading up to World War I may recall that intricate networks of alliances had been set up among the nations of Europe. When an attack was made on one of the nations so allied, it became the *casus foederis*, obliging all the other nations in one way or another to commit their resources to the tragic war that followed. *Foedus* is not restricted in meaning to alliances between nations. Cicero spoke of **foedus amorum** (ah-MOH-ruum), "a love pact," surely a happier and more narrowly intended agreement.

causa sine qua non
KOW-sah SIH-neh kwah nohn
a necessary condition

Causa sine qua non is literally "a cause without which not," so we can readily understand the meaning of the phrase. *Causa* occurs in other phrases as well: **causa causans** (KOW-sahns) can be translated as "an initiating cause," and **causa causata** (kow-SAH-tah) as "a cause owing its existence to a *causa causans* or, perhaps, to another *causa causata*," thus giving us a way to use Latin in arguing the eternal question of who did what to whom first. Theologians use these terms in describing God and His works, God being *causa causans*, and creation *causa causata*.

caveant consules ne quid detrimenti respublica capiat
KAH-way-ahnt KAWN-suu-lays nay kwid
day-tree-MEN-tee rays-POO-blih-kah KAH-pee-aht
beware, consuls, that the republic is not harmed

Usually abbreviated *caveant consules*, "consuls beware," this elegant sentence was the formula used by the Roman Senate to invite the consuls—the two chief magistrates of the republic—to designate a dictator in times of crisis. Presumably there was no time available for the ordinary processes of government, involving time-consuming debate. In modern use, this formula becomes ominous, alerting a legally constituted government to the threat of replacement by a dictatorship if the people's dissatisfaction with that government is not recognized and reversed.

caveat emptor
KAH-way-aht EMP-tawr
let the buyer beware

The rule of law warning potential purchasers of goods or services that they are not protected during a transaction against failure of the sellers to live up to the bargain except to the extent that the sales contract stipulates. By this rule, the purchaser, not the seller, is responsible for protecting the purchaser in the transaction. *Caveat emptor* is the opposite of **caveat venditor** (WEN-dih-tawr). Whereas *caveat emptor* has a long history in common law, *caveat venditor* is just now coming into prominence as a result of the consumer rights movement. Under *caveat venditor*, the seller is assumed to be more sophisticated than the purchaser and so must bear responsibility for protecting the unwary purchaser. The purchaser, *emptor*, is a child who must be protected against his own mistakes, while the seller, *venditor*, is the big, bad wolf lying in wait for Little Red Riding Hood. So while the two rules struggle for preeminence, attorneys gleefully watch—and litigate.

cave canem
KAH-weh KAH-nem
beware of the dog

This friendly warning, commonly inscribed on doors of Roman homes, was found on the door of a house in Pompeii during excavation of that ancient city, rediscovered in 1748. Pompeii had been buried during an eruption of Mount Vesuvius in A.D. 79. Finding a homely reminder of the day-to-day lives of an ancient people whose lives were snuffed out suddenly by catastrophe reinforces the validity of the warning found on old clocks: ULTIMA FORSAN (UUL-tih-mah FAWR-sahn), "perhaps the last hour." The inhabitants of Pompeii had little warning their time had come. How many of them had followed the injunction CARPE DIEM?

cave quid dicis, quando, et cui
KAH-weh kwid DEE-kis, KWAHN-doh, et KOO-ee
beware what you say, when, and to whom

Excellent advice for all of us. (See VIR SAPIT QUI PAUCA LOQUITUR.)

cedant arma togae
KAY-dahnt AHR-mah TOH-gī
military power must be subordinate to civil authority

The motto of Wyoming, literally "let arms yield to the gown." Cicero, discussing in *De Officiis* his term as consul, used these words to affirm the primacy of civil authority under his rule, giving us a maxim we may cite to warn against military dictatorship. *Arma*, "arms," represents the military; *toga* (TOH-gah), the garment worn by Roman citizens in their peacetime lives, represents civil authority. (See TOGA.)

certiorari
KEHR-tee-oh-RAH-ree
to be made certain

A writ of *certiorari*, in English pronounced sur-shee-ə-RAIR-ee, is a legal document calling for delivery to a higher court of the record of a proceeding before a lower court. The purpose of calling for the record is to enable judicial review of the action taken by the lower court. The basis for issuing the writ is a complaint that an injustice has been done by the lower court.

certum est quia impossibile est
KEHR-tuum est KWEE-ah im-paw-SIH-bih-leh est
it is certain because it is impossible

A maxim of Tertullian (third century A.D.), in *De Carne Christi*, warning us that in matters of faith we are not to believe the evidence presented to us by our eyes and ears. In light of our limited understanding as mere mortals, the apparent impossibility of the truth of the supernatural is an argument for acceptance, rather than for rejection, of the supernatural.

cessante causa cessat et effectus
keh-SAHN-tay KOW-sah KEH-saht et ef-FEK-tuus
when the cause is removed, the effect disappears

The validity of *cessante causa cessat et effectus*, literally "the cause ceasing, the effect also ceases," is demonstrable in most of life's activities, but not in human behavior, if we are to believe the psychoanalyst. For example, while pain caused by an aching tooth may disappear once the tooth is treated, pain suffered in childhood may plague adults all through their lives.

cetera desunt
KAY-teh-rah DAY-suunt
the rest are missing

This scholarly notation (also given as **caetera desunt**) is used to indicate that parts of a work have not been found despite careful research. "The full text of the verse by Sappho has never been found, so the missing portions are marked *cetera desunt*."

ceteris paribus
KAY-teh-rees PAH-rih-buus
other things being equal

See CAETERIS PARIBUS.

cf.

See CONFER.

circa
KIHR-kah
about

This scholar's term, in English pronounced SUR-kə, and abbreviated *c* or *ca*., indicates uncertainty about a date. "It is generally assumed that Chaucer was born *c* A.D. 1340." "The vase was dated *ca*. fourth century B.C."

codex
KOH-deks
a manuscript parchment; a code of laws

Codex, originally spelled **caudex** (KOW-deks), first meant "tree trunk," but eventually acquired additional meanings. For example, Juvenal used *codex* to mean "a wooden block," to which men were tied as punishment. Terence used *codex* as a term of derision, the equivalent of "blockhead." Finally *codex* came to mean a book made of bound wooden slabs, with printing scratched into wax coatings on the slabs. But *codex* also has the meaning of "a code of laws." Two famous **codices**, plural of *codex* and pronounced KOH-dih-kays (in English KOHD-ǝ -seez), are the **Codex Alexandrinus** (ah-lek-sahn-DREE-nuus) and the **Codex Sinaiticus** (see-NĪ-tih-kuus), but there are many others, including the **Codex Juris Canonici** (YUU-ris kah-NOH-nih-kee), the official collection of ecclesiastical laws of the Roman Catholic Church.

coelum non animum mutant qui trans mare currunt
KOY-luum nohn AH-nih-muum MOO-tahnt kwee
trahns MAH-reh KUUR-ruunt
those who cross the sea change the sky, not their
spirits

In this delightful sentence from Horace's *Epistles*, we are cautioned that a change of scene—here *coelum*, "the heavens," also given as **caelum** (KĪ-luum)—does not change us: As we travel from one place to another, what we see with our eyes may change dramatically, but we are the same people we were when we started our journey. If we are to credit Horace, then, we cannot flee our destinies, nor by flight can we change what is fundamental to our nature: The grass is not greener on the other side of the street. Fortunately, in *Paradise Lost* Milton sends a happier message:

> The mind is its own place, and in itself
> Can make a Heav'n of Hell, a Hell of Heav'n.

cogito ergo sum
KOH-gih-toh EHR-goh SUUM
I think, therefore I exist

One of the most famous of all philosophic axioms, known—perhaps imperfectly—by every freshman student of philosophy. Descartes, in his *Discourse on Method*, used it as the starting point for his philosophic system.

coitus interruptus
koh-EE-tuus in-tehr-RUUP-tuus
interrupted coitus

collegium
kawl-LAY-gee-uum
colleagueship

A *collegium*—in Roman times the word described the connection between a pair of colleagues as well as within a group of colleagues—can be applied now to members of any group united by common interest or pursuits: a college faculty or department, a society of scholars, an ecclesiastical group living together to pursue a common purpose, etc.

compos mentis
KAWM-paws MEN-tis
of sound mind

A person in his right mind is adjudged *compos mentis*, translated more literally as "in full possession of mental powers," while a person not of sound mind is said to be **non** (nohn) **compos mentis**. The two terms are used loosely today by people unqualified to make either judgment. More properly the two expressions find use in legal writing and court testimony.

compos sui
KAWM-paws SOO-ee
master of himself

Compos sui is a condition few of us can aspire to in this world of big government and big corporations. Unlike the English poet W. E. Henley (1849–1903), we cannot declaim:

> I am the master of my fate:
> I am the captain of my soul.

conditio sine qua non
kawn-DEE-tee-oh SIH-neh kwah nohn
indispensable condition

When an agreement stands or falls on the inclusion of a particular condition, that condition may be called a *conditio sine qua non*, literally "a condition without which not." (See CAUSA SINE QUA NON.)

confer
KAWN-fehr
compare

The abbreviation of *confer*, cf., is seen in English most often in scholarly writing. The abbreviation may be used, for example, to invite readers to compare an author's discussion with that presented in another work, but the important fact to bear in mind is that *cf.* does not mean merely "see" or "see also." The full Latin word *confer* is never seen in modern texts.

confiteor
kawn-FIH-tay-awr
I confess

The opening word of the Catholic general confession said at the beginning of the mass.

Congregatio de Propaganda Fide
kawn-greh-GAH-tee-oh day praw-pah-GAHN-dah
FIH-deh
Congregation for the Propagation of the Faith

The committee that supervises messages and missions for the Vatican. The committee members are cardinals and other church officials.

coniunctis (or conjunctis) viribus
kawn-YUUNK-tees WEE-rih-buus
with united powers

Anyone acting in concert with others can be said to be acting *conjunctis viribus* toward a common goal. "The Allied Powers pledged to act *conjunctis viribus* when an attack was directed at any of the several nations."

consensus
kawn-SEN-suus
agreement

This word, taken into English with the same meaning as its Latin ancestor, bedevils poor spellers of English, who fail to associate *consensus* with the English word "consent." Thus, we often see the misspelling "concensus," reflecting a confusion with the word "census." The Latin word **census** (KEN-suus) has a meaning somewhat like that of our English "census": The Romans registered all citizens and their property for purposes of taxation, calling the registration a *census*. "Consent," as one already knows, has little to do with taxation. The word "consent" derives from **consentire** (kawn-sen-TIH-reh), "to agree," whose past participle is *consensus*. While it is primarily to help poor spellers that *consensus* is given its own entry here, *consensus*, as soon will be seen, is central—forgive me—to several useful Latin expressions.

consensus audacium

kawn-SEN-suus ow-DAH-kee-uum

a conspiracy

Cicero used this phrase, literally "agreement of rash (men)," to describe conspiracies by people intent on some nefarious purpose. In his time, Cicero acted as self-appointed watchdog of men in government and frequently held forth in the Senate to accuse his political enemies of conspiracy.

consensus facit legem

kawn-SEN-suus FAH-kit LAY-gem

consent makes law

The principle that an agreement between two parties is binding if the agreement does not in any way violate existing law.

consensus gentium

kawn-SEN-suus GEN-tee-uum

widespread agreement

This phrase, literally "unanimity of the nations," is used to describe perfect or nearly perfect agreement on some matter by everyone concerned. So a generally accepted belief or opinion may be described as a *consensus gentium*.

consensus omnium

kawn-SEN-suus AW-mnee-uum

agreement of all

A happy situation, in which all parties involved in a discussion of policy, procedure, or the like have reached unanimity. Another form of this phrase is **consensu** (kawn-SEN-soo) **omnium**, with the meaning "by general consent." "We acted *consensu omnium* in all decisions affecting our members' welfare." Tacitus, in his *Annales*, made telling use of *consensu omnium* in describing an inept politician: **Omnium consensu capax imperii nisi imperasset** (KAH-pahks im-PEH-ree-ee NIH-sih im-peh-RAHS-set), "By general consent, he would have been considered capable of governing if he had never governed." A classic putdown.

consilio manuque
kawn-SIH-lee-oh mah-NOO-kweh
by stratagem and manual labor

The motto of Figaro in Beaumarchais's *Barber of Seville*. Figaro was a barber who used wit and resourcefulness in struggling against the abuses of government. *Consilio manuque* could well serve also as the motto of the unfortunate intellectual who must make his living by practicing a trade because he cannot find employment more suitable for his true talent and education.

consule Planco
KAWN-suu-leh PLAHN-koh
in the good old days

The literal translation of this phrase is "in the consulship of Plancus." Two consuls held office in Rome at any time. Their term of office under the republic was one year, but under the empire the term was reduced to a few months. Romans often referred to past years by the names of the consuls who then held office. Thus, Horace in his *Odes* referred to the carefree days of his youth as *consule Planco*. Plancus was consul in 42 B.C., when Horace was twenty-three and serving on the wrong side —under Brutus—at Philippi, where Augustus and Antony defeated Brutus and Cassius. Horace returned to Italy after the defeat to find that his family's property had been confiscated, his own prospects diminished. The phrase *consule Planco* has survived in the sense of "in the good old days." Since, justifiably or not, most people look back upon their early years as good times, Horace has given us a handy alternative for lectures to

our juniors that begin too often with "When I was young.
. . ." Nonetheless, recalling the experience of Plancus, we must
recognize the irony in *consule Planco*. The good old days too
often are good only in retrospect.

consummatum est
kawn-suum-MAH-tuum est
it is completed

Christ's last words on the cross, John 19:30.

contra bonos mores
KAWN-trah BAW-nohs MOH-rays
against the best interests of society

This phrase, literally "contrary to good morals," is used in law
to describe an action or a contract considered harmful to the
moral welfare of society. Thus, a contract to commit a crime, for
example, is a contract *contra bonos mores* and therefore legally
void. Lawyers pronounce the phrase KAHN-trə BOH-nohs
MOH-reez. (See PRO BONO PUBLICO, a happier legal phrase.)

contraria contrariis curantur
kawn-TRAH-ree-ah kawn-TRAH-ree-ees
koo-RAHN-tuur
opposites are cured by opposites

The principle of allopathic medicine, the traditional form of
medicine, which seeks to fight disease by using remedies—an-
tibiotics are a good example—that produce effects totally different from the effects produced by the disease under treatment.
This principle is the direct opposite of that of homeopathic
medicine. (See SIMILIA SIMILIBUS CURANTUR.)

coram iudice (or judice)
KOH-rahm YOO-dih-keh
before a judge who has jurisdiction

This phrase, literally "in the presence of a judge," is used by lawyers to describe a hearing before a court that has the authority to act in the case. Lawyers pronounce *coram judice* (their preferred spelling) KOH-ram JOO-di-see.

coram nobis
KOH-rahm NOH-bees
before us

The legal phrase *coram nobis* denotes a writ intended to correct an injury caused by a mistake of the court. The phrase originated in English law, thus explaining the royal plural *nobis*. Lawyers pronounce *coram nobis* KOH-ram NOH-bis.

coram non iudice (or judice)
KOH-rahm nohn YOO-dih-keh
before a judge who does not have jurisdiction

This phrase, literally "in the presence of one not a judge," is used by lawyers to describe a hearing before a court that lacks authority or competence to rule in the matter. (See CORAM IUDICE.)

coram populo
KOH-rahm PAW-puu-loh
in public

This phrase, literally "in the presence of the people," was used by Horace in his *Ars Poetica*, in suggesting that a dramatist, in deference to sensibilities of audiences, should not depict murder on stage.

cornu copiae
KAWR-noo KOH-pee-ī
horn of plenty

Cornu copiae is also written in Latin as **cornucopia** (kawr-noo-KOH-pee-ah). The legend of Amalthea, the nymph who nursed Zeus when he was an infant, has it that she fed the young god with goat's milk. (Another version of the story has it that Amalthea was a goat that suckled the young Zeus.) Zeus endowed the horn of the goat with the capability of producing whatever the owner of the horn desired. Since Amalthea was the possessor of this *cornu copiae*, she could get from it whatever she wanted. Even today, the cornucopia is the symbol of abundance.

corpus delicti
KAWR-puus day-LIK-tee
the terrible evidence that a crime has been committed

The *corpus delicti*, literally "the body of the crime," is the fact or set of facts needed to establish that a crime has been committed. In murder, for example, it is proof that a person has been murdered. When we hear this phrase in old Hollywood detective movies, the district attorney is usually the character who complains to the chief of police that there is no *corpus delicti*, pronouncing it KOR-pəs də-LIK-tī, of course, and therefore there can be no prosecution of the heavy we all suspect. The audience squirms at the familiar complaint, believing the D.A. means the police cannot find the body of the victim. The confusion is with the English word "corpse," but what is really meant is that the district attorney cannot prove that a crime has been committed, even though a hacked-up corpse might be a good beginning. If the crime in question is arson, to take another example, the *corpus delicti* may be proof of arson, not merely a burned-out building; if the crime is burglary, evidence that a safe has been rifled, rather than merely an empty safe.

corpus iuris (or **juris**)
KAWR-puus YOO-ris
body of law

The collected laws of a nation, state, or city are its *corpus iuris*. Church law is **corpus iuris canonici** (kah-NOH-nih-kee), and civil law is **corpus iuris civilis** (KEE-wee-lis).

corrigenda
kawr-rih-GEN-dah
items to be corrected

The singular form, **corrigendum**, literally "that which is to be corrected," is ample evidence of the frailty of human beings: Because it is a singular form, it is almost never used. By contrast, the plural, *corrigenda*, is frequently found in manuscripts as well as in published books and journals. *Corrigenda* in its modern meaning calls attention to corrections that must be made here and there throughout a work before it is published (or republished).

Cras amet qui nunquam amavit;
Quique amavit, cras amet.
krahs AH-met kwee NUUN-kwahm ah-MAH-wit
KWEE-kweh ah-MAH-wit, krahs AH-met
May he love tomorrow who never has loved before;
And may he who has loved, love tomorrow as well.

This couplet forms the refrain of the *Pervigilium Veneris* (per-wih-GIH-lee-uum WEH-neh-ris), "The Night Watch of Love," written by an anonymous poet who obviously believed in love: yesterday, today, and tomorrow, as well as every day before and after. Samuel Butler, in *The Way of All Flesh*, expressed the same confidence in the desirability of love: " 'Tis better to have loved and lost than never to have loved at all."

credo quia absurdum est

KRAY-doh KWEE-ah ahb-SUUR-duum est

I believe it because it is unreasonable

A justification of faith on the basis that there is no need to understand: It is the essence of faith not to seek a rational explanation in matters spiritual. This profound statement of belief is also given as **credo quia impossibile** (im-paw-SIH-bih-leh) **est**, "I believe it because it is impossible."

crescite et multiplicamini

KREH-skih-teh et muul-tih-plih-KAH-mih-nee

increase and multiply

Motto of Maryland.

crescit eundo

KRAY-skit ay-UUN-doh

it grows as it goes

Motto of New Mexico.

cui bono?

KOO-ee BOH-noh

who stands to gain?

This expression, attributed by Cicero to a Roman judge and literally meaning "to whom for a benefit?" is mistakenly taken to mean "what good will it do?" Rather, it must be understood to be the question raised by anyone wise in the ways of the world: A new bridge is proposed for which there is no apparent need. Which contractor wants to make a fat profit from the project? A new weapon program is said to be essential to our national defense. Whose turn is it now in the military-industrial cost-overrun labyrinth? Both questions may be replaced by *cui bono?*

cuius regio eius religio
KOO-yuus RAY-gee-oh EH-yuus reh-LIH-gee-oh
the ruler of a territory chooses its religion

Historically, the religion practiced by the ruler of a region determined the religion practiced by his or her subjects. Today, *cuius regio eius religio*, literally "whose the region, his the religion," may be used in a broader sense. For example, the white shirt, striped tie, and vested dark suit dictated for male employees of certain corporations; the spectacle of football players, under compulsion, bowing their heads in prayer before a game (and then being told to "get out there and hit them hard").

cum grano salis
kuum GRAH-noh SAH-lis
with a grain of salt

One of the most familiar Latin expressions. When one does not fully believe something or someone, *cum grano salis* implies a certain caution or reserve. Salt was a valuable commodity in the ancient world, so a grain of salt is not be taken as a trivial matter. It is worth noting that the English word "salary" derives ultimately from the Latin: **Salarium** (sah-LAH-ree-uum) was the money allotted to Roman soldiers for purchase of salt, hence, their pay.

cum laude
kuum LOW-deh
with praise

A university degree awarded *cum laude* is the third rank of honors, **magna** (MAHG-nah) **cum laude**, "with great praise," is second in rank, while **summa** (SUUM-mah) **cum laude**, "with greatest praise," is the top rank. A student who has staggered through to a degree with barely passing grades is said jocularly to be graduated **summa cum difficultate** (dih-fih-kuul-TAH-teh), "with greatest difficulty."

cum privilegio
kuum pree-wih-LAY-gee-oh
with privilege

An authorized or licensed edition of a book is an edition *cum privilegio* or an **editio** (eh-DIH-tee-oh, "edition") **cum privilegio**.

cum tacent clamant
kuum TAH-kent KLAH-mahnt
silence is an admission of guilt

This expression, literally "when they remain silent they cry out," is from the first of Cicero's orations against Catiline, one of Cicero's political opponents. Despite the tradition of Western justice that a person accused of crime is not required to give evidence against himself, the popular view is that silence is an admission of guilt. Thus, *cum tacent clamant* is a powerful argument outside a court of law (and sometimes inside a jury room).

curae leves loquuntur ingentes stupent
KOO-rī LEH-ways loh-KWUUN-tuur in-GEN-tays STUU-pent
minor losses can be talked away, profound ones strike us dumb

This maxim of Seneca's, from his play *Phaedra*, is more literally translated as "slight griefs talk, great ones are speechless." Seneca's observation may be tested at a wake, when conversation of the most inane sort occupies many of the people present, yet others speak not at all.

currente calamo
kuu-REN-teh KAH-lah-moh
with pen running on

Anything written without care or forethought can be described as having been written *currente calamo*: A writer who never stops to reflect need not take his pen from the page.

curriculum vitae
kuu-RIH-kuu-luum WEE-tī
a résumé

An academic who is asked to submit a written account of his qualifications usually compiles his *curriculum vitae*, literally "the course of (one's) life." Using the Latin expression instead of the mundane, albeit once-glamorous, word *résumé*, a French adoption, avoids association with the world of commerce. Because *curriculum vitae* is a mouthful, it is often referred to as a **c.v.** or as a **vita**, and the latter is pronounced VĪT-ə (in Latin WEE-tah).

custos morum
KUUS-tohs MOH-ruum
a censor

Custos means "guardian" or "watchman." Thus, a **custos incorruptissimus** (in-kaw-ruup-TIHS-sih-muus) is "a young man's guardian," since such a person can be trusted never to stray in any way; he is superlatively incorruptible. **Mores** (MOH-rays) means "morals," so *custos morum* is "the guardian of morals" and a Latin term for "censor."

dabit deus his quoque finem
DAH-bit DAY-uus hees KWAH-kweh FEE-nem
God will grant an end even to these (troubles)

This saying from Virgil's *Aeneid* counsels hope, even in the darkest hour. (For a similarly optimistic observation from Virgil, see FORSAN ET HAEC OLIM MEMINISSE IUVABIT.)

dabit qui dedit
DAH-bit kwee DEH-dit
he who has given will give

A suitable maxim for the professional fund-raiser: Those who once have contributed to a worthwhile cause can be counted upon to reach down deep again. It is for this reason that those of us who give even once to charity—or who buy once by mail order—soon find ourselves inundated with requests that we do so once again and again and again.

damnant quod non intelligunt
DAHM-nahnt kwawd nohn in-TEHL-lih-guunt
they condemn what they do not understand

The perennial cry of the obscure poet or struggling avant-gardist.

damnum absque iniuria (or injuria)
DAHM-nuum AHBS-kweh ihn-YOO-ree-ah
sorry, no basis for a lawsuit

This legal term, literally "loss without harm," refers to loss of property or violation of a right without possibility of legal redress. Not exactly the sort of thing on which attorneys thrive.

de asini umbra disceptare
day AH-sih-nee UUM-brah dih-skeh-PTAH-reh
"little things affect little minds"

This Latin phrase, freely rendered above in a line quoted from Disraeli's novel *Sybil*, may be translated literally as "to argue about the shadow of an ass." The phrase finds ready use in derogating the work of a lesser scholar who spends a lifetime explicating the unimportant, as well as in hushing the disputatious bore ever ready to quibble over the trivial.

de bono et malo
day BAW-noh et MAH-loh
come what may

The literal translation of this phrase is "of good and bad." When one has decided to forge ahead come what may, for better or for worse, the decision is made *de bono et malo*.

deceptio visus
day-KEH-ptee-oh WEE-soos
an optical illusion

Literally "a deception of vision."

de die in diem
day DEE-ay in DEE-em
continuously

Literally "from day to day," and also given as **diem ex die** (DEE-em eks DEE-ay), with the same meaning. "Those of us who are happily employed work *de die in diem*, never looking up from our work until we finish the task in hand." An apt rendering of either of the Latin phrases would be "day in, day out."

de duobus malis, minus est semper eligendum
deh doo-OH-buus MAH-lees MIH-nuus est SEM-pehr eh-lih-GEN-duum
choose the lesser of two evils

Recognizing the realities facing those who must often choose between less than perfect alternatives, Thomas à Kempis, the fifteenth-century theologian, adjures us in this Latin phrase to make the best of a bad situation, saying literally, "of two evils, the lesser is always to be chosen."

de facto
day FAH-ktoh
in reality

This common expression, pronounced di FAK-toh in English, is literally translated as "from the fact." It differentiates that which exists in fact (*de facto*) from that which exists legally (*de iure* or *de jure*, day YOO-reh). Thus, *de facto* rulers, in contrast with *de iure* rulers, are calling the signals even though no legal process has been employed in establishing their power. Again, *de facto* segregation may reflect custom or practice, rather than the law of the land, yet segregation it is.

de gustibus non est disputandum
day GUU-stih-buus nohn est dih-spuu-TAHN-duum
there's no accounting for tastes

This widely used expression, literally "about tastes there is no disputing," wisely tells us that taste is a personal matter. Since no amount of persuasion can succeed in changing a person's taste—and rightfully so—it is better not to argue about matters of personal preference. In time, a person's taste may change, but not because of anything others may say. This saying is sometimes given as **de gustibus et coloribus** (et kaw-LOH-rih-buus, "and colors") **non disputandum**, more often merely as *de gustibus*, "concerning tastes."

Dei gratia
DAY-ee GRAH-tee-ah
by the grace of God

Found in such expressions as **Regina** (ray-GEE-nah) **Dei Gratia**, "Queen by the Grace of God," and **Imperator** (im-peh-RÁH-tawr) **Dei Gratia**, "Emperor by the Grace of God." The implication is that anyone functioning *Dei gratia* has direct access to the Divinity.

de integro
day IN-teh-groh
anew

Anything that commences with the past obliterated from memory begins *de integro*. (See DE NOVO.)

de iure (or de jure)
day YOO-reh
sanctioned by law

See DE FACTO.

delenda est Carthago
day-LEN-dah est kahr-TAH-goh
Carthage must be destroyed

The story behind this phrase is well worth recounting. For two centuries or so, Carthage was the only real rival to Rome in the western Mediterranean. In fact, until the two superpowers came into conflict in Sicily in 264 B.C.—war broke out because Rome feared Carthaginian expansionism in southern Italy —Carthage had been the dominant power. Rome prevailed in the First Punic War (264–261), but the peace terms left Carthage still strong enough to threaten Rome. Sure enough, there was a Second Punic War (218–201). This time, Hannibal's brilliant strategy nearly destroyed Rome, but Scipio Africanus, the Roman general, defeated Hannibal—perhaps at Zama, an ancient town in present-day Tunisia—in the decisive battle of that war, and Carthage was no longer a power to reckon with. Half a century later, when Carthage still was not a threat to Rome, war broke out once again, in part because of the influence of Cato the Elder, who repeatedly egged the Roman Senate on with his ominous phrase *delenda est Carthago*: "Carthage must be destroyed." Since Carthage was not a match for Rome's military power, the outcome of this Third Punic War (149–146) was predictable: Soon enough the Carthaginians, led to believe they would be given generous peace terms, were tricked into surrendering. But once peace prevailed, the great city of Carthage was destroyed by the Romans, and a century was to pass before Carthage was resettled and became a prosperous city once more. Cato's *delenda est Carthago* survives as an ironic reminder that a ruling clique in a powerful nation can have its way in crushing a helpless rival if it musters the rhetoric to stir irrational passions.

delineavit
day-lee-nay-AH-wit
he (or she) drew (this)

An indication, along with the artist's name, of the creator of a painting, drawing, or sculpture: *delineavit Publius* or *del. Publius*, "drawn by Publius."

delirium tremens
day-LEE-ree-uum TREH-mens
the d.t.'s

Literally "trembling delirium," *delirium tremens* is the mental disorder associated with overindulgence in drinking. The afflicted person characteristically trembles excessively and hallucinates. *Delirium tremens* is commonly given the English pronunciation də-LIR-ee-əm TREE-mənz.

de minimis non curat praetor
day MĪH-nih-mees nohn KOO-raht PRĪ-tawr
don't bother me with petty matters

The literal translation of this expression is "a praetor does not occupy himself with petty matters." A praetor—the English word is pronounced PREET-ər—in ancient Rome was a magis-

trate who assisted the consuls by administering justice and commanding armies. In Caesar's time, there were sixteen **praetores**
(prī-TOH-rays). Since a praetor was a busy man, we can appreciate his insistence on saving his time for important matters.
Today, anyone wanting to suggest that he or she is above small
matters may use this phrase, inevitably with the intention of
impressing others with the importance of the concerns that
normally occupy an important person's time. A related expression is the legal precept **de minimis non curat lex** (leks), "the law
does not concern itself with trifles," which is used to justify
refusal by a court, particularly an appellate court, to hear a suit,
on the basis that a court's time must not be taken up with
matters of small import. This phrase, often abbreviated *de minimis*, explains why income tax payments that are a few dollars
short of what they should be are sometimes accepted without
complaint.

de mortuis nihil nisi bonum
day MAWR-too-ees NIH-hil NIH-sih BAW-nuum
speak kindly of the dead

Tradition has it that Chilon of Sparta, one of the wise men of
sixth-century B.C. Greece, is the author of this saying, literally
"of the dead, (say) nothing but good." (Of course, Chilon used
Greek rather than Latin, so what we have here is the Latin
translation.) The advice to all of us that one should speak well
of the recently dead or remain silent is at least as old as Homer.
Nihil, "nothing," is also given as a contraction, nil (neel).

de nihilo nihil
day NIH-hih-loh NIH-hil·
nothing comes from nothing

Persius, the first-century A.D. Roman poet, advises us in his
Satires that effort is required to produce anything of value.
He goes on to tell us that anything once produced cannot be-
come nothing again: **in nihilum nil posse reverti** (in NIH-

hih-luum neel PAW-seh reh-WEHR-tee). Persius is believed to have been parodying Lucretius (first century B.C.), who propounded the physical theories of Epicurus (fourth century B.C.). As a cynical comment, *de nihilo nihil* can be distorted to denigrate a failed work as the product of a person of little talent. The implication is, "How can we expect better from such a source?"

de novo
day NAW-woh
anew

Like DE INTEGRO, *de novo* is an expression used in describing a fresh start. "Let's forget the past and begin *de novo*."

Deo favente
DAY-oh fah-WEN-teh
with God's favor

An expression used to invoke God's cooperation in ensuring success for an action about to begin or to express gratitude for the success of an activity completed successfully. "*Deo favente*, I will pass my examination." "I have always been able to make a good living, *Deo favente*."

Deo gratias
DAY-oh GRAH-tee-ahs
thanks to God

When an enterprise has turned out well, one may say *Deo gratias* or DEO FAVENTE. *Deo gratias* appears frequently in Latin prayers, but it is also used jocularly. "As the curtain came down on the opera after five long hours, some were shouting *bravo* while others were muttering *Deo gratias*."

Deo iuvante (or **Deo juvante**)
DAY-oh yoo-WAHN-teh
with God's help

This expression, also given as **Deo adiuvante** or **Deo adjuvante** (ahd-yoo-WAHN-teh), has the same intent and is used in the same manner as DEO FAVENTE.

de omni re scibili et quibusdam aliis
day AWM-nee ray SKIH-bih-lee et KWIH-buus-dahm AH-lee-ees
I know everything worth knowing, and more

De omni re scibili, literally "of all the things one can know," was the pretentious title of a work by a fifteenth-century Italian scholar, Pico della Mirandola, who prided himself on being able to debate with anyone on any subject. In derision, someone (perhaps Voltaire) added to it *et quibusdam aliis*, literally "and even of several other things." The result is an elegant phrase one can use to puncture the pomposity of a self-proclaimed expert on everything under the sun.

Deo optimo maximo
DAY-oh AW-ptih-moh MAH-ksih-moh
to God, the best, the greatest

Once a favorite dedication (abbreviated **D.O.M.**) for a work of art. (See DOMINO OPTIMO MAXIMO.)

Deo volente
DAY-oh waw-LEN-teh
God willing

Yet another expression (abbreviated **D.V.**) used to enlist the aid of the deity when initiating an enterprise or looking forward to the future. "*Deo volente*, we will all be here next year to celebrate our fifty-first anniversary."

de pilo pendet
day PIH-loh PEN-det
we've reached the critical stage

This expression, literally "it hangs by a hair," is used to describe the tense moment when a sickness, a sports event, a military action, or the like appears to be in the lap of the gods. *De pilo pendet* derives from the situation in which Damocles found himself: Dionysius I, the tyrant of Syracuse, in order to demonstrate that the life of a ruler was no bed of roses, had Damocles, a fawning member of the court, seated at a royal banquet with a sword suspended over his head by a single hair. We recall Damocles in the phrase "sword of Damocles," with the meaning "an impending disaster," and our word "impending" has its origin in **pendere** (PEN-deh-reh), the Latin word for "hang."

de profundis
day praw-FUUN-dees
out of the depths (of despair)

A cry of deepest anguish, from the opening words of Psalm 130: "Out of the depths have I cried unto thee, O Lord." This psalm is often read in the Catholic burial service, but *de profundis* has other associations: Oscar Wilde, after being imprisoned in 1895 for homosexual practices, wrote an essay called "De Profundis," which was published posthumously.

de proprio motu
day PRAW-pree-oh MOH-too
spontaneously

Literally "of one's (or its) own motion." "Everything happened *de proprio motu* from then on; we played no further part in shaping events."

De Rerum Natura
day REH-ruum nah-TOO-rah
On the Nature of Things

A philosophic poem by Lucretius, first century B.C., outlining a science of the universe based on the philosophies of Democritus and Epicurus, and attempting to prove that all things in nature operate without reliance on the supernatural.

desipere in loco
day-SIH-peh-reh in LAW-koh
to play the fool on occasion

Horace, in his *Odes*, wrote **dulce est** (DUUL-keh est) **desipere in loco**, literally "sweet it is (*dulce est*) to relax at the proper time." Students who complete their examinations successfully and writers who finish a book on schedule, for example, know how to shuck off their dignity and enjoy themselves fully, knowing their work is done. The rest of us, who spend our time in idleness when faced with pressing obligations, never know the restorative value of that great delight, earned leisure.

deus ex machina
DAY-uus eks MAH-kih-nah
an unlikely and providential intervention

Deus ex machina, literally "a god out of a machine," describes an unexpected occurrence that rescues someone or something from an apparently hopeless predicament: An impoverished widow about to be evicted receives a legacy from a long-lost aunt or wins first prize in a million-dollar lottery. This is the stuff that bad fiction or drama is made of, so it is no surprise that *deus ex machina* is usually applied to narrative works, especially to the work of playwrights and novelists who find themselves enmeshed in complexities of their own devising and incapable of bringing their plots to a close without relying on improbable coincidence. Thus, when the U.S. Cavalry—in vintage Hollywood style—comes over the hill just as the long-lost brother of its commanding officer is about to be scalped, the writer has resorted to *deus ex machina*. The expression has its origin in ancient Greek theater, especially in certain plays of Euripides. When the complexities of plot and character appeared incapable of resolution, a god was set down on stage by a mechanical crane to sort out things and make them right. Greek gods could do anything.

Deus Misereatur
DAY-uus mih-seh-ray-AH-tuur
May God Have Mercy

The title of Psalm 67, which begins *Deus misereatur* and continues (in English) "and bless us, and cause His countenance to shine upon us."

Deus vobiscum
DAY-uus woh-BEES-kuum
God be with you

An appropriate saying, literally "God with you," to use when taking one's leave. The singular form is **Deus tecum** (TAY-kuum).

Deus vult
DAY-uus wuult
God wills it

Battle cry of the First Crusade, in the final years of the eleventh century, which resulted in recovery of the Holy Land from the Muslims: The people who had gathered to hear an address by Pope Urban II at the Council of Clermont in 1095 responded *Deus vult*. Since most armies normally proceed on the basis that God favors them or orders them to fight, it is not surprising that the Crusaders used *Deus vult* as a battle cry. The motto of the German armies during the two great wars of the twentieth century was *Gott Mitt Uns*, "God (is) with us."

diem ex die
DEE-em eks DEE-ay
continuously

See DE DIE IN DIEM.

diem perdidi
DEE-em PEHR-dih-dee
another day wasted

Titus, emperor of Rome, having passed an entire day without performing a good deed, is reported to have said, *Diem perdidi*, literally "I have lost a day." Anyone who has a job to do that requires sustained effort in order to meet a tight deadline may use the phrase to express despair at the end of an unproductive day, another day down the tube.

dies faustus
DEE-ays FOW-stuus
an auspicious day

The Romans paid a great deal of attention to omens. For example, a Roman who saw a meteor or a flight of birds would look upon the display as an indication of a ***dies faustus***, literally "a day bringing good fortune." (***Faustus*** is the perfect passive participle of **faveo** (FAH-weh-oh), "favor.") **Dies infaustus** (in-FOW-stuus) has the opposite meaning.

Dies Irae
DEE-ays EE-rī
Day of Wrath

A thirteenth-century Latin hymn on the Day of Judgment, sung at the requiem mass.

dii penates
DEE-ee peh-NAH-tays
guardians of the household

Dii penates were the household gods of the ancient Romans, a people given to a plethora of gods. *Dii*, the plural of **deus** (DAY-uus), "god," is also written **dei** (DAY-ee) and **di** (dee). *Penates* alone also means "household gods." However expressed, the intention is clear: Roman families and their homes were looked after by special deities. (See LARES ET PENATES.)

dirigo
DEE-rih-goh
I direct

Motto of Maine, there pronounced də-REE-goh, and also translated as "I guide" or "I lead the way." The implication is that God directs, despite the popular wisdom that New Englanders—witness "As Maine goes, so goes the nation"—take direction from no one but themselves.

dis aliter visum
dees AH-lih-tehr WEE-suum
man proposes, God disposes

A literal translation for Virgil's *dis aliter visum*, in the *Aeneid*, is "it seemed otherwise to the gods." An appropriate expression for rationalizing a failed effort.

disiecta (or disjecta) membra
dih-SYEH-ktah MEM-brah
fragments

A phrase, literally "scattered limbs," used to describe brief quotations from literary works. Horace wrote of **disiecti** (dih-SYEH-ktee) **membra poetae** (poh-AY-tī), "limbs of a dismembered poet," suggesting that one can perceive the quality of good poets even in brief quotations from their works.

disputandi pruritus ecclesiarum scabies
dih-spuu-TAHN-dee proo-REE-tuus
ek-KLAY-see-AH-ruum SKAH-bee-ays
the theologian's urge to debate is an incurable disease

Sir Henry Wotton, 1568–1639, an English poet and diplomat, wrote this sentence, literally "an itch for disputation is the mange of the churches," in *A Panegyric to King Charles*, and it was later used as part of Wotton's own tombstone inscription. (Wotton is also recalled for his definition of an ambassador: "an honest man sent to lie abroad for the good of his country.")

ditat Deus
DEE-taht DAY-uus
God enriches

Motto of Arizona.

divide et impera
DEE-wih-deh et IHM-peh-rah
divide and rule

This ancient political maxim, adopted by Machiavelli, is also given as **divide ut regnes** (uut REH-gnays) and as **divide ut imperes** (IHM-peh-rays), all of which mean "divide in order to rule." One stratagem of a wily leader is to encourage his follow-ers to squabble continually among themselves, making it easy for him to have his own way.

divina natura dedit agros, ars humana aedificavit urbes
dih-WEE-nah nah-TOO-rah DEH-dit AH-grohs ahrs
hoo-MAH-nah ī-dih-fih-KAH-wit UUR-bays
God made the country, and man made the town

A maxim, literally "godlike nature gave us the fields, human skill built the cities," of Marcus Terentius Varro, first-century B.C. Roman scholar, in *De Re Rustica*.

Divinitatis Doctor
dee-wee-nih-TAH-tis DAWK-tawr
Doctor of Divinity

Abbreviated **D.D.** It is worth mentioning that the Latin word *doctor* means "teacher," not "physician."

dixi
DEE-ksee
that settles the matter

This word, literally "I have spoken," signals that "I will say no more on the matter, and no one else may speak further."

docendo discimus
daw-KEN-doh DIH-skih-muus
we learn by teaching

A maxim well understood by inspired teachers and leading to the advice **doce ut discas** (DAW-kay uut DIH-skahs), "teach in order to learn."

doctus cum libro
DAW-ktuus kuum LIH-broh
having book learning

This expression, literally "learned with a book," describes those of us who lack practical knowledge.

Domine, dirige nos
DAW-mih-neh DEE-rih-geh nohs
Lord, direct us

Motto of London.

Domino optimo maximo
DAW-mih-noh AW-ptih-moh MAH-ksih-moh
to the Lord God, supreme ruler of the world

This phrase, literally "to the Lord, best and greatest," is the motto of the Benedictine Order. It is included here for the edification of those who are fond of an after-dinner glass of Benedictine and brandy. On the label of a bottle of Benedictine, a liqueur originally made by monks of the Benedictine Order, appears **D.O.M.**, the abbreviation of *Domino optimo maximo*. (See DEO OPTIMO MAXIMO.)

Dominus illuminatio mea
DAW-mih-nuus ih-LOO-mih-NAH-tee-oh MAY-ah
the Lord is my light

Motto of Oxford University.

Dominus vobiscum
DAW-mih-nuus woh-BEES-kuum
God be with you

Another way to bid farewell. The singular form is **Dominus tecum** (TAY-kuum). (See DEUS VOBISCUM.)

donec eris felix, multos numerabis amicos
DAW-nek EH-ris FAY-liks MUUL-tohs
nuu-meh-RAH-bis ah-MEE-kohs
when you're successful, everyone wants to be your friend

This observation, literally "as long as you are fortunate, you will have many friends," from Ovid's *Tristia* reflects bitterly on human nature. It concludes with **tempora si fuerint nubila, solus eris** (TEM-paw-rah see FOO-eh-rint NOO-bih-lah SOH-luus EH-ris), literally "if clouds appear, you will be alone." Even in ancient Rome, there were fair-weather friends.

dramatis personae
DRAH-mah-tis per-SOH-nī
cast of characters

This familiar expression, literally "the persons of the drama," although primarily denoting the characters or actors in a play, can be taken also as the characters in a novel, poem, film, etc., as well as the participants in the events of everyday life. "The hostages and their captors constituted a familiar *dramatis personae*."

ducit amor patriae
DOO-kit AH-mawr PAH-tree-ī
love of country guides me

The motto of the patriot, literally "love of country guides." (See DULCE ET DECORUM . . .)

dulce est desipere in loco
DUUL-keh est day-SIH-peh-reh in LAW-koh
sweet it is to relax at the proper time

See DESIPERE IN LOCO.

dulce et decorum est pro patria mori
DUUL-keh et deh-KOH-ruum est proh PAH-tree-ah
MAW-ree
there's no greater honor than to die for one's country

We meet these words in Horace's *Odes*, literally "it is sweet
and fitting to die for the fatherland."

dum spiro spero
duum SPEE-roh SPEH-roh
while I breathe, I hope

A motto of South Carolina. (See ANIMIS OPIBUSQUE PARATI.)

dum tacent clamant
duum TAH-kent KLAH-mahnt
their silence speaks volumes

The literal meaning of this saying is "though they are silent
they cry aloud." Silence may have great significance, in certain
situations even constituting an admission of guilt.

dum vita est spes est
duum WEE-tah est SPAYS est
while there's life, there's hope

dum vivimus vivamus
duum WEE-wih-muus wee-WAH-muus
while we live, let us live

The motto of the Epicureans, followers of Epicurus, who taught that pleasure is the goal of morality, but defined a life of pleasure as one of honor, prudence, and justice—in short, advocating living one's life to make for tranquility of body and mind. These teachings were corrupted later—epicureanism today is equated with self-indulgence and luxurious tastes.

dura lex sed lex
DOO-rah leks sed leks
the law is hard, but it is the law

Just about the only thing one can say when trying to convince others to pay their income tax or to obey a law generally considered unfair or harsh.

dux femina facti
duuks FAY-mih-nah FAH-ktee
cherchez la femme

We have Virgil, in the *Aeneid*, to thank for this Latin phrase, literally "a woman was the leader in the deed." We must also bow in the direction of countless fictional detectives for their adoption of Dumas's advice, *cherchez la femme* if you want to get to the bottom of things.

ecce homo
EK-keh HAW-moh
behold the man

The Latin translation of the words Pontius Pilate (John 19) used in showing the people the bound Christ wearing the crown of thorns. *Ecce homo* is the title taken for many paintings depicting Christ in this condition.

ecce signum
EK-keh SIH-gnuum
look at the proof

This phrase, literally "behold the sign," adjures us to examine the evidence, the proof. In *Henry IV, Part I*, Falstaff boasts of his encounter with a small army of attackers bent on his destruction: "I am eight times thrust through the doublet, four through the hose; my buckler cut through and through; my sword hacked like a handsaw—*ecce signum!*"

e contrario
ay kawn-TRAH-ree-oh
on the contrary

editio cum notis variorum
ay-DIH-tee-oh kuum NOH-tees wah-ree-OH-ruum
an edition with the notes of various persons

An edition of a literary text, called in English a "variorum (va-ree-OHR-əm) edition," that offers variant readings of the text as well as notes and commentary by scholars. (See VARIORUM.)

editio princeps
ay-DIH-tee-oh PRIN-keps
first edition

Of ancient texts, the first printed edition.

editio vulgata
ay-DIH-tee-oh wuul-GAH-tah
common edition

See TERRA ES, TERRAM IBIS.

e.g.
for example

See EXEMPLI GRATIA.

eheu fugaces labuntur anni
eh-HEHOO fuu-GAH-kays lah-BUUN-tuur AHN-nee
alas, the fleeting years glide by

A sad line from Horace's *Odes*, reminding us—as though we need help in remembering—that Maxwell Anderson was on the money when he told us that our "days dwindle down to a precious few." *Eheu*, alas! (Turn quickly to CARPE DIEM.)

eiusdem (or **ejusdem**) **farinae**
ay-YUUS-dem fah-REE-nī
birds of a feather

This expression, literally "of the same flour," is used to characterize people of the same nature—"cut from the same cloth"—usually in a pejorative sense.

e libris
ay LIH-brees

See EX LIBRIS.

emeritus
ay-MEH-rih-tuus
having served his time

This word has its origins in Roman military tradition, with the meaning of "a soldier who has served his time honorably." In modern usage, it is applied to a university officer who is rewarded for faithful service with the rank, for example, of "emeritus professor." The designation, pronounced ə-MER-ə-təs in English, carries no formal obligation to the institution, but usually entitles the person so designated to continue to use the facilities of the institution and to attend ceremonies as an honored member of the academic community. Emeritus rank is the academic equivalent of the gold watch given to good old what's-his-name upon retirement. University women who retire from academic life may be given **emerita** (ay-MEH-rih-tah; in English, ə-MER-ə-tə) rank, although some institutions eschew this feminine form.

ense et aratro
EN-seh et ah-RAH-troh
serving in war and in peace

The motto, literally "with sword and plow," of the farmer who serves his country by putting down the plow, **aratrum** (ah-RAH-truum), in time of war to take up the sword, **ensis** (EN-sees), for his country. In time of peace, he returns to his farm to serve his country once again. The motto applies equally well to any civilians who leave their peacetime jobs to take up arms for their country. Isaiah looks forward to the time when "They shall beat their swords into plowshares, and their spears into pruning hooks; nation shall not lift up sword against nation, neither shall they learn war any more."

ense petit placidam sub libertate quietem
EN-seh PEH-tit PLAH-kih-dahm suub
lee-behr-TAH-teh kwee-AY-tem
by the sword she seeks peaceful quiet under liberty

Motto of Massachusetts, making the case for military preparedness for the sake of ensuring peace.

e pluribus unum
ay PLOO-rih-buus OO-nuum
one out of many

Motto of the United States of America, indicating that a single nation was made by uniting many states.

ergo
EHR-goh
therefore

errare humanum est
ehr-RAH-reh hoo-MAH-nuum est
to err is human

The recognition, also given as **errare est humanum**, that erasers are attached to pencils for good reason. Alexander Pope, in "An Essay on Criticism": "To err is human, to forgive, divine."

erratum
ehr-RAH-tuum
error

An error in printing or writing is given the dignified appellation *erratum*, plural **errata** (ehr-RAH-tah). An *errata* (English pronunciation e-RAHT-ə) is a list of such errors.

esse quam videri
ES-seh kwahm wih-DAY-ree
to be rather than seem

Motto of North Carolina.

est modus in rebus
est MAW-duus in RAY-buus
choose the middle ground

With these words from Horace's *Satires*, literally "there is a proper measure in things," we are advised against extremes.

esto perpetua
EH-stoh per-PEH-too-ah
may she live forever

Motto of Idaho. Said to be the dying words of Fra Paolo Sarpi (1552–1623), historian and philosopher, speaking of his native Venice.

et al.
abbreviation of **et alii, et aliae, et alia**

This abbreviation is used in writing to avoid a lengthy listing. **Et alii** (et AH-lee-ee) is masculine, so it is properly used in speech to mean "and other men" when preceded by the name of a male or to mean "and other people." **Et aliae** (AH-lee-ī) is feminine, so it is properly used in speech to mean "and other women." **Et alia** (AH-lee-ah) is neuter, so it is properly used in speech to mean "and other things." Educated persons do not pronounce the abbreviation *et al.* "And others" is said for *et al.*

et cetera
et KAY-teh-rah
and so on

This familiar phrase, pronounced et SET-ər-ə in English and used only when speaking of things, not people, literally means "and the rest." In speech, its abbreviation, **etc.**, is given the pronunciation of the full phrase.

et hoc genus omne
et hawk GEH-nuus AWM-neh
and all that sort

This expression, literally "and everything of the kind," is used to indicate others of a class of persons or things. It finds use as a pretentious substitute for *et cetera*.

etiam atque etiam
EH-tee-ahm AHT-kweh EH-tee-ahm
again and again

et nunc et semper
et nuunk et SEM-pehr
from now on

Literally "now and forever."

et sic de similibus
et seek day sih-MIH-lih-buus
and that goes for the others too

This phrase, literally "and so of similar (people or things)," is used to suggest that whatever has been said of one person or topic under discussion holds true for related matters as well. (See AB UNO DISCE OMNES.)

et tu, Brute
et too BROO-teh
so you're mixed up in this too

According to tradition, reflected in Shakespeare's *Julius Caesar*, the final words of Caesar, falling before the conspirators' knives: "*Et tu Brute!* (literally "You also Brutus") Then fall Caesar." The line, memorized by all schoolchildren, reflects Plutarch's account of the death of Caesar. Caesar resisted his attackers until he realized that Brutus, his trusted ally, had joined in the attack. Blessed with this provenance, *et tu Brute* has become the classic recognition of betrayal by a trusted friend.

et ux.
and wife

The lawyer's abbreviation for **et uxor** (et UUK-sawr): "John Smith *et ux.*" "And wife" is said for *et ux.*

ex aequo et bono
eks Ī-kwoh et BAW-noh
equitably

A principled person does everything *ex aequo et bono*, literally "according to what is just and good."

ex animo
eks AH-nih-moh
sincerely

A person who speaks from the bottom of his heart speaks *ex animo*, literally "from the heart."

ex cathedra
eks KAH-teh-drah
with authority

When a pope speaks *ex cathedra*, literally "from the chair," he is considered to speak infallibly, and the chair he speaks from is the papal throne. Thus, when experts speak authoritatively on matters in their fields of knowledge, we may say that they speak *ex cathedra* (in English, eks kə-THEE-drə) or that they have made *ex cathedra* statements. We may also apply *ex cathedra* ironically to dogmatic pronouncements by the pretentious self-proclaimed expert. It must be pointed out that before the *cathedra* was the pope's chair —indeed, before there were popes—it was the chair of a teacher.

excelsior
eks-KEHL-see-awr
ever upward

Literally "higher," *excelsior* is pronounced ek-SEL-see-ər in English and serves as the motto of the State of New York.

exceptio probat regulam
eks-KEH-ptee-oh PRAW-baht RAY-guu-lahm
the exception establishes the rule

This proverb, shortened from the legal maxim **exceptio probat regulam in casibus non exceptis** (in KAH-sih-buus nohn eks-KEH-ptees, "in the cases not excepted"), is mistakenly taken as "the exception proves the rule," leading the unwary to think that any self-respecting rule must have an exception. What is meant is that the existence of an exception to a rule provides an opportunity to test the validity of a rule: Finding an exception to a rule enables us to define the rule more precisely, confirming its applicability to those items truly covered by the rule.

excudit
eks-KOO-dit
made by

A printer or engraver's mark, literally "he (or she) struck (this)," used to identify the person who executed the work. The abbreviation for *excudit* is **excud**.

exeat
EKS-ay-aht
permission to be absent

An *exeat*, literally "let him (or her) go forth," is an official permission granted to a priest to leave a diocese or monastery. In British universities, an *exeat* is permission granted for temporary absence from a college.

exegi monumentum aere perennius
eks-AY-gee MAW-nuu-MEN-tuum AH-eh-reh
pehr-EHN-nee-uus
I have raised a monument more durable than bronze

Horace started his final ode with these words, suggesting that his *Odes* would bring him immortality. Only the likes of a Horace should apply this sentence to their own work.

exempli gratia
eks-EHM-plee GRAH-tee-ah
for instance

This expression, literally "for the sake of example," is always abbreviated **e.g.** in English. It is used correctly to introduce an example, incorrectly to mean "that is." (See ID EST.)

exeunt
EKS-ay-uunt
they leave the stage

We are accustomed to seeing *exeunt*, literally "they go out," as a stage direction in old plays, with the meaning "two or more actors leave the stage." When *exeunt* is followed by **omnes** (AWM-nays), the playwright is telling us that all the actors on stage at the time are to leave. The singular of *exeunt* is the familiar **exit** (EKS-it), a stage direction meaning "he (or she) leaves the stage."

exit

See EXEUNT.

exitus acta probat
EKS-ih-tuus AH-ktah PRAW-baht
the end justifies the means

Literally "the result validates the deeds." This proverb avers that any means—no matter how foul—may be used if the intended result is a good one. But take care.

ex libris
eks LIH-brees
from the library of

This familiar legend, also given as **e** (eh) **libris**, translated literally as "from the books," commonly appears on book plates. The phrase is followed by the owner's name.

ex mero motu
eks MEH-roh MOH-too
spontaneously

Literally "out of pure, simple impulse." "He insisted that no one had exerted pressure on him, that he acted *ex mero motu*."

ex more
eks MOH-reh
according to custom

ex nihilo nihil fit
eks NIH-hih-loh NIH-hihl fit
nothing comes from nothing

Lucretius, the first-century Roman poet, wrote in *De Rerum Natura* of the creation of the world: **Nil posse creari de nilo** (neel PAWS-seh kray-AH-ree day NEE-loh), "nothing can be created out of nothing," which is also rendered as *ex nihilo nihil fit*, suggesting that every effect must have a cause. Lucretius agreed with the fifth-century B.C. Greek philosophers who theorized that the world could not have been made from nothing. They thought it had been created from the accidental joining of atoms falling from space. The Latin **atomus** (AHT-awm-uus) means "atom" or—remember that this theory antedated quarks and mesons by more than two millennia—"that which is indivisible." But there is ambiguity in *ex nihilo nihil fit* and in its English translation. Thus, the Latin phrase is applied rather broadly today, and *ex nihilo nihil fit* may be used to suggest that a dull mind cannot be expected to produce great thoughts, anything worth doing requires hard work, you can't get bet blood from a stone, and the like. (See DE NIHILO NIHIL.)

ex officio
eks awf-FIH-kee-oh
by virtue of an office

Officers of an institution usually serve on many of its committees not because they have personal qualifications needed on the committees, but because they hold certain offices. Thus, the chief executive officer of a corporation usually is a member *ex officio* of all the important committees of the corporation. The phrase is so thoroughly part of the English language that it has an English pronunciation, eks ə-FISH-ee-oh.

ex parte
eks PAHR-teh
from one side only

A legal expression, literally "from a party," applied to a proceeding in which only one side of the case is presented, and the opposing side is absent. Naturally, there is the presumption of partisan testimony in an *ex parte* proceeding.

ex pede Herculem
eks PEH-deh HEHR-kuu-lem
from a sample we can judge the whole

This expression, literally "from the foot, a Hercules," means we can extrapolate accurately when we know a single pertinent fact. The phrase is an allusion to Pythagoras, the sixth-century B.C. Greek mathematician and philosopher, who calculated the height of Hercules by measuring and comparing the length of many Greek stadiums. Since Hercules' stadium at Olympia was longest by far, Pythagoras deduced that Hercules' foot was longer than the foot of lesser men (or gods). Knowing that a man's height is proportional to the length of his foot, Pythagoras was able to establish a credible height (the whole) for Hercules from the length of his foot (the sample). Inspector Maigret, Sherlock Holmes, Hercule Poirot, and Nero Wolfe may owe a great deal to Pythagoras. (See EX UNGUE LEONEM.)

experto credite
eks-PEHR-toh KRAY-dih-teh
trust me

In the absence of evidence to the contrary, we are adjured by Virgil, in the *Aeneid*, literally to "believe one who has experience." The fragility of this advice is implicit in its use: *Experto credite* is too often cited by the person who may understand little and have even less evidence to offer but has spent a long time practicing his trade. "That stock is a good buy, *experto credite*," said the broker.

ex post facto
eks pawst FAH-ktoh
from what is done afterward

We are all experts *ex post facto*, Monday morning quarterbacks who can always give the correct answers to all problems once we know how things have worked out. An *ex post facto* law, normally not permitted in United States constitutional law, is one that can be applied retroactively; even though such a law is passed after a particular case has been settled, it would be deemed applicable even to previously closed cases.

ex proprio motu
eks PRAW-pree-oh MOH-too
voluntarily

Anyone who acts entirely without encouragement or coercion does so *ex proprio motu*, literally "of one's own accord."

ex tempore
eks TEM-paw-reh
extemporaneously

Anyone speaking *ex tempore*, Cicero's phrase, with the meaning "without preparation," is winging it: "Two of the speakers were well prepared, but one surely spoke *ex tempore* and made a fool of himself." The phrase can also be used in the sense of "without premeditation."

extinctus amabitur idem
eks-TIN-ktuus ah-MAH-bih-tuur EE-dem
how quickly we forget

A marvelously insightful observation from the *Epistles* of Horace, with the literal meaning "the same man will be loved after he's dead." Horace understood how quickly a person's bad reputation is forgotten once he's safely underground, and we have ample evidence of the aptness of *extinctus amabitur idem* in the work of revisionist biographers and historians.

ex ungue leonem
eks UUN-gweh lay-OH-nem
from a sample we can judge the whole

Another way of saying that we can tell the whole from a single part, with the literal meaning "from a claw, the lion." (See EX PEDE HERCULEM.)

ex uno disce omnes
eks OO-noh DIH-skeh AWM-nays
from one example you may deduce the rest

This maxim, literally "from one, learn of all," advises us to generalize from one example, a precept that must be applied intelligently. *Ex uno disce omnes* may be useful for certain cases —if one oak leaf turns brown, they all will; if one quart of milk in a batch is sour, the entire batch will not be potable; if one war is hell, all wars will be hell—but if one child . . . others may not. . . . After all, S. I. Hayakawa long ago taught us that $rose_1$ is not $rose_2$ is not $rose_3$ despite Gertrude Stein's claim to the contrary, and we more recently identified the flaw in "if you've seen one ghetto, you've seen them all."

fabas indulcet fames
FAH-bahs in-DUUL-ket FAH-mays
hunger makes everything taste good

Literally "hunger sweetens beans," beans, of course, being the poor man's fare. *Fabas indulcet fames* is another way of saying *fames optimum condimentum*, "hunger is the best seasoning."

facile princeps
FAH-kih-leh PRIHN-keps
number one

A felicitous phrase, literally "easily first," used to designate the acknowledged leader in any field.

facilis descensus Averno
FAH-kih-lis deh-SKEHN-suus ah-WEHR-noh
the descent to hell is easy

Avernus (ah-WEHR-nuus), a lake in Campania, was considered by the Romans to be an entrance to hell. *Avernus*, literally "without a bird," is said to have been so named because poisonous vapors arose from it and were said to draw birds down into its waters, where they perished. Thus, *facilis descensus Averno*, a line from Virgil's *Aeneid*, cautions us that it is easy to fall, but once fallen, difficult to make one's way back up. Beware that first misstep!

facta non verba
FAH-ktah nohn WEHR-bah
actions speak louder than words

Facta non verba, literally "deeds, not words," holds that protestations of good intentions count for little: Action is what we need.

fama semper vivat
FAH-mah SEM-pehr WEE-waht
may his (or her) good name live forever

A useful expression when invoking the name of an illustrious or revered person. "This good woman, *fama semper vivat*, saw fit to remember us in a bequest that will help our cause for many years to come." (Notice the difference in the translation of *fama* in the next entry. In Latin, as in any other language, words acquire additional meanings through use.)

fama volat
FAH-mah WAW-laht
rumor travels fast

In the *Aeneid*, Virgil tells us that nothing travels faster than scandal: **Fama malum quo non aliud velocius ullum** (FAH-mah MAH-luum kwoh nohn AH-lee-uud way-LOH-kee-uus UUL-luum). *Fama volat*, another phrase from the *Aeneid*, provides a handier way to convey the same thought.

fames optimum condimentum
FAH-mays AW-ptih-muum kawn-dih-MEN-tuum
hunger is the best seasoning

See FABAS INDULCET FAMES.

Fata obstant
FAH-tah AWB-stahnt
the gods willed otherwise

The *Fata* were the three Roman goddesses of fate or destiny: Nona, Decuma, and Morta. Any human action that went amiss was blamed on the opposition of the *Fata*, "the Fates." So Virgil's phrase in the *Aeneid*, *Fata obstant*, literally "the Fates oppose," could be cited. Similarly, anything that concluded happily was ascribed to the cooperation of the Fata. Thus, the Romans had a foolproof device for refusing to take action or for turning down a request. *Fata obstant* beats "my hands were tied."

Fata viam invenient
FAH-tah WEE-ahm in-WEHN-ee-ent
the gods will find a way

Another saying (see the preceding entry) from Virgil's *Aeneid*, literally "the Fates will find a way," but this time an expression of optimism. Yet it is worth noting that the Romans here reveal once again their inclination to leave things in the laps of the gods. Modern man is more apt to say: "God helps those who help themselves." The Romans had more fun.

favete linguis
fah-WAY-teh LIHN-gwees
hold your tongue

This expression from Horace's *Odes*, with the literal meaning "favor with your tongues," is a warning to utter no words of bad omen during a religious rite: "Say nothing lest what you say hurt another or bring down on us an unfavorable act of the gods." The Latin for telling someone to keep silent under ordinary circumstances is **quin taces** (kween TAH-kays).

fecit
FAY-kit
made by

Fecit, literally "he or she made (it)," was an artist's way of signing a work. *Fecit* is followed by the artist's name. (See EXCUDIT.)

felicitas habet multos amicos
fay-LEE-kih-tahs HAH-bet MUUL-tohs ah-MEE-kohs
prosperity has many friends

When things are going well for us, we never lack for friends. When our fortunes turn . . .

felix qui nihil debet
FAY-liks kwee NIH-hil DAY-bet
happy is he who owes nothing

If this proverb is accurate, Americans are among the unhappiest people of all time.

felix qui potuit rerum cognoscere causas
FEH-liks kwee PAW-too-it REH-ruum
kaw-GNAW-skeh-reh KOW-sahs
fortunate is he who has been able to learn the causes of things

This line from Virgil's *Georgics* praises those of superior intelligence who can grasp the secrets of nature and so raise themselves above reliance on superstition.

festina lente
feh-STEE-nah LEN-tay
make haste slowly

Suetonius, in *Divus Augustus*, attributes this bit of wisdom to the emperor Augustus, who moved cautiously, step by step, to transform Rome from a republic to an empire ruled virtually by one man. Thus, what appears to be salutary advice worthy of our own Ben Franklin may have Machiavellian overtones.

fiat iustitia (or justitia) ruat caelum
FEE-aht YUUS-tih-tee-ah ROO-aht KĪ-luum
let justice be done though the heavens fall

The unyielding precept that the law must be followed precisely, regardless of the circumstances and eventualities.

fiat lux
FEE-aht luuks
let there be light

The Latin version of one of the opening verses of Genesis.

fiat voluntas Tua
FEE-aht waw-LUUN-tahs TOO-ah
Thy will be done

Familiar words from the Latin version of the Lord's Prayer, from Matthew.

fide et amore
FIH-deh et ah-MOH-reh
by faith and love

fide et fiducia
FIH-deh et fee-DOO-kee-ah
by faith and confidence

Fidei Defensor
fih-DAY-ee day-FEN-sawr
Defender of the Faith

Fidei Defensor, abbreviated **F.D.**, is one of the many titles of British monarchs. Henry VIII was the first to have this one.

fides Punica
FIH-days POO-nih-kah
a double cross

This expression, literally "Punic faith," refers to the Carthaginians—the Latin name **Punicus** (POO-nih-kuus) means "Phoenician," and it was the Phoenicians who founded Carthage. The Punic Wars resulted in the destruction of Carthage by the Romans. The distrust of the Carthaginians by the Romans exemplified in *fides Punica*—the Romans intended the same meaning when they spoke of **ars** (ahrs) **Punica**, "the Punic art"; **fraus** (frows) **Punica**, "Punic deceit"; and **perfidia** (pehr-FEE-dih-ah) **Punica**, "Punic treachery"—may be a world-class proof of the aptness of "it takes one to know one." (See DELENDA EST CARTHAGO for an illustration of the trustworthiness of Rome.)

fidus Achates
FEE-duus ah-KAH-tays
bosom pal

In the *Aeneid*, Virgil characterized Achates, companion of Aeneas, as *fidus Achates*, literally "faithful Achates," giving us a convenient Latin substitute for "best friend."

finem respice
FEE-nem REH-spih-keh
look to the end

Appropriate advice for anyone about to take an irreversible step or launch a risky venture.

finis coronat opus
FEE-nis kaw-ROH-naht AW-puus
the end crowns the work

Easily understood by anyone who has completed a major project and rejoiced in its completion.

floruit
FLOH-roo-it
he [she] flourished

Floruit, often abbreviated fl., is used to date the period of a person's prime, particularly when exact birth and death dates are unknown: "Somadeva (*fl.* 11th century) was a Sanskrit author."

fluctuat nec mergitur
FLUUK-too-aht nek MEHR-gih-tuur
unsinkable

Fluctuat nec mergitur, literally "it is tossed by the waves but does not sink," is the motto of Paris, which has a ship as its emblem. Like any other city that has existed for a long time, Paris has had its ups and downs. In ancient times, for example, Paris was called **Lutetia** (luu-TEH-tee-ah), from the Latin word lutum (LUU-tuum), meaning "mud," reflecting the fact that the City of Lights was then only an aggregation of mud hovels. Anyone for Paris in the spring?

fons et origo
fawns et aw-REE-goh
the source and origin

forsan et haec olim meminisse iuvabit

FAWR-sahn et hĭk OH-lim meh-mih-NIS-seh
yuu-WAH-bit

perhaps this will be a pleasure to look back on one day

Virgil, in the *Aeneid*, knowing that time cures all (see TEMPORIS ARS MEDICINA FERE EST), gives us this formula for surviving difficult times by looking ahead to what surely will be happier days.

fortes fortuna iuvat (or juvat)

FAWR-tays fawr-TOO-nah YUU-waht

fortune helps the brave

A proverb of Terence, in *Phormio*, given by others as **fortuna favet fortibus** (FAH-wet FAWR-tih-buus), "fortune favors the brave." We make our own luck.

fortiter in re, suaviter in modo

FAWR-tih-tehr in ray SWAH-wih-tehr in MAW-doh

resolutely in action, gently in manner

A characterization of the estimable person who does unhesitatingly what must be done, but accomplishes the deed as inoffensively as possible. An excellent motto for personnel managers.

fortuna favet fortibus

fawr-TOO-nah FAH-wet FAWR-tih-buus

fortune favors the brave

See FORTES FORTUNA IUVAT.

fronti nulla fides
FRAWN-tee NUUL-lah FIH-days
never judge a book by its cover

This advice from Juvenal's *Satires*, more literally "no reliance can be placed on appearance," warns us against hasty judgments of character made solely on what the eyes perceive.

fugaces labuntur anni
foo-GAH-kays lah-BUUN-tuur AHN-nee
you wake up one morning and find you are old

Literally "the fleeting years glide by." (See the next two entries and EHEU FUGACES LABUNTUR ANNI.)

fugit hora
FUU-git HOH-rah
time flies

Persius, a first-century A.D. Roman poet, used this expression, literally "the hour flies," to tell us that it's later than we think.

fugit irreparabile tempus
FUU-git ihr-reh-pah-RAH-bih-leh TEM-puus
we cannot stop time in its tracks

Tempus fugit, an expression we employ to mean "time flies" (in English pronounced TEM-pəs FYOO-jət), is taken from *fugit irreparabile tempus*—itself a slightly shortened form of a line from Virgil's *Georgics*—with the literal meaning "time irretrievably is flying." (See EHEU FUGACES LABUNTUR ANNI.)

fuit Ilium
FOO-it EE-lee-uum
Troy has had it

Virgil, declaring that Troy—called Ilium by the Romans—no longer existed, wrote *fuit Ilium*, literally "Troy has been," but better rendered as "Troy is no more." We now know a great deal about the riches of Troy, thanks to the work of Heinrich Schliemann, the gifted amateur archaeologist, so the lesson we learn from *fuit Ilium* is that if such a gem can fall, the rest of civilization—even IBM—had better watch out. What Virgil implied in *fuit Ilium* was "and now Rome is number one," that is, from a world destroyed a new world is created. But now that the Roman Empire is gone. . . .

furor
FUU-rawr
madness

This word concludes the entries for the sixth letter of the alphabet, but it is not to be taken as an indication that *furor* itself is of interest. Rather, *furor* combines with other Latin words to give us some useful phrases: **furor loquendi** (law-KWEN-dee), "a rage for speaking"; **furor poeticus** (poh-AY-tih-kuus), "poetic frenzy"; and **furor scribendi** (skree-BEN-dee), "a rage for writing."

gaudeamus igitur
gow-day-AH-muus IH-gih-tuur
let us therefore rejoice

The opening words of a student song of German origin, sung sometimes at academic exercises. Even without knowing what the words mean, anyone who looks back fondly at undergraduate life—proving that absence makes the heart grow fonder—will automatically choke up on hearing this song. After all, the words following are **iuvenes** (or **juvenes**) **dum sumus** (YUU-weh-nays duum SUU-muus), meaning "while we are young." (See EHEU FUGACES LABUNTUR ANNI for a bit of irony.) But to put college life in perspective, it is worthwhile to know that the English word "gaudeamus" (gaw-dee-AY-məs) means a revel by university students, who traditionally imbibe spirits and otherwise carouse to celebrate successful completion of their examinations. Those of us who are unfamiliar with the melody of *gaudeamus igitur* may hear it in the Brahms *Academic Festival Overture*.

genius loci
GEH-nee-uus LAW-kee
the guardian spirit of a place

The Romans believed that everybody born into this world was assigned a *genius*, a guardian spirit that accompanied that person from then on, determining the character and fortunes of the person until death—and beyond. The Romans also believed that every house and every institution had the same arrangement, a *genius loci*. The modern use of this term is intended to be taken as "the character of a place," for example, the *genius loci* (in English, JEEN-yəs LOH-sī) of one's alma mater.

genus irritabile vatum
GEH-nuus ihr-rih-TAH-bih-leh WAH-tuum
the irritable race of poets

Horace used this phrase in his *Epistles*, giving us a way to chide testy men of letters. The usual word for "poet" is **poeta** (POH-ay-tah). In replacing *poeta* with a form of **vates** (WAH-tays), which means "a prophet or seer who makes divine utterances," Horace—later poets also applied *vates* to members of their profession—was using a more honorific term, but one that conveys a vaguely sinister sense.

Gesta Romanorum
GEH-stah roh-mah-NOH-ruum
Deeds of the Romans

Title of a medieval collection of stories in Latin, with each
story intended to teach a moral lesson.

Gloria in Excelsis Deo
GLOH-ree-ah in eks-KEL-sees DAY-oh
Glory be to God on high

The first words of the familiar hymn, from Luke.

Gradus ad Parnassum
GRAH-duus ahd pahr-NAHS-suum
a step to Parnassus

The title of a dictionary of prosody much used by past generations of English schoolboys learning to write Latin verse. A
gradus (in English, GRAY-dəs), as any work of its type is known,
supplies the length of syllables in spoken Latin, as well as suggesting poetic phraseology. Parnassus, a mountain in Greece,
has two summits, one of which was consecrated to the Muses by
the ancient Greeks. For this reason Parnassus is thought of as
the seat of poetry.

grammatici certant
grahm-MAH-tih-kee KEHR-tahnt
grammarians dispute

The beginning of a line from Horace's *Ars Poetica*, concluding **et adhuc sub iudice** (or **judice**) **lis est** (et AHD-huuk suub
YOO-dee-keh lees est), thus giving us: "Grammarians discuss,
and the case is still before the courts." *Grammatici certant*, by
itself, can be used to characterize any problem that is still to be
resolved by the experts, in particular disagreement among critics over the quality of a work of art.

gratias tibi ago
GRAH-tee-ahs TIH-bee AH-goh
thank you

habeas corpus
HAH-beh-ahs KAWR-puus
you may have the body

Devotees of Hollywood movies know *habeas corpus* as something magical that a lawyer threatens to obtain when a district attorney appears to have the upper hand in a case. What the lawyer usually means is that he intends to apply to a court to obtain a judicial writ, fully described as a writ **habeas corpus ad subiciendum** (ahd suub-ih-kee-EN-duum), requiring the prosecutor in the case to bring the accused before a court to undergo (*ad subiciendum*) the action of the law. A "habeas corpus" (HAY-bee-əs KAWR-pəs), as this legal writ is commonly called in English—other writs carry these same opening words, but they are too numerous to list here—is a feature of British and United States law that protects an individual against arbitrary imprisonment by requiring that any person arrested be brought before a court for formal charge. When the writ is executed, the court hears the complaint under which the person has been detained and rules on the validity of the arrest. If the charge is considered valid, the person must submit to trial; if not, the person goes free. So when a Perry Mason or Joyce Davenport threatens, "I'll slap a habeas corpus on you so fast, it'll make your head swim," full protection of the law is being sought for the accused.

haec olim meminisse iuvabit (or **juvabit**)
hīk OH-lim meh-mih-NIS-seh yuu-WAH-bit
time heals all wounds

See FORSAN ET HAEC OLIM MEMINISSE IUVABIT.

Hannibal ad portas

HAHN-nih-bahl ahd PAWR-tahs

the Russians are coming

This expression, literally "Hannibal is at the gates," was used to alert the citizens of Rome to imminent danger. Hannibal, the commanding general of Carthaginian armies during the Second Punic War, was so feared by the Romans that *Hannibal ad portas* became a proverbial expression, in use well after Hannibal and his armies no longer were a threat, and carrying the meaning "our country's in danger." Comparable warnings—"missile gap" and "window of vulnerability" spring to mind—are not unknown today. (See DELENDA EST CARTHAGO.)

haud ignota loquor

howd ih-GNOH-tah LAW-kwawr

you know as well as I that . . .

A rhetorical expression, literally "I speak of things by no means unknown," implying that an audience understands—and agrees with—a speaker's interpretation of some aspect of the subject under discussion, thus giving the speaker license to gloss over the putative merits of the point being made.

hic et nunc

heek et nuunk

here and now

A person who demands immediate action, such as repayment of a debt, would say he wants it *hic et nunc*.

hic et ubique

heek et oo-BEE-kweh

here and everywhere

hic iacet (or jacet)
heek YAH-ket
here lies

The opening words of many an old tombstone inscription.

hinc illae lacrimae
hihnk IHL-lī LAH-krih-mī
so that's what's eating you!

In the play *Andria*, Terence used this phrase, literally "hence those tears," to mean "so that is the true offense, the underlying reason for the annoyance." The rare modern father who finally grasps the reason for a child's display of moodiness might say, "*Hinc illae lacrimae*, you want to spend all your weekends with your mother."

hoc age
hawk AH-geh
get with it!

Literally "do this," but used to adjure people to apply themselves to their work.

hoc anno
hawk AHN-noh
in this year

hoc erat in votis
hawk EH-raht in WOH-tees
this is what I once longed for

These words from Horace's *Satires*, more literally "this was what I wished," introduce a listing of things he once wanted. The sense is that passage of time has altered his desires, so we use this phrase when looking back at our abandoned dreams.

hoc est vivere bis vita posse priore frui
hawk est wee-WEH-reh bihs WEE-tah PAWS-seh pree-OH-reh FROO-ee
to live twice is to make useful profit from one's past

This epigram by Marcus Valerius Martialis (*c* A.D. 100), known today as Martial, may be interpreted in a variety of ways, all of them positive: Experience is the best teacher. Plan ahead. Don't look back, but capitalize on what you have been through. Who would dispute the efficacy of any of these?

hoc genus omne
hawk GEH-nuus AWM-neh
all this sort

A phrase from Horace's *Satires* that can be applied to people with the meaning "all people of that type," as well as in broader senses: "I quickly tire of discussions of home computers, word processors, and *hoc genus omne*."

hoc loco
hawk LAW-koh
in this place

hoc opus, hic labor est
hawk AW-puus hik LAH-bawr est
this is the tough part

Virgil, in the *Aeneid*, tells in this phrase, literally "this is work, this is labor," that once we go wrong, we will find it difficult to get back on the right track. Virgil was referring to how easy it is to fall into Avernus, the lower depths, and then how hard to

make one's way back. (See FACILIS DESCENSUS AVERNO.) But
we can use his phrase aptly to prescribe behavior for many
difficult situations we encounter in life on earth.

hoc volo, sic iubeo (or jubeo), sit pro ratione voluntas
hawk WAW-loh seek YUU-bay-oh sit proh
rah-tee-OH-neh WAW-luun-tahs
the fact that I wish it is reason enough for doing it

This statement from Juvenal's *Satires* translates more literally
as "this I will, thus I command; let my will serve as reason."
Excellent text for a sampler destined for hanging at home or in
the office of an editor or business executive.

hodie mihi, cras tibi
HAW-dee-ay MIH-hee krahs TIH-bee
my turn today, yours tomorrow

These words, literally "today to me, tomorrow to you," reflect
the inevitability of change, so they are used in old epitaphs to
remind viewers of their own mortality.

homo doctus in se semper divitias habet
HAW-moh DAW-ktuus in say SEM-pehr
dee-WIH-tee-ahs HAH-bet
a learned man always has wealth within himself

homo homini lupus
HAW-moh HAW-mih-nee LUU-puus
"man's inhumanity to man"

The bitter translation quoted above from Robert Burns has
persisted in our culture with the same meaning as *homo homini
lupus*, literally "man is a wolf to man," an observation adapted
from the play *Asinaria*, by Plautus, and appropriate whenever
one reads a newspaper.

honoris causa
haw-NOH-ris KOW-sah
honorary

An academic degree granted *honoris causa*, literally "for the sake of honor," is bestowed as recognition of merit without formal examination. As we know well, degrees awarded *honoris causa* too often are rewards for financial generosity: **pecuniae** (peh-KOO-nee-ī) **causa**, "for the sake of wealth." (For another point of view, see PECUNIA NON OLET.)

hora fugit
HAW-rah FUU-git
the hour flies

One of several Latin expressions reminding us that life passes all too quickly.

horas non numero nisi serenas
HAW-rahs nohn NUU-meh-roh NIH-sih seh-RAY-nahs
I do not count the hours unless they are bright

A favorite inscription for sundials.

horresco referens
hawr-REH-skoh reh-FEH-rens
I shudder to relate

In Virgil's *Aeneid*, Aeneas says these words as he recounts the death of Laocoön. A priest of Apollo, Laocoön saw that his sons were being attacked by serpents sent by Apollo or Athena. Good father that he was, Laocoön went to his children's defense and was killed along with them, supposedly for his role in attempting to dissuade the Trojans from accepting the horse the Greeks used to penetrate Troy. The only good thing about *horresco referens* is that it gives us a welcome relief from "you wouldn't believe it," "I kid you not," and "too horrible for words."

horribile dictu
hawr-RIH-bih-leh DIH-ktoo
horrible to relate

In describing a particularly bloody automobile accident, for example, one might interject *horribile dictu* just before launching into the most shocking details of the narrative. (See MIRABILE DICTU.)

hostis humani generis
HAW-stihs huu-MAH-nee GEH-neh-rihs
enemy of the human race

Few qualify for this appellation, suitable in our time for the likes of Adolf Hitler.

humanum est errare
hoo-MAH-nuum est ehr-RAH-reh
to err is human

See ERRARE HUMANUM EST.

iacta (or jacta) alea est
YAH-ktah AH-lay-ah est
the die is cast

See ALEA IACTA EST.

ianuis (or januis) clausis
YAH-noo-ees KLOW-sees
behind closed doors

Any private meeting can be called a meeting *ianuis clausis*, literally "with closed doors," the most celebrated examples being the meetings held by the college of cardinals in the Sistine Chapel to elect a pope.

ibid.

See next entry.

ibidem
IH-bih-dem (also ih-BEE-dem)
in the same place

A weapon in the arsenal of scholarly terms, used so often that it has acquired the English pronunciation IB-ə-dem. Abbreviated **Ibid.** in a footnote, and often italicized (underscored in manuscript) because it is Latin, *Ibid.* makes reference to an identical source cited in an immediately preceding footnote. For example, in the footnote "[16] *Ibid.*, p. 77," the source referred to in footnote 15 is being referred to again, but this time citing page 77 of that source. Small wonder the young scholar complains: "Half my life is spent writing *Ibid.*, *op. cit.*, and *loc. cit.*"

idem
EE-dem
the same

Sometimes abbreviated **id.**, this scholarly term appears in footnotes containing more than one reference to works by the same author. It is used in place of the author's name after the initial reference. *Idem* has the English pronunciation ĪD-em.

id est
id est
that is

This scholarly term, abbreviated **i.e.**, is used in identical fashion as its English translation: to clarify a statement just made. The abbreviation *i.e.* is heard more and more in the speech of those who do not know the Latin phrase—nor even the meaning of the term—so misuse is almost as common as correct use.

The most frequent mistake reflects confusion of *i.e.* with **e.g.**, the abbreviation of *exempli gratia*, "for example." Perhaps we are better advised to use the English equivalents in place of these abbreviations.

id genus omne
id GEH-nuus AWM-neh
all that sort

Used in the same way as HOC GENUS OMNE.

i.e.

See ID EST.

Iesus (or Jesus) Nazarenus Rex Iudaeorum (or Judaeorum)
YAY-suus nah-zah-RAY-nuus reks yoo-dī-OH-ruum
Jesus of Nazareth, King of the Jews

Abbreviated **I.N.R.I.**

ignis aurum probat, miseria fortes viros
IH-gnis OW-ruum PRAW-baht mih-SEH-ree-ah
FAWR-tays WIH-rohs
life is not a bowl of cherries

Seneca, in *De Providentia*, warns us that there will be trouble in our lives and we must learn to come to grips with it, telling us literally: "Fire tests gold; adversity (tests) strong men." (Seneca apparently knew something of the differential melting points of metals.)

ignis fatuus
IH-gnis FAH-too-uus
will-o'-the-wisp

Ignis fatuus, literally "foolish fire," signifying any misleading or deluding goal, is so called for the phosphorescent light sometimes seen at night above marshy ground and thought to be caused by the combustion of methane rising from decaying vegetable matter. Anyone who attempts to follow such light is misled, hence the meaning "will-o'-the-wisp."

ignorantia legis neminem excusat
ih-gnoh-RAHN-tee-ah LAY-gihs NEH-mih-nem
eks-KOO-saht
ignorance of the law excuses no one

Also given as **ignorantia iuris** (or **juris**) **non** (YOO-rees nohn) **excusat**, "ignorance of the law does not excuse." An even broader expression is **ignorantia non excusat**, "ignorance does not excuse," which goes beyond the realm of law, enabling us to upbraid an unfortunate who says, "But I didn't know. . . ."

ignoti nulla cupido
ih-GNOH-tee NUUL-lah kuu-PEE-doh
we don't want what we can't see

Ovid's thought in *Ars Amatoria*, literally "no desire (exists) for a thing unknown," is excellent for young parents to keep in mind if they want to preclude unreasonable requests from their children.

imo pectore
EE-moh PEH-ktaw-reh

See AB IMO PECTORE.

in absentia
in ahb-SEN-tee-ah
in (one's) absence

Pronounced in ab-SEN-shə in English. One may be awarded a university degree *in absentia* or convicted of a crime *in absentia*, in the former case because of inability to appear for the academic ceremony, in the latter because one is beyond the reach of the law.

in aeternum
in ī-TEHR-nuum
forever

in articulo mortis
in ahr-TIH-kuu-loh MAWR-tihs
at the point of death

A statement made *in articulo mortis*, literally "in the grasp of death," carries special weight, since it is believed that a person about to die has nothing to gain, perhaps much to lose, from lying.

in bello parvis momentis magni casus intercedunt
in BEL-loh PAHR-wees moh-MEN-tees MAH-gnee KAH-soos ihn-tehr-KAY-duunt
in war great events are the results of small causes

Anyone who has participated in war can affirm this observation, made by Caesar in his *Bellum Gallicum*: Battles are usually won by the armies that blunder least. Applied more broadly, Caesar's words tell us to pay attention to detail in any enterprise.

in camera

in KAH-meh-rah

in private

Literally "in a chamber," and applied especially to a hearing held by a judge in chambers or in a courtroom with public and press excluded.

in cauda venenum

in KOW-dah weh-NAY-nuum

watch out for the part you can't see

The Romans knew that the scorpion's sting was in its tail, so *in cauda venenum*, literally "in the tail is the poison," warns us to look beyond the obvious in judging potential danger. Thus, a speech that starts out innocuously may gather spite as it proceeds and climax in a malicious peroration: *in cauda venenum*.

incidis in Scyllam cupiens vitare Charybdim

IHN-kih-dihs ihn SKIH-lahm KUU-pee-ens

wee-TAH-reh kah-RIH-bdim

out of the frying pan into the fire

Scylla was a nymph who was changed into a sea monster, in Homer's *Odyssey* said to inhabit a rock in the strait of Messina —it separates Italy from Sicily—opposite the whirlpool that was the home of Charybdis, another sea monster. Scylla and Charybdis may be thought of as our modern rock and a hard place, because sailors careful to avoid one threat usually ended up being caught by the other: *incidis in Scyllam cupiens vitare Charybdim*, literally "you fall into Scylla in trying to avoid Charybdis." The message is clear: Although life usually demands that you face problems to attain any reasonable goal, exercise due caution lest you be blind-sided. In short, don't jump from the frying pan into the fire. But remember to see Italy before you die.

incipit
IN-kih-pit
here begins

The first word in many medieval manuscripts.

Index Librorum Prohibitorum
IN-deks lih-BROH-ruum praw-hih-bih-TOH-ruum
List of Prohibited Books

A list published by church authorities naming books currently out of bounds for most Catholics.

in dubio
in DUU-bee-oh
in doubt

in esse
in ES-seh
in being

Used to contrast things actually existing with those in **posse** (in PAWS-seh), literally "in potentiality."

in extenso
in ek-STEN-soh
word for word

An unabridged text is given *in extenso*, literally "in full."

in extremis
in ek-STRAY-mees
at the point of death

This unhappy phrase, also given as IN ARTICULO MORTIS, designates the final moments of a person's life.

in flagrante delicto
in flah-GRAHN-teh day-LIH-ktoh
red-handed

When someone is caught in the act of committing a crime, he has been caught *in flagrante delicto*, literally "while the crime is blazing." (The phrase is also applied to situations involving lesser embarrassments.) Our own "red-handed" is almost as vivid, if the red hands are thought of as hands covered with blood.

infra
IN-frah
below

A scholarly term used to call the reader's attention to something that follows in a text. It is usually preceded by **vide** (WIH-day, "see"). The opposite of **vide infra**, "see below," is **vide supra** (SOO-prah, "see above").

infra dignitatem
IN-frah dih-gnih-TAH-tem
undignified

This phrase, literally "beneath (one's) dignity," is used to indicate that a suggested or contemplated act does not befit one's character or standing. The phrase is shortened to *infra dig* by those in the know, who pronounce it in-frə dig.

in futuro
in fuu-TOO-roh
in the future

in hoc signo vinces
in hawk SIH-gnoh WIN-kays
in this sign thou shalt conquer

Emperor Constantine, on his way to battle, is said to have seen a cross appear in the sky, carrying these words. He had the message painted on his standard and went on to victory.

in limine
in LEE-mih-neh
on the threshold

Used to describe something that is about to happen or is beginning to happen.

in loco parentis
in LAW-koh pah-REN-tees
in the place of a parent

Anyone who serves *in loco parentis* may be considered to have responsibilities of guardianship, either formal or informal, over minors.

in lumine tuo videbimus lumen
in LOO-mih-neh TOO-oh wih-DAY-bih-muus LOO-men
in thy light shall we see light

Motto of Columbia University.

in medias res
in MEH-dee-ahs rays
into the thick of it

Authors who eschew slow beginnings for their stories, but plunge right into the action, put their readers *in medias res*, literally "into the middle of things."

in medio tutissimus ibis
in MEH-dee-oh too-TIH-sih-muus EE-bis
you shall go safest in the middle course

Ovid counseling conservatism in *Metamorphoses*, and providing the prevailing political wisdom for candidates for high office in the United States.

in memoriam
in meh-MAW-ree-ahm
to the memory of

This expression, literally "in memory," is widely used in inscriptions, epitaphs, etc.

in naturalibus
in nah-too-RAH-lih-buus
stark naked

This phrase, literally "in a state of nature," fails to come to grips with its true meaning, just as the French *au naturel*, in its primary sense, plays games with the unclothed state—oops! with nakedness.

in nomine Patris et Filii et Spiritus Sancti
in NOH-mih-neh PAH-trihs et FEE-lee-ee et SPEE-rih-toos SAHN-ktee
in the name of the Father and of the Son and of the Holy Spirit

in omnia paratus
in AWM-nee-ah pah-RAH-tuus
ready for anything

This phrase, literally "prepared for all things," echoes
SEMPER PARATUS.

in ovo
in OH-woh
immature

This expression, literally "in the egg," can be used to characterize anything that is still in an undeveloped state. "Modern
education too often leaves its beneficiaries just as it found them,
in ovo."

in pace, ut sapiens, aptarit idonea bello
in PAH-keh uut SAH-pee-ens ah-PTAH-rit
ih-doh-NAY-ah BEL-loh
in peace, like a wise man, he appropriately prepares
for war

The advice of Horace in his *Satires*, used by modern advocates of a strong war machine as the best strategy for guarantee-
ing peace, even though it has been followed for centuries and
has yet to produce lasting peace. (See QUI DESIDERAT PACEM
PRAEPARET BELLUM.)

in partibus infidelium
in PAHR-tih-buus in-fih-DAY-lee-uum
in the lands of the infidels

This phrase, usually abbreviated *in partibus*, is used in English as part of an ecclesiastical title. For example, "Bishop *in
partibus*" designates a bishop who bears the title of the office

but has no religious jurisdiction, since he serves in an area under religious control of another group.

in pectore
in PEH-ktaw-reh
in secret

Anything done *in pectore* is done literally "in the breast," such as designation of a cardinal by a pope without public announcement. The designation is said to be *in pectore*.

in perpetuum
in pehr-PEH-too-uum
forever

Also given as **in perpetuo** (pehr-PEH-too-oh).

in pleno
in PLAY-noh
in full

Payment *in pleno* is payment in full.

in posse
in PAWS-seh
potentially

See IN ESSE.

in praesenti
in prī-SEHN-tee
at present

In praesenti means now rather than IN FUTURO.

in re
in ray
regarding

This phrase, literally "in the matter of," finds correct use in legal documents and notices.

in rerum natura
in REH-ruum nah-TOO-rah
in the nature of things

in saecula saeculorum
in SĪ-kuu-lah sī-kuu-LOH-ruum
forever and ever

Anything that has continued for a very long time can be said to have existed *in saecula saeculorum*, literally "for ages of ages."

insalutato hospite
in-sah-loo-TAH-toh HAW-spih-teh
without saluting one's host

This phrase refers to taking one's leave in a great hurry, for example, leaving a party without saying proper goodbyes. It also may be interpreted as "taking French leave," an old expression for leaving without announcement, for example, skipping town without paying one's debts. The French call this doubtful practice *filer à l'anglaise*, "to take English leave," an instance of the not-too-infrequent linguistic phenomenon of ascribing doubtful practices to the members of cultures other than one's own.

insanus omnis furere credit ceteros
in-SAH-nuus AWM-nis FOO-reh-reh KRAY-dit
KAY-teh-rohs
every madman thinks everybody else is mad

Syrus gave us this penetrating observation in his *Maxims*.
Who among us can see their own faults? The thief accuses
everybody else of dishonesty; the adulterer says we are all un-
faithful.

in se
in say
in itself

See PER SE.

in situ
in SIH-too
in its natural location

In situ, literally "in place," is an expression used by scholars,
who may say, for example, that an observation or experiment
was performed *in situ*, signifying that it was made in the natural
or original location of the material or process under study. "A
field examination of the archaeological find was performed *in
situ* before the shards were removed." The opposite of *in situ*
would be **in vitro** (WIH-troh), literally "in glass"—think of a test
tube, for example—and indicating a laboratory, hence artificial,
setting to which the material or process has been moved. "A
great deal is heard these days about *in vitro* fertilization." A
third expression, **in vivo** (WEE-woh), literally "in that which is
alive," is encountered in the writings of scientists. It describes
experiments performed in or on a living organism. All three
expressions have English pronunciations: *in situ* (in SĪ-too), *in
vitro* (in VEE-troh), *in vivo* (in VEE-voh).

instar omnium
IN-stahr AWM-nee-uum
worth all of them

Instar omnium is the expression Cicero used in speaking of Plato, to indicate that one Plato is worth all other men combined. The rest of us should be cautious in characterizing anyone as *instar omnium*.

in statu quo
in STAH-too kwoh
in the same state

In statu quo, literally "in the state in which," is used to refer to the condition of something at a particular time, for example, **in statu quo ante bellum** (AHN-teh BEL-luum), "in the same state as before the war," and **in statu quo ante**, "in the same state of things before they were changed." (See STATUS.)

integer vitae
IN-teh-gehr WEE-tī
blameless of life

These are the opening words of a beautiful sentence in Horace's *Odes*: **Integer vitae scelerisque purus non eget mauris iaculis neque arcu** (skeh-leh-REES-kweh POO-ruus nohn AY-get MOW-rees YAH-kuu-lees NAY-kweh AHR-koo), with the meaning "An upright man, free of guilt, needs no weapon to defend himself." The initial words, *integer vitae*, may be used alone to describe a person who lives an honorable life.

intelligenti pauca
in-tehl-lih-GEN-tee POW-kah
a word to the wise

This useful phrase, literally "to the intelligent, few words," is also expressed as **verbum sapienti** (WEHR-buum sah-pee-EN-tee), "a word is enough for a wise man," implying that the unwise will not heed even a lengthy, explicit warning.

in tempore opportuno
in TEM-paw-reh awp-pawr-TOO-noh
at the opportune time

inter alia
IN-tehr AH-lee-ah
among other things

"His views on women's rights and nuclear disarmament *inter alia* finally turned me against him."

inter alios
IN-tehr AH-lee-ohs
among other persons

inter nos
IN-tehr nohs
between or among us

The Latin equivalent of *entre nous*.

inter pares
IN-tehr PAH-rays
between or among equals

A discussion *inter pares* is one in which the participants consider one another peers.

inter pocula
IN-tehr POH-kuu-lah
over drinks

Literally "between cups." "Why don't we discuss this *inter pocula*?"

interregnum
in-tehr-REH-gnuum
a period between rulers

Now an English word (in-tər-REG-nəm), used to indicate a period in which there is no ruling authority. In the days of the Roman republic, it meant the time during the absence of the consuls or the time between the retirement or the death of the consuls and the election of their successors.

inter se
IN-tehr say
between or among themselves

inter vivos
IN-tehr WEE-wohs
between living persons

This legal phrase is used to designate a gift that is given by one living person to another, taking effect during their lifetimes. The English pronunciation is IN-tər VEE-vohs.

in toto
in TOH-toh
entirely

In toto can also be translated as "on the whole," "altogether," "in all," and "completely." The English pronunciation is the same as the Latin.

intra muros
IN-trah MOO-rohs
within the walls

In ancient times, sturdy walls built on the perimeters of cities protected their inhabitants against invasion, and the day-to-day life of the city was conducted *intra muros*.

in transitu
in TRAHN-sih-too
on the way

In transitu has its English counterpart in the phrase "in transit."

intra vires
IN-trah WEE-rays
within the powers

A matter that is *intra vires* is within the legal power or authority of an institution or individual, as opposed to one that is **ultra** (UUL-trah) **vires**, beyond the legal powers. The English pronunciation of *intra vires* is IN-trə VĪ-reez.

in utrumque paratus
in uu-TRUUM-kweh pah-RAH-tuus
ready, come what may

Regardless of the possible outcome for any human endeavor —success or defeat, life or death—the wise person is in **utrumque paratus,** Virgil's phrase in the *Aeneid*, with the literal meaning "prepared for either alternative."

in vacuo
in WAH-koo-oh
isolated

Physicists may study phenomena *in vacuo*, literally "in a vacuum," but the rest of us use the term in an extended meaning —just as we use the phrase *in a vacuum*—to indicate complete absence of communication with others, or separation from reality.

in vino veritas
in WEE-noh WAY-rih-tahs
wine loosens the tongue

There are sleeping drunks and fighting drunks and quiet drunks and talkative drunks. *In vino veritas*, an old Roman proverb, with the literal meaning "in wine the truth," tells us that people under the influence of wine or other spirits will say things they ordinarily try to conceal.

invita Minerva
in-WEE-tah mih-NEHR-wah
uninspired

Minerva, the Roman goddess of wisdom and patroness of all the arts, obviously is someone to have on your team at all times if you work in the arts. If she deserts you on a given day, your work will suffer, but you can put the blame on her by saying *invita Minerva*, literally "Minerva being unwilling." The phrase may also be used by critics to characterize an artist or a work of art lacking inspiration.

in vitro
in WIH-troh

See IN SITU.

in vivo
in WEE-woh

See IN SITU.

ipsa quidem pretium virtus sibi
IH-psah KWIH-dem PREH-tee-uum WIHR-tuus
SIH-bee
virtue is its own reward

A saying of Claudian, a late-classical, fourth-century Roman poet, who has been called the last of the Roman poets.

ipse dixit
IH-pseh DEE-ksit
an unsupported assertion

This phrase, literally "he himself said so" and pronounced IP-see DIK-sit in English, labels a statement as authoritative only to the extent that the reputation of its author merits trust, with the implication that there is no other guarantee of its validity: "All we have is his *ipse dixit*." When Cicero used this phrase, he was referring to Pythagoras himself, and when Pythagoras is the *ipse* in *ipse dixit*, the authority cannot be questioned.

ipsissima verba
ih-PSIHS-sih-mah WEHR-bah
verbatim

Literally "the very words." "Did she say that?" "Yes, that is what she said, *ipsissima verba*."

ipso facto
IH-psoh FAH-ktoh
by that very fact

Ipso facto has the meaning of "absolutely, regardless of all other considerations of right and wrong." "By ordering troops into the presidential palace, the general was *ipso facto* guilty of treason."

ira furor brevis est
EE-rah FOO-rawr BREH-wis est
anger is brief madness

Horace uses these words in his *Epistles* to tell us that anger is a momentary departure from rationality, and goes on to caution control over our passions lest they control us.

ite, missa est
EE-teh MEES-sah est
go, the mass is ended

The celebrant of the mass concludes with these words, literally "go, it has been sent on its way."

ius (or jus) est ars boni et aequi
yoos est ahrs BAW-nee et Ī-kwee
law is the art of the good and the just

An elegant characterization of the law, that much maligned profession. Contrast *ius est ars boni et aequi* with the characterization offered by Mr. Bumble in *Oliver Twist*: "The law is a ass, a idiot."

ius (or jus) primae noctis
yoos PREE-mī NAW-ktis
droit du seigneur

A feudal lord had the right, literally "right of the first night," to share the bed of his vassal's bride on her wedding night. This custom, not always practiced, one must believe, gave way to requiring payment of a sum of money to the lord in lieu of exercise of *ius primae noctis*.

iustitia (or justitia) omnibus
yuu-STIH-tee-ah AWM-nih-buus
justice for all

Motto of the District of Columbia.

jacta alea est
See ALEA IACTA EST.

januis clausis
See IANUIS CLAUSIS.

Jesus Nazarenus Rex Judaeorum
See IESUS NAZARENUS REX IUDAEORUM.

jus est ars boni et aequi
See IUS EST ARS BONI ET AEQUI.

jus primae noctis
See IUS PRIMAE NOCTIS.

justitia omnibus
See IUSTITIA OMNIBUS.

labor omnia vincit
LAH-bawr AWM-nee-ah WIHN-kiht
work conquers all things

Motto of Oklahoma, affirming that our pioneers knew how to tame the wilderness and, apparently, how to farm successfully. (Of course, there's nothing like an oil strike to make a farm really pay off.) The phrase is a shortened form—with the tense of the verb changed from *vicit* (perfect) to *vincit* (present)—of Virgil's statement in his *Georgics*: **labor omnia vicit improbus** (WIH-kiht ihm-PRAW-buus): "never-ending work conquered all things." Virgil was describing the harshness of life following the Golden Age, when the earth had yielded its fruits without labor. Jupiter then decided to change everything, making life hard so that men would learn and become independent. No welfare state from then on.

lacrima Christi
LAH-krih-mah KRIH-stee
the tear of Christ

This mournful expression is often given as **lacrimae** (LAH-krih-mī, "tears") **Christi** and as **Lachryma Christi**. In the latter spelling, we see the triumph of commercialism, Lachryma Christi being a sweet wine produced in Italy.

lapsus calami
LAH-psuus KAH-lah-mee
a slip of the pen

An error made through carelessness in writing is a *lapsus calami*. A calamus (KAH-lah-muus) was a reed that found use as a pen.

lapsus linguae
LAH-psuus LIHN-gwī
a slip of the tongue

lapsus memoriae
LAH-psuus meh-MAW-ree-ī
a lapse of memory

lares et penates
LAH-rays et peh-NAH-tays
Roman gods of the household

The *lares et penates* looked after the safety and well-being of the home. The *lares* were usually deified heroes or ancestors; the *penates* were the gods of the storeroom, with the special duty of keeping the house free of danger. Images of these gods were kept in a shrine in every home, and offerings were made to them on family occasions. Today, the phrase "lares and penates" (LAY-reez and pǝ-NAY-teez in English) has the meaning of "household effects and personal possessions."

laudator temporis acti
low-DAH-tawr TEHM-paw-rihs AH-ktee
a praiser of time past

Horace's expression in *Ars Poetica* for the bore who looks back always on the good old days, telling us that present times have nothing to recommend them. Revisionists of this stripe are always with us. Today's **laudatores** (low-dah-TOH-rays) **temporis acti** recall the good times we all enjoyed during the Great Depression; what will be said fifty years from now about the Glorious Eighties?

laudem virtutis necessitati damus
LOW-demwihr-TOO-tisneh-keh-sih-TAH-teeDAH-muus
we give to necessity the praise of virtue

Marcus Fabius Quintilianus, known as Quintilian, was a Roman rhetorician of the first century A.D. In this marvelous saying, he recognized that people give themselves the courage to face adversity by finding some benefit in it. Chaucer spoke of making "vertue of necessitee," and Shakespeare followed with "there is no virtue like necessity." Without the ability to face our troubles this way, many more of us might founder.

laus Deo
lows DAY-oh
praise (be) to God

lex loci
leks LAW-kee
the law of the place

The Latin equivalent of "the law of the land."

lex non scripta
leks nohn SKRIH-ptah
the unwritten law

Lex non scripta refers to what we call common law, the body of law derived in the English tradition from precedent without the formality of statutes and regulations, but nonetheless binding. *Lex scripta*, it follows logically, is the body of written, or statutory, law.

lex salica
leks SAH-lih-kah
Salic law

Lex salica is the law of the ancient Salian Franks, a people who inhabited a region in the Rhine valley near the North Sea. *Lex salica* became part of the French legal tradition, and the aspect of Salian law that became particularly well known is that forbidding the inheritance of an estate by female members of a family. It was because of an interpretation of this law that the French monarchy never had women as rulers.

lex scripta
leks SKRIH-ptah

See LEX NON SCRIPTA.

lex talionis
leks tah-lee-OH-nis
an eye for an eye, a tooth for a tooth

Lex talionis, literally "the law of retaliation," is the practice of punishment in kind, dating back at least to the Old Testament, yet much in vogue today in some societies.

licentia vatum
lih-KEN-tee-ah WAH-tuum
poetic license

Literally "the license of poets." (See GENUS IRRITABILE VATUM.)

licet
LIH-keht
it is allowed

Licet, pronounced LĪ-set in English, is the formal expression used in granting permission. "May I be relieved of my academic responsibilities during the coming semester?" "*Licet*." (Or "*Non licet*.")

ligonem ligonem vocat
lih-GOH-nem lih-GOH-nem WAW-kaht
he or she calls a spade a spade

A *ligo* (LIH-goh) is really a hoe, but the phrase is construed as a compliment regardless of the tool employed. Many of us prefer people who are outspoken even to the point of rudeness, compared with pussyfooters who never let us know where they stand.

lis sub iudice (or judice)
lees suub YOO-dih-keh
a case not yet decided

A matter before the courts that has not yet been disposed of is a *lis sub iudice*, literally "a lawsuit before the judge." (See ADHUC SUB IUDICE LIS EST.)

litterae humaniores
LIHT-teh-rī huu-mah-nee-OH-rays
the humanities

The Latin phrase, literally "the more humane letters (or learning)," designating the Greek and Latin classics, grammar, poetry, and rhetoric—all considered polite learning conducive to culture, contrasted with **litterae divinae** (dee-WEE-nī), "theology."

Litterarum Doctor
lih-teh-RAH-ruum DAW-ktawr
Doctor of Letters

An honorary degree, abbreviated **Litt.D.**

loco citato
LAW-koh kih-TAH-toh
in the place cited

This phrase, in English pronounced LOH-koh sī-TAY-toh, is a tool of the scholar. Abbreviated **loc. cit.**, it is used in footnotes to refer the reader to a passage previously cited: "Morrison, *loc. cit.*"

locum tenens
LAW-kuum TEH-nens
a substitute or deputy

Locum tenens, pronounced LOH-kəm TEN-enz in English, and literally "one holding the place," refers to someone who is filling in temporarily for another person. The expression is said most often of pinch-hitting physicians and clergymen.

locus classicus
LAW-kuus KLAHS-sih-kuus
the most authoritative or most frequently cited passage

A *locus classicus*, pronounced LOH-kəs KLAS-si-kəs in English, and literally "a classical source," is a passage commonly cited to explain or illustrate a subject.

locus delicti
LAW-kuus day-LIH-ktee
the scene of the crime

A CORPUS DELICTI establishes that a crime has been committed. A *locus delicti*, pronounced LOH-kəs də-LIK-tī in English, is the place where the crime occurred. Now all we need is the perpetrator.

locus in quo
LAW-kuus in kwoh
the place in question

A *locus in quo*, literally "the place in which," refers to a place where something of interest has occurred, or where a passage under discussion may be found.

locus poenitentiae
LAW-kuus poy-nih-TEN-tee-ī
a place or opportunity for repentance

A legal expression, pronounced LOH-kəs pen-ih-TEN-shih-ee in English, denoting the period within which a person may withdraw from an assumed obligation before it becomes binding.

locus sigilli
LAW-kuus sih-GIHL-lee
the place of the seal

The *locus sigilli*, abbreviated l.s., is the place on a document for affixing the seal of the notary public or other official.

loquitur
LAW-kwih-tuur
he or she speaks

A stage direction, abbreviated **loq.**

lucri causa
LUU-kree KOW-sah
for the sake of gain

Anything done in hope of financial reward or profit is done *lucri causa*. Before leaving the subject of money, it is worthwhile to cite Juvenal, in his *Satires*: **Lucri bonus est odor** (BAW-nuus est AW-dawr), "sweet is the smell of money," and the line concludes **ex re qualibet** (eks ray KWAH-lih-bet), "obtained from any source."

lucus a non lucendo
LOO-kuus ah nohn loo-KEN-doh
a paradoxical or absurd etymology

This expression, literally "(called) a grove from the absence of light," can be used to characterize anything whose essence is the opposite of what its name suggests, but it is most frequently used to describe a paradoxical or false word derivation. It has this latter use because the words *lucus* and *lucendo* are not derived from the same root, even though the unwary may assume that they are.

lupus est homo homini
LOO-puus est HAW-moh HAW-mih-nee
man is a wolf to man

Plautus, in his *Asinaria*, recognized man's inhumanity to man in this phrase, suggesting that pride and avarice are the cause of lupine behavior in humans. The wolf epitomizes predatory behavior, of course, but we must regretfully take note that while wolves are not known to attack one another, human beings too often do.

lusus naturae
LOO-suus nah-TOO-rī
a freak

Literally "a sport of nature."

lux et veritas
luuks et WAY-rih-tahs
light and truth

Motto of Yale University.

macte virtute
MAH-kteh wihr-TUU-teh
well done!

This phrase, literally "be increased in merit," gives us a Latin equivalent for "bravo" or "hooray." *Macte virtute*, like its English counterparts, commends and encourages.

magis mutus quam piscis
MAH-gihs MOO-tuus kwahm PIH-skis
silent as the grave

Literally "quieter than a fish."

magister artis ingeniique largitor venter
mah-GIH-stehr AHR-tihs in-gen-ee-EE-kweh lahr-GEE-tawr WEN-tehr
necessity is the mother of invention

The Roman satirist Aulus Persius Flaccus, known as Persius, gave us this maxim, literally "the belly is the teacher of art and the bestower of genius."

Magister Artium
mah-GIH-stehr AHR-tee-uum
Master of Arts

The intermediate university degree, abbreviated **M.A.** or **A.M.**

magister dixit
mah-GIH-stehr DEEK-sit
the master has spoken

Medieval scholastics used this phrase as an irrefutable argument, invoking Aristotle.

magister ludi
mah-GIH-stehr LOO-dee
schoolteacher

Literally "master of public games in honor of the gods." A **ludus litterarius** (LOO-dis liht-teh-RAH-ree-uus) was an elementary school. Modern readers know *Magister Ludi* as the title of a novel by Hermann Hesse.

magna cum laude
MAH-gnah kuum LOW-deh
with great praise

Second honors in a university degree. (See CUM LAUDE.)

magna est veritas et praevalet
MAHG-nah est WEH-rih-tahs et PRĪ-wah-let
great is truth, and it prevails

A proverb from Esdras, also given with **praevalebit** (PRĪ-wah-lay-bit, "will prevail") as the final word.

magnificat
mah-GNIH-fih-kaht
it magnifies

A hymn to the Virgin Mary, "My soul doth magnify the Lord," begins in Latin: **Magnificat anima mea Dominum** (AH-nih-mah MAY-ah DAW-mih-nuum). Any song of praise may be called a *magnificat*, pronounced mag-NIF-i-kat in English.

magni nominis umbra
MAH-gnee NAW-mih-nihs UUM-brah
an unworthy descendant of an illustrious family

Literally "the shadow of a great name," an unfortunate appellation for anyone who struggles unsuccessfully to emulate the achievements of senior members of his family. The expression is from Lucan's *Pharsalia*.

magnum bonum
MAH-gnuum BAW-nuum
a great good

magnum opus
MAH-gnuum AW-puus
one's crowning achievement

An artist's or a writer's masterpiece may be called his *magnum opus*, literally "a great work." The English pronunciation for this happy expression is MAG-nəm OH-pəs.

maior (or **major**) **e longinquo reverentia**
MAH-yawr ay lawn-GIHN-kwoh reh-weh-REN-tee-ah
no man is a hero to his valet

Literally "greater reverence from afar," *maior e longinquo reverentia* calls attention to our inclination to fail to observe faults when we consider people or things from a distance—distance lends enchantment—and our inclination to find fault with everyone and everything close at hand. And, conversely, familiarity breeds contempt—faults are exaggerated when we observe them often, as in someone we love.

mala fide
MAH-lah FIH-deh
in bad faith

Anything done *mala fide*, as opposed to BONA FIDE, is done fraudulently.

mala in se
MAH-lah in say
inherently bad

Literally "bad in themselves."

malesuada fames
mah-leh-SWAH-dah FAH-mays
hunger that leads to crime

In a description of Hell in the *Aeneid*, Virgil tells us that outside Hell's doors live Grief, Suffering, Disease, Age, Fear, Hunger, and Want. Hunger (*fames*) is described as *malesuada*, literally "persuading to evil." A sobering thought for those who make social policy.

malis avibus
MAH-lees AH-wih-buus
under unfavorable signs

The Roman propensity for employing soothsayers when planning an important move is nowhere better illustrated than in this phrase, literally "with bad birds." The birds referred to are birds of divination, and since they are **malae** (MAH-lī), the omens are bad. *Avibus bonis*, literally "with good birds," means "under favorable signs." Roman soothsayers often based their predictions and advice on their observations of birds, particularly birds in flight.

malo animo
MAH-loh AH-nih-moh
with evil intent

The legal phrase "with malice aforethought" is based on the Latin *malo animo*.

malum in se
MAH-luum in say
inherently bad

> Literally "bad in itself." (See MALA IN SE.)

mandamus
mahn-DAH-muus
we command

> A writ of *mandamus*, pronounced man-DAY-məs in English, is an order of a higher court directing a lower court to enforce performance of a legal duty.

manibus pedibusque
MAH-nih-buus peh-dih-BUUS-kweh
with all one's might

> Literally "with the hands and feet." This colorful expression reminds one of the expression "jumping in with both feet."

manu propria
MAH-noo PRAW-pree-ah
with one's own hand

> Anything done without assistance is accomplished *manu propria*. Medieval artists who affixed this legend to a work were telling the world they had done their work without help from apprentices.

mare clausum
MAH-reh KLOW-suum
a closed sea

This phrase describes a body of navigable water entirely within the jurisdiction of a nation, therefore closed to foreign shipping.

mare liberum
MAH-reh LEE-beh-ruum
an open sea

Mare liberum is a body of navigable water open to ships of all nations.

mare nostrum
MAH-reh NAW-struum
the Mediterranean

The Romans referred to the Mediterranean as *mare nostrum*, literally "our sea."

margaritas ante porcos
mahr-gah-REE-tahs AHN-teh PAWR-kohs
pearls before swine

Matthew cautions against offering the uncultured anything of quality: "Give not that which is holy to dogs; neither cast ye your pearls before swine." Serving Mexican cocktails to those who habitually swill six-packs is a more modern application of *margaritas ante porcos*.

mater dolorosa
MAH-tehr daw-law-ROH-sah
sorrowful mother

Any mother who has lost her child is a *mater dolorosa*, but the term is applied particularly to the Virgin Mary, mourning the death of her son.

materfamilias
mah-tehr-fah-MIH-lee-ahs
matriarch

This term can be used to describe the mistress of a household or a matron. The meaning "matriarch" is more appropriate for *materfamilias* because the Latin word *familia* is usually applied to an extended family. (See PATERFAMILIAS.)

materia medica
mah-TEH-ree-ah MEH-dih-kah
substances used as medicine

Materia medica, literally "medical material," comprises the drugs and other substances physicians prescribe to cure illness. *Materia medica*, pronounced mə-TEE-ri-ə MED-i-kə in English, is also used to mean "pharmacology."

mea culpa
MAY-ah KUUL-pah
I am to blame

This phrase, literally "through or by my fault," is heard in the confessional and in certain Christian prayers. When **maxima** (MAH-ksih-mah) is added, the resulting phrase, **mea maxima culpa**, literally means "through or by my very great fault."

medice, cura te ipsum
MEH-dih-keh KOO-rah tay IH-psuum
physician, heal thyself

Excellent advice from Luke for those who give advice they themselves should heed.

Medicinae Doctor
meh-dih-KEE-nī DAW-ktawr
Doctor of Medicine

The familiar university degree, abbreviated **M.D.**

medio tutissimus ibis
MEH-dee-oh too-TIHS-sih-muus IH-bihs
avoid extremes

This proverb from Ovid's *Metamorphoses* translates literally as "you will go safest in the middle," typically Roman advice and the conventional political wisdom for those who aspire to high office in the United States. (See IN MEDIO TUTISSIMUS IBIS.)

me iudice (or judice)
may YOO-dih-keh
in my opinion

membrum virile
MEHM-bruum wih-REE-leh
the male member

A euphemism for **penis** (PAY-nihs), with the meaning of our own word spelled identically but pronounced PEE-nis. The Latin word *penis* also means "tail."

memento, homo, quia pulvis es et in pulverem revertis
meh-MEN-toh HAW-moh KWEE-ah PUUL-wihs es et in PUUL-weh-rem reh-WEHR-tees
remember, man, that dust thou art, and to dust shalt thou return

A Latin rendering of words in Genesis spoken by God to Adam. They are repeated on Ash Wednesday each year by priests marking the foreheads of the faithful. (See TERRA ES, TERRAM IBIS.)

memento mori
meh-MEN-toh MAW-ree
remember that you must die

A grim reminder, literally "remember to die," telling all of us that we must be prepared for death. A *memento mori* (mə-MEN-toh MOHR-ee in English) is a human skull or any other object serving as a reminder of the inevitability of death: It's later than you think.

memoriter
meh-MAW-rih-tehr
by rote

Literally "by or from memory." When we learn something *memoriter*, we learn it by heart.

mendacem memorem esse oportet
men-DAH-kem MEH-maw-rem ES-seh aw-PAWR-tet
liars should have good memories

This saying of Quintilian's, literally "it is fitting that a liar should be a man of good memory," recognizes a difficulty the inveterate liar faces every day of his life, that of keeping his fabrications consistent. "Oh, what a tangled web we weave . . . ."

mens sana in corpore sano
mens SAH-nah in KAWR-paw-reh SAH-noh
a sound mind in a sound body

Juvenal, in his *Satires*, suggests to us that we must pray for attainment of *mens sana in corpore sano*, and his phrase has found use for many centuries as the stated educational goal of many schools: to train the body as well as the mind. Public statements by some near-illiterate college athletes suggest that the sound body is too often achieved without accompanying improvement of mind.

miles gloriosus
MEE-lehs gloh-ree-OH-suus
A Boastful Soldier

Title of a comedy by Plautus.

minima de malis
MIH-nih-mah day MAH-lees
choose the lesser of two evils

A proverb, literally "of evils, the least," to bear in mind when we are forced to choose between less than desirable alternatives.

mirabile dictu
mih-RAH-bih-leh DIH-ktoo
wonderful to relate

The phrase to use when one wishes to express astonishment while recounting an event of overwhelming significance or accomplishment or irony. "Then, as the child watched, the figure, *mirabile dictu*, rose high in the air and vanished." "As he left the penitentiary, where he had just completed a two-year sentence for stealing public funds, he announced, *mirabile dictu*, that he would be a candidate for a second term in the United States Senate."

mirabile visu
mih-RAH-bih-leh WEE-soo
wonderful to behold

A companion phrase for MIRABILE DICTU. "There before me, *mirabile visu*, stood Bethlehem itself. My dream had been fulfilled."

mirabilia
mih-rah-BIH-lee-ah
wonders

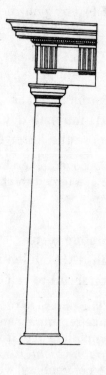

misericordia
mih-seh-rih-KAWR-dee-ah
mercy

The classic plea.

Missa solemnis
MIHS-sah saw-LEM-nihs
High Mass

Literally "solemn mass."

mobile perpetuum
MAW-bih-leh pehr-PEH-too-uum
something perpetually in motion

The impossible dream of the inventor who rejects the laws of thermodynamics.

mobile vulgus
MAW-bih-leh WUUL-guus
the fickle crowd

A phrase, literally "the movable public," that recognizes the inconstancy of popular taste and the ease with which adroit politicians can influence the great mass of voters—and can lose the support of the same voters when circumstances turn against them. It is interesting to note that the English word "mob" is a contraction of *mobile vulgus*.

modus operandi
MAW-duus aw-peh-RAHN-dee
manner of working

Every devotee of crime stories knows this phrase and the police abbreviation for it, **M.O.**, designating the pattern a criminal typically follows in pursuing his felonious ways. But *modus operandi* is not restricted to police use. Any work plan or scheme for doing a job may be termed a *modus operandi*, pronounced MOHD-əs ahp-ə-RAN-dee in English.

modus vivendi
MAW-duus wee-WEN-dee
a way of getting along together

When partners in any human enterprise must somehow manage to get along with one another despite the fact that they are not on the best of terms, they reach an accommodation, a *modus vivendi*, literally "a way of living," which makes possible the continuing relationship. The English pronunciation of *modus vivendi* is MOHD-əs vi-VEN-dee.

montani semper liberi
mawn-TAH-nee SEM-pehr LEE-beh-ree
mountaineers are always freemen

Motto of West Virginia.

morituri te salutamus
maw-rih-TOO-ree tay sah-loo-TAH-muus
we who are about to die salute you

See AVE CAESAR, MORITURI TE SALUTANT.

mors tua, vita mea
mawrs TOO-ah WEE-tah MAY-ah
you must die so that I may live

One who can preserve his own life only by taking the life of another—think of the hired assassin or the desperately ill patient awaiting an organ transplant from a dying donor—may employ this dismal expression, literally "your death, my life."

mortis causa
MAWR-tihs KOW-sah
in prospect of death

A legal expression, literally "because of death," used to describe a decision made in anticipation of one's death. The phrase is seen in old wills.

mortui non mordent
MAWR-too-ee nohn MAWR-dent
dead men carry no tales

In its literal meaning, "dead men don't bite," an especially colorful expression.

mox nox in rem
mawks nawks in rem
let's get on with it

For anyone who believes that things are moving too slowly, an excellent call to action, akin to "let's get this show on the road," but literally "soon night, to the business."

multi sunt vocati, pauci vero electi

MUUL-tee suunt waw-KAH-tee POW-kee WAY-roh
eh-LEH-ktee

many are called, but few are chosen

The words of Matthew.

multum in parvo

MUUL-tuum in PAHR-woh

much in little

A useful phrase for praising a message or a reference book
that conveys much information in few words.

mundus vult decipi

MUUN-duus wuult DAY-kih-pee

there's a sucker born every minute

Mundus vult decipi, literally "the world wants to be deceived," concludes **et decipiatur** (et day-kih-pee-AH-tuur), "and
let it be deceived." This thought, from an unknown Roman P.
T. Barnum, shows that twentieth-century man did not invent
cynicism or opportunism.

mutatis mutandis

moo-TAH-tees moo-TAHN-dees

after making the necessary changes

This phrase can be rendered as "when what must be changed
has been changed," or translated more literally as "things having been changed that had to be changed," in the sense "with
alterations to fit the new circumstances." Thus, we may write
a sentence such as: "The new regulations governing our men's
athletic teams are to apply as well to our women's teams, *muta-
tis mutandis*."

mutato nomine
moo-TAH-toh NAW-mih-neh
with the name changed

Literally "the name having been changed." This phrase becomes more interesting when we add the rest of Horace's line from his *Satires*: **de te fabula narratur** (day tay FAH-buu-lah NAHR-rah-tuur). Now we have "with the name changed, the story applies to you." Can you see the opportunities *mutato nomine* offers?

nam et ipsa scientia potestas est
nahm et IH-psah skee-EN-tee-ah paw-TES-tahs est
knowledge is power

Francis Bacon's much repeated and often borrowed aphorism, literally "for knowledge too is itself power."

nascentes morimur
nah-SKEN-tays maw-REE-muur
every day we die a little

This sobering thought from Manilius, in *Astronomica*, translates literally as "from the moment of birth we begin to die." It concludes **finisque ab origine pendet** (fih-NIHS-kweh ahb aw-REE-gih-neh PEN-det), "and the end hangs from the beginning."

naturam expelles furca tamen usque recurret
nah-TOO-rahm ek-SPEL-lays FUUR-kah TAH-men UUS-kweh reh-KUUR-ret
the leopard cannot change its spots

This proverb from Horace's *Epistles*, literally "you may drive nature out with a pitchfork, but it will still return," states the nature side of the nature vs. nurture debate.

191 nec pluribus impar 191

natura non facit saltum
nah-TOO-rah nohn FAH-kiht SAHL-tuum
nature makes no leaps

This aphorism suggests the continuity and consistency of natural phenomena. Great changes that become evident as time goes by are achieved slowly and gradually, and always in consonance with underlying natural principles. Alexander Pope, in *An Essay on Man*: "Order is heaven's first law."

ne Aesopum quidem trivit
nay Ī-saw-puum KWIH-dem TREE-wit
he doesn't know beans about anything

Aesop's *Fables* was used as a primer for Roman schoolboys, so *ne Aesopum quidem trivit*, literally "he has not even thumbed through Aesop," is strong condemnation.

ne cede malis
nay KAY-deh MAH-lees
do not yield to misfortunes

nec pluribus impar
nek PLOO-rih-buus IHM-pahr
a match for anyone

The motto, literally "not unequal to most," of Louis XIV of France, who used the sun as his emblem and was known as *le Roi Soleil*, "the sun king." "Not unequal to most" and its Latin counterpart are good examples of litotes, understatement in which an affirmative thought is expressed by stating the negative of the contrary thought.

nefasti dies
neh-FAH-stee DEE-ays
legal holidays

Certain days in the Roman religious calendar were *nefasti dies*, days in which official business of any kind was proscribed.

nemine contradicente
NAY-mih-neh kawn-trah-dih-KEN-teh
unanimously

Literally "no one contradicting."

nemine dissentiente
NAY-mih-neh dihs-sen-tih-EN-teh
unanimously

Literally "no one dissenting."

nemo liber est qui corpori servit
NAY-moh LEE-behr est kwee KAWR-paw-ree
SEHR-wit
no one is free who is a slave to his body

Seneca's observation may have been intended for those who indulged in the unbridled pursuit of pleasure (and other excesses), but it can just as easily be applied to frenzied dieters, dogged joggers, natural food faddists, and those who enrich manufacturers of vitamins.

nemo malus felix
NAY-moh MAH-luus FAY-liks
"there is no peace unto the wicked"

Isaiah provides this observation, literally "no bad man is happy."

nemo me impune lacessit
NAY-moh may im-POO-neh lah-KES-sit
no one provokes me with impunity

Motto of the kings of Scotland.

nemo repente fuit turpissimus
NAY-moh reh-PEN-teh FOO-it tuur-PIHS-sih-muus
no one ever became extremely wicked suddenly

Juvenal, in his *Satires*, telling us we can always find a history of mischief in anyone who goes wrong in a big way.

ne plus ultra
nay ploos UUL-trah
perfection

Ne plus ultra may be translated formally as "the acme" or "the highest attainable point," literally as "not more beyond." The literal sense of the phrase enables it to be used as a term expressing prohibition, in the sense of "no further may you go," but its primary use remains that of indicating the supremacy of a product, a literary work, a system, and the like.

ne quid nimis
nay kwid NIH-mihs
nothing in excess

Yet another Roman expression advocating the middle ground in all things.

ne supra crepidam sutor iudicaret (or judicaret)
nay SUU-prah KREH-pih-dahm SOO-tawr
yoo-dih-KAH-ret
cobbler, stick to your last

These wise words, literally "the cobbler should not judge above the sandal," of Pliny the Elder, first-century A.D. Roman naturalist and writer, advise us not to make judgments in areas in which we have no special competence. The story behind the expression concerns a cobbler's encounter with Apelles, a Greek painter, fourth century B.C. The cobbler correctly criticized the representation of a sandal in a painting Apelles was working on. Unfortunately, he went on to criticize the way in which the subject's legs were being painted. This was too much for Apelles, who responded with his memorable rebuke: *ne supra crepidam sutor iudicaret* (also given as *sutor, ne supra crepidam*).

nigro notanda lapillo
NIH-groh naw-TAHN-dah lah-PIHL-loh
marking (a day) with a black pebble

In ancient Rome, a sad day or an unlucky day was marked with a black pebble, **niger lapillus** (NIH-gehr lah-PIHL-luus), a happy or lucky day with a white pebble, **albus** (AHL-buus) **lapillus**. (See ALBO LAPILLO NOTARE DIEM.) Black pebbles were also used at Roman trials to signify a guilty verdict, white stones acquittal.

nihil agendo homines male agere discunt
NIH-hihl ah-GEN-doh HAW-mih-nays MAH-lay
AH-geh-reh DIH-skuunt
the devil finds mischief for idle hands

Literally "by doing nothing, men learn to act wickedly."

nihil obstat
NIH-hihl AWB-staht
nothing stands in its way

Nihil obstat—the complete expression is **nihil obstat quo-minus imprimatur** (KWOH-mih-nuus ihm-prih-MAH-tuur), "nothing hinders it from being published"—are the words used by a Roman Catholic censor to indicate that a book has been found to contain nothing morally offensive or contrary to the faith. A *nihil obstat*, therefore, is a clean bill of health.

nil admirari
neel ahd-mee-RAH-ree
to wonder at nothing

According to Horace's *Epistles*, *nil admirari*, which also translates as "to admire nothing," may be the only way a person can become happy and remain happy. Stolid indifference is strange counsel, but is not *nil admirari* the slogan of the truly cool?

nil desperandum
neel deh-spay-RAHN-duum
never say die

The old college spirit, as expressed by Horace in his *Odes*, meaning literally "nothing is to be despaired of." As Yogi Berra so aptly puts it, "The game ain't over until it's over."

Nil habet infelix paupertas durius in se,
Quam quod ridiculos homines facit.
neel HAH-bet in-FAY-liks POW-pehr-tahs DOO-ree-uus
in say
kwahm kwawd ree-DIH-kuu-lohs HAW-mih-nays
FAH-kit
"Nothing in poverty so ill is borne
As its exposing men to grinning scorn."

The translation of two lines from Juvenal's *Satires* is by John Oldham, 1653–1683, sometimes called the English Juvenal. The thought is as apt today—uncaring politicians take note—as it was in ancient Rome.

nil nisi bonum
neel NIH-sih BAWN-uum
nothing unless good

See DE MORTUIS NIHIL NISI BONUM.

nil novi sub sole
neel NAW-wee suub SOH-leh
nothing new under the sun

This well-known phrase from Ecclesiastes reads fully: "That which hath been is that which shall be, and that which hath been done is that which shall be done; and there is nothing new under the sun."

nil sine numine
neel SIH-neh NOO-mih-neh
nothing without divine will

Motto of Colorado.

nolens, volens

NOH-lens WAW-lens

whether willing or not

Literally "being unwilling, willing." Anyone who does something he really does not want to do does it *nolens, volens*. The phrase is used also to mean "willy-nilly," in the sense of "haphazardly."

noli me tangere

NOH-lee may TAHN-geh-reh

touch me not

John has it that Christ said these words when he was approached by Mary Magdalene after the resurrection. Today, a picture representing this scene is called a *noli me tangere*, and the impatiens plant is also called by this name, as well as by "touch-me-not."

nolo contendere

NOH-loh kawn-TEN-deh-reh

I do not wish to contend

The plea of a defendant in a criminal proceeding who does not admit guilt but states that he will offer no defense against the charges. The defendant may then be declared guilty, yet retain the right to deny the validity of that finding in related proceedings. "Spiro Agnew pled *nolo contendere* to a charge of income tax evasion."

non bis in idem

nohn bihs in IH-dem

not twice for the same thing

The Latin expression proscribing double jeopardy in the courts. Also a boy's defense against further punishment by his father after being punished by his mother.

non compos mentis
nohn KAWM-paws MEN-tihs
not of sound mind

The legal expression used for any form of mental unsoundness. (See COMPOS MENTIS.)

non erat his locus
nohn EH-raht hees LAW-kuus
that was inappropriate

Literally "that was not the place for these things."

non est tanti
nohn est TAHN-tee
it's no big deal

Literally "it is not of such great importance."

non est vivere sed valere vita est
nohn est WEE-weh-reh sed wah-LAY-reh WEE-tah est
life is more than just being alive

From Martial's *Epigrams*, literally "life is not being alive but being well." A suitable motto for those who value physical fitness. (But see NEMO LIBER EST QUI CORPORI SERVIT.)

non ignara mali, miseris succurrere disco
nohn ih-GNAH-rah MAH-lee mih-SEH-rees
suuk-KUUR-reh-reh DIH-skoh
I've been there myself

One rationale for helping people in distress, from Virgil's *Aeneid*. Dido, Queen of Carthage, greets Aeneas and his companions, who are in exile: *Non ignara mali*, "no stranger to misfortune myself," *miseris succurrere disco*, "I learn to relieve the sufferings of others."

non licet omnibus adire Corinthum
nohn LIH-ket AWM-nih-buus ahd-EE-reh
kaw-RIHN-tuum
circumstances deny us certain pleasures

From Horace's *Epistles*, literally "not everyone is permitted to go to Corinth." Why? Corinth was the Paris of its day, but its pleasures were too costly for the pocketbooks of many people. The expression is also given as **non cuivis homini contingit** (nohn KOOEE-wihs HAW-mih-nee kawn-TIHNG-it) **adire Corinthum**, "it does not fall to every man's lot to go to Corinth."

non mihi, non tibi, sed nobis
nohn MIH-hee nohn TIH-bee sed NOH-bees
not for you, not for me, but for us

non nova sed nove
nohn NAW-wah sed NAW-way
not new things but in a new way

non obstante
nohn awb-STAHN-teh
notwithstanding

non omnia possumus omnes
nohn AWM-nee-ah PAWS-suu-muus AWM-nays
we cannot all do everything

Virgil, in the *Aeneid*, gives us this way to acknowledge a fact of life: No one can reasonably be expected to become expert in all things.

non omnis moriar
nohn AWM-nihs MAW-ree-ahr
I shall not wholly die

This was Horace's way, in the *Odes*, of telling the world that his works would live forever. Not a bad call.

non placet
nohn PLAH-ket
nay

A formal way of indicating dissent, literally translated as "it does not please."

non possumus
nohn PAWS-suu-muus
no way!

The answer, literally "we cannot," given by Peter and John when they were asked to stop preaching, and now used by a pope to reject a suggested innovation in doctrine. *Non possumus* may be used by the rest of us in pleading inability to honor a request.

non semper ea sunt quae videntur
nohn SEM-pehr AY-ah suunt kwī wih-DEN-tuur
things are not always what they appear to be

Phaedrus, first-century A.D. Roman fabulist, came up with this gem to warn the unwary. In *H.M.S. Pinafore*, William S. Gilbert put it this way: "Things are seldom what they seem, Skim milk masquerades as cream."

non semper erit aestas
nohn SEM-pehr EH-rit Ī-stahs
be prepared for hard times

Literally "it will not always be summer." A similar bit of advice, this one from Seneca, is **non semper Saturnalia erunt** (sah-tuur-NAH-lee-ah EH-ruunt), literally "the Saturnalia will not last forever," more freely "every day is not a holiday." The Saturnalia, one of the principal festivals of the Romans, was celebrated in December. A time of merrymaking—often debauchery—the period of the Saturnalia saw suspension of all public business: Schools and courts were shut down, criminals were not punished, and even slaves enjoyed a taste of liberty. But the implication of Seneca's words and of *non semper erit aestas* is not lost on us: The day of reckoning will come.

non sequitur

nohn SEH-kwih-tuur

it does not follow

A familiar way of indicating a logical fallacy: A conclusion offered cannot justly be inferred from the premises. The English pronunciation of *non sequitur* is non SEK-wə-tər.

non sum qualis eram

nohn suum KWAH-lihs EH-rahm

I'm a different person today

Horace gave us this line in his *Odes*, literally translated as "I am not the sort of person I was," and we may use it whenever there is a need to explain why our character and behavior have changed. The full line from Horace is **non sum qualis eram bonae sub regno Cinarae** (BAW-nī suub REH-gnoh kih-NAH-rī), literally "I am not what I was under the reign of good Cynara." The poet is pleading with Venus, the goddess of love, to stop tempting him with love, since he is no longer the man he once was. It is worthwhile to recall Cynara now for reasons that soon will become clear. In the poem "Cynara," the nineteenth-century English poet Ernest Dowson used as a refrain "I have been faithful to thee, Cynara, in my fashion"—recall the song from *Kiss Me, Kate*—and in one of the stanzas wrote: "I have forgot much, Cynara! gone with the wind. . . ." Need one say more?

non teneas aurum totum quod splendet ut aurum
nohn TEH-nay-ahs OW-ruum TOH-tuum kwawd
SPLEN-det uut OW-ruum
all that glitters is not gold

Literally "do not take as gold everything that shines like gold." In *The Merchant of Venice*, Shakespeare gave the line as "All that glisters is not gold."

nosce te ipsum
NAW-skeh tay IH-psuum
know thyself

Plutarch attributed this advice to Plato, but a score of candidates may claim original authorship. Plutarch reported that *nosce te ipsum* was inscribed—in Greek, of course—at the oracle at Delphi.

nota bene
NAW-tah BEH-neh
take notice

The familiar way of calling attention to something of importance in a letter or other document one is writing, and abbreviated **N.B.** The literal meaning is "note well." "*N.B.* The alliance had already begun to fall apart by that time."

notatu dignum
naw-TAH-too DIH-gnuum
worthy of note

novissima verba

naw-WIHS-sih-mah WEHR-bah

final words

Latin for a person's last utterance.

novus homo

NAW-wuus HAW-moh

a Johnny-come-lately

Literally "a new man," but used to describe a *parvenu*. In the days of the Roman republic, a *novus homo* was the first man in a family to hold a consulship, thus ennobling both himself and his family.

novus ordo seclorum

NAW-wuus AWR-doh seh-KLAW-ruum

a new order of the ages (is created)

Motto on the great seal of the United States. (See ANNUIT COEPTIS and any one-dollar bill.)

nudum pactum

NOO-duum PAH-ktuum

an invalid agreement

Literally "a nude pact." This legal phrase describes a contract made without a consideration—that is, without passing something of value sufficient to make the contract binding and therefore resulting in no contract at all. In Roman law, **nudus** (NOO-duus) was used either to describe a promise made without formal agreement or to describe a type of ownership that did not include the right to convey a property to others.

nulla dies sine linea
NUUL-lah DEE-ays SIH-neh LIH-nay-ah
you've got to keep at it

This expression, applied by Pliny to the Greek painter Apelles (see NE SUPRA CREPIDAM SUTOR IUDICARET), described the painter's admirable steadfastness in practicing his art, and is translated literally as "not a day without a line."

nulli secundus
NUUL-lee seh-KUUN-duus
second to none

nullius filius
NUUL-lee-uus FEE-lee-uus
a bastard

Literally "no one's son."

nullum quod tetigit non ornavit
NUUL-luum kwawd TEH-tih-giht nohn awr-NAH-wiht
he touched nothing he did not adorn

From Dr. Johnson's epitaph on Goldsmith: "To Oliver Goldsmith, A Poet, Naturalist, and Historian, who left scarcely any style of writing untouched, and touched none [a better translation of *nullum*] he did not adorn."

numerus clausus
NUU-meh-ruus KLOW-suus
a quota

This ugly phrase, literally "closed number," veils in Latin the idea of limiting membership of classes of people deemed undesirable for a club, school, or the like. "When a *num-*

erus clausus is condoned for any group, your group may be next."

nunc aut nunquam
nuunk owt NUUN-kwahm
now or never

An excellent phrase for anyone to use when trying to force someone into making a decision.

nunc dimittis
nuunk dee-MIHT-tihs
permission to leave

From Luke: **nunc dimittis servum tuum, Domine** (SEHR-wuum TOO-uum DAW-mih-neh), "Lord, now let thy servant depart." To receive one's *nunc dimittis* is, therefore, to receive permission to depart.

nunc est bibendum
nuunk est bih-BEN-dum
break out the champagne

Horace's call to merrymaking, literally "now it's time to drink," from the *Odes*.

nunc pro tunc
nuunk proh tuunk
now for then

A wage settlement or other agreement made *nunc pro tunc* is retroactive to some time prior to the date of the settlement.

nunc scripsi totum pro Christo da mihi potum
nuunk SKRIH-psee TOH-tuum proh KRIH-stoh dah
MIH-hee PAW-tuum
Now I have written so much for Christ, give me a
drink!

With this inscription, monk-copyists marked the end of a
manuscript or perhaps the end of a day's work.

nunquam non paratus
NUUN-kwahm nohn pah-RAH-tuus
never unprepared

A less direct way to say SEMPER PARATUS.

obiit
AWB-ih-iht
he or she died

An inscription found on tombstones and in church records.
All that remains to be done is to supply the date of the unhappy
event.

obiit sine prole
AWB-ih-iht SIH-neh PROH-leh
he or she died without issue

Even unhappier than the preceding entry.

obiter dictum
AW-bih-tehr DIH-ktuum
an incidental remark

A legal phrase, designating a statement made in passing by a
judge on a tangential matter in connection with a judicial opin-

ion he is rendering. While an *obiter dictum*—the plural is **obiter dicta** (DIH-ktah)—has no legal bearing on the opinion to which it is appended, it may have considerable effect in later cases, since it may be read and considered along with the full opinion, and in some circumstances become even more important than the opinion itself. The English pronunciation of *obiter dictum* is OH-bit-ər DIKT-əm.

obsta principiis
AWB-stah prihn-KIH-pee-ees
nip it in the bud

Ovid advises in *Remedia Amoris* that we take immediate steps, literally that we "resist the beginnings," once we know we have fallen into difficulties: It is much easier to root out evil as soon as it appears than to try to do so after its effects have become pervasive.

obstupui, steteruntque comae, et vox faucibus haesit
awb-STUU-poo-ee steh-teh-RUUNT-kweh KAW-mī et wawks FOW-kih-buus HĪ-siht
I was scared stiff

A description of the physical effects of fear, from Virgil's *Aeneid*, literally "I was stupefied, and my hair stood on end, and my voice stuck to my throat." How about that?

occasionem cognosce
awk-kah-see-OH-nem kaw-GNAW-skeh
strike while the iron is hot

Literally "recognize opportunity."

oderint dum metuant
OH-deh-rihnt duum MEH-too-ahnt
let them hate, provided they fear

A motto attributed to Emperor Tiberius, now appropriate for any despot or misguided business executive.

odi et amo
OH-dee et AH-moh
I hate and I love

Catullus, verbalizing the love-hate relationship. His thoughts continue: "I don't know why, and I am in agony."

odium
AW-dee-uum
hatred

This word, in English pronounced OHD-ee-əm, plays a part in several Latin phrases of interest. **Odium aestheticum** (ī-STEH-tih-kuum) designates the bitter rivalry among artists and writers; **odium medicum** (MEH-dih-kuum), the hatred of physicians for one another—consider the attitude of the medical establishment toward radical practitioners; **odium theologicum** (tay-aw-LAW-gih-kuum), mutual hatred among theologians, the result of differences in doctrinal interpretation.

O fortunatos nimium, sua si bona norint, agricolas.
oh fawr-too-NAH-tohs NIH-mee-uum SOO-ah see
BAW-nah NOH-rihnt ah-GRIH-kaw-lahs
Oh, blessed beyond all bliss, the farmers—did they but know their happiness.

Virgil, in the *Georgics*, apparently expressing a romantic view of bucolic life. In fairness to Virgil, the farmers he had in mind in this characterization were not perceived as blessed because of the nature of their work or their surroundings, but because they were far removed from the dangers experienced by warriors.

oleo tranquillior
AW-lay-oh trahn-KWIHL-lee-awr
smoother than oil

An interesting phrase from the Psalms: "His mouth was as smooth as butter, but his heart was war; his words were smoother than oil, yet they were drawn swords."

olet lucernam
AW-let luu-KEHR-nahm
it smells of the lamp

Any labored literary work may be condemned with this phrase, also given as **redolet** (REH-daw-let) **lucernam**. So while students are advised to burn the midnight oil, poets and other creative writers must avoid giving the impression that they have labored too long over a piece of work. (See OLEUM PERDISTI.)

oleum addere camino
AW-lay-uum AHD-deh-reh kah-MEE-noh
to make bad things worse

Literally "to pour fuel on the stove."

oleum perdisti
AW-lay-uum pehr-DIH-stee
you've wasted your time

Like *olet lucernam*, this phrase refers to the oil lamps used by Romans, this time in the literal meaning "you have lost oil," telling a writer that whatever oil he burned while working on a manuscript was ill spent. A useful phrase for anyone intent on critical attack.

olim meminisse iuvabit (or juvabit)
OH-lihm meh-mih-NIHS-seh yuu-WAH-biht
it will be pleasant to look back on things past

> Shades of Shakespeare and Proust:
>
>> When to the sessions of sweet silent thought
>> I summon up remembrance of things past. . . .
>
> (See FORSAN ET HAEC OLIM MEMINISSE IUVABIT.)

omne ignotum pro magnifico est
AWM-neh ih-GNOH-tuum proh mah-GNIH-fih-koh est
distance lends enchantment

Tacitus, in *Agricola*, gives us this useful phrase, literally "everything unknown is thought magnificent." But it can also be interpreted as "everything unknown is thought to be more difficult or challenging than it really is."

omnem movere lapidem
AWM-nem maw-WAY-reh LAH-pih-dem
keep trying

This saying, literally "to move every stone" or "to leave no stone unturned" adjures us to do our level best in any enterprise.

omnes deteriores sumus licentia
AWM-nays day-teh-ree-OH-rays SUUM-uus
lih-KEN-tee-ah
too much freedom debases us

A saying attributed to Terence. Applied to child rearing, today sometimes called "mothering" or "fathering," these words recall "spare the rod and spoil the child."

omne trinum est perfectum
AWM-neh TREE-nuum est pehr-FEH-ktuum
everything in threes is perfect

An old adage, reflecting the mystical power ascribed to the number three. Three fates, three graces, three muses, the trinity, three kings, Jonah in the whale's belly for three days and three nights, three cardinal colors, three cheers—the list is a long one.

omne tulit punctum qui miscuit utile dulci
AWM-neh TUU-liht PUUN-ktuum kwee MIH-skoo-iht
OO-tih-leh DUUL-kee
he has gained every point who has combined the useful with the agreeable

Horace, in *Ars Poetica*.

omnia mutantur nos et mutamur in illis
AWM-nee-ah moo-TAHN-tuur nohs et moo-TAH-muur
in IHL-lees
all things change, and we change with them

Unless we want to be left behind.

omnia vincit amor
AWM-nee-ah WIHN-kiht AH-mawr
love conquers all

See AMOR VINCIT OMNIA.

omnia vincit labor
AWM-nee-ah WIHN-kiht LAH-bawr
work conquers all things

See LABOR OMNIA VINCIT.

onus probandi
AW-nuus praw-BAHN-dee
the burden of proof

Literally "the burden of proving."

op. cit.

See OPERE CITATO.

ope et consilio
AW-peh et kawn-SIH-lee-oh
with help and counsel

opere citato
AW-peh-reh kih-TAH-toh
in the work cited

Known better in its abbreviated form, **op. cit.**, this scholarly
phrase is used in a footnote to indicate reference to a work
previously cited. For example, "Flexner, *op. cit.*, p. 242."

opere in medio
AW-peh-reh in MEH-dee-oh
in the midst of work

A useful phrase: "You caught me *opere in medio*."

optat supremo collocare Sisyphus in monte saxum
AW-ptaht suu-PRAY-moh kawl-law-KAH-reh
SIH-sih-puus in MAWN-teh SAH-ksuum
someone up there doesn't love me

The literal translation of this phrase is "Sisyphus tries to place the boulder atop the mountain," but the phrase does not end there: **sed vetant leges Iovis** (sehd WEH-tahnt LEH-gays YOH-wihs), "but Jove's decrees forbid." Poor Sisyphus (in English pronounced SIS-ə-fəs), mythological ruler of Corinth, was known for his cunning. In one version of the myth, the gods decided to punish him for showing disrespect to Zeus. They compelled him forever to push a boulder to the top of a mountain. Each time Sisyphus tried, he moved it closer to the top, but at the last moment the boulder would slip from his grasp and roll farther down the mountain from where he had started. Thus, when anyone is confronted with a task that seems to become harder and harder to complete, the task is termed Sisyphean (sis-ə-FEE-ən). Have the gods taken offense?

opus magnum
AW-puus MAH-gnuum
a masterpiece

Literally "a great work." Also given as *magnum opus*.

ora et labora
OH-rah et lah-BOH-rah
pray and work

ora pro nobis
OH-rah proh NOH-bees
pray for us

orator fit, poeta nascitur

AWR-ah-tawr fiht PAW-eh-tah NAHS-kih-tuur

poets are born, not made

Literally "an orator is made, a poet is born."

origo mali

aw-REE-goh MAH-lee

the source or origin of evil

Choose your own uses for this phrase.

O si sic omnia

oh see sihk AWM-nee-ah

oh, if everything were thus

A happy phrase for those rare times when one completes a task without a hitch, enjoys an ideal vacation, or. . . .

O tempora! O mores!

oh TEM-paw-rah oh MOH-rays

these are bad times

Literally, "Oh, the times! Oh, the habits!" Speaking in the Roman Senate, Cicero opened an attack on Catiline—he was accusing Catiline of conspiracy—with a rhetorical question, "How long will you abuse our patience, Catiline?" and then exclaimed, "*O tempora! O mores!*" The phrase has become a legacy for all who wish to decry the times they live in.

otium cum dignitate

OH-tee-uum kuum dih-gnih-TAH-teh

leisure with dignity

The best kind.

pace tua
PAH-keh TOO-ah
with your permission

Paete, non dolet
PĪ-teh nohn DAW-leht
don't worry, it doesn't hurt

Literally "Paetus, it does not hurt." The classic way to firm up the wavering resolve of the second principal in a double-suicide team to fulfill the rest of the agreement after the first member has taken the irretrievable step. **Paetus** (PĪ-tuus), who had made the mistake of criticizing Emperor Nero, was number two in a husband-and-wife suicide team. He watched while **Arria** (AHR-ree-ah), his wife, opened a vein in her arm. She then handed him the dagger and said, "*Paete, non dolet.*" It is an obvious advantage to know the right words to say under such circumstances.

pallida Mors
PAH-lih-dah mawrs
pale Death

The opening words of a sobering observation from Horace's *Odes*: "Pale Death with impartial foot knocks at the doors of poor men's lodgings and of king's castles."

panem et circenses
PAH-nehm et kihr-KEN-says
bread and circus games

Juvenal said that the Romans, once rulers of the world, had come to care for nothing but handouts and spectacles, and *panem et circenses* was the favorite formula for Roman leaders who wanted to keep the allegiance of the masses.

pares cum paribus
PAH-rays kuum PAH-rih-buus
birds of a feather

   The full expression is **pares cum paribus facillime congregan-tur** (fah-KIHL-lih-may kawn-greh-GAHN-tuur), with the literal meaning "like persons most readily crowd together."

pari passu
PAH-ree PAHS-soo
at an equal pace

   Two or more projects being worked on simultaneously and receiving an equal degree of attention—or inattention—may be said to be worked on *pari passu*.

pari ratione
PAH-ree rah-tih-OH-neh
by equally valid reasoning

   Literally "for a like reason." "Having explained at length why neither candidate was acceptable to her, she concluded her statement with, '*Pari ratione*, I am forced to stay home this November.'"

par pari refero
pahr PAH-ree REH-feh-roh
tit for tat

   Literally "I return like for like." (See LEX TALIONIS.)

particeps criminis
PAHR-tih-keps KREE-mih-nihs
an accomplice

   Literally "a partner in the crime."

parturient montes, nascetur ridiculus mus
pahr-TUU-ree-ehnt MAWN-tays nah-SKAY-tuur
ree-DIH-kuu-luus moos
all that work and nothing to show for it

Literally "mountains will be in labor, and an absurd mouse will be born," Horace's pungent line from *Ars Poetica*. An apt way to derogate a long-awaited novel, an expensive Broadway production, a much-discussed new building, a monumental piece of sculpture, or the like that fails to live up to expectations.

parva leves capiunt animas
PAHR-wah LEH-wehs KAH-pih-uunt AHN-ih-mahs
small minds concern themselves with trifles

Literally "small things occupy light minds," one of Ovid's lines in *Ars Amatoria*, and an apt comment when one is offended by pettiness.

passim
PAHS-sihm
here and there

A scholarly reference, also translated as "in various places" or "in many places." *Passim* informs the reader that the topic under discussion is treated in various places in a book or article that has been cited. For example, "Chapter 4 *passim*" indicates that the topic is discussed here and there in the entire chapter; "Chapter 4 *et passim*" indicates that the topic is discussed in Chapter 4 as well as here and there throughout the rest of the work.

paterfamilias
PAH-tehr-fah-MIH-lih-ahs
a patriarch

Literally "father of a family." *Paterfamilias* can also be taken as "head of a household." (See MATERFAMILIAS.)

pater noster
PAH-tehr NAW-stehr
our father

The opening words of the Lord's Prayer, in Latin called the *Paternoster*: "Our Father, which art in heaven . . ."

pater patriae
PAH-tehr PAH-tree-ī
father of his country

The Romans sometimes used this expression to designate distinguished statesmen.

patris est filius
PAH-trihs est FEE-lee-uus
a chip off the old block

Literally "he is his father's son."

pauca sed bona
POW-kah sed BAWN-ah
few things, but good

An excellent precept for Christmas shoppers.

paucis verbis
POW-kees WEHR-bees
in brief

Literally "in few words."

paupertas omnium artium repertrix
POW-pehr-tahs AWM-nee-uum AHR-tee-uum
reh-PEHR-trihks
necessity is the mother of invention

Literally "poverty is the inventor of all the arts."

pax
pahks
peace

This Latin word gives us the core of many expressions. **Pax Britannica** (brih-TAHN-nih-kah), literally "the peace of Britain," reflects the terms imposed by the British—a British peace —on members of their colonial empire. **Pax in bello** (in BEL-loh) is "peace in war," a peace in which fighting continues but at a reduced rate. **Pax regis** (REH-gihs) is "the king's peace." **Pax Romana** (roh-MAH-nah), literally "the Roman peace," denotes the peace dictated by the impressive strength of the Roman military. **Pax vobiscum** (woh-BEES-kuum) is a greeting, literally "peace be unto you." Christ greeted the apostles with these words on the first Easter morning. **Pax tecum** (TAY-kuum), literally "peace be unto you," is the singular form of *pax vobiscum*.

peccavi
pehk-KAH-wee
I have sinned

The pleasurable aspect of this frank admission, normally made in the confessional (see MEA CULPA), lies in its use in a dispatch by Sir Charles Napier, a British general, while on campaign in 1843 in northwest India. Having taken Miani, in central Sind, he wrote the single word *Peccavi* as his entire message to his superiors, announcing conquest—in actuality at that point still incomplete—of the entire region. Listen closely: *Peccavi*. (I have sinned? No, I have Sind.)

pecuniae obediunt omnia
peh-KOO-nee-ī awb-AY-dee-uunt AWM-nee-ah
money makes the world go round

Literally "all things yield to money." *Obediunt* is also seen as **oboediunt**, pronounced awb-OY-dee-unt.

pecunia non olet
peh-KOO-nee-ah nohn AW-leht
money doesn't smell

A Roman proverb counseling us not to concern ourselves with the source of any money that may come our way: Don't look a gift horse in the mouth.

penates
peh-NAH-tays
household gods

See LARES ET PENATES.

pendente lite
pehn-DEHN-teh LEE-teh
while the suit is pending

A legal phrase. "*Pendente lite*, I shall say make no public statements." Unless I see a way to help my cause by speaking out?

penetralia mentis
peh-neh-TRAH-lee-ah MEN-tihs
heart of hearts

Literally "the innermost recesses of the mind."

per acria belli
pehr AH-kree-ah BEL-lee
through the harshness of war

The word *acria* may also be translated as "bitterness" or "savagery."

per angusta ad augusta
pehr ahn-GUU-stah ahd ow-GUU-stah
through difficulties to honors

Also given as AD AUGUSTA PER ANGUSTA.

per annum
pehr AHN-nuum
annually

Literally "by the year." The English pronunciation of *per annum* is pər AN-əm.

per ardua ad astra
pehr AHR-doo-ah ahd AH-strah
through difficulties to the stars

Motto of the Royal Air Force. The thought is also conveyed by *per aspera ad astra*. (See AD ASTRA PER ASPERA.)

per capita
pehr KAH-pih-tah
individually

Literally "by the head." The English pronunciation of *per capita* is pər KAP-ət-ə.

per centum
pehr KEHN-tuum
on each hundred

Literally "by the hundred." The English pronunciation of *per centum* is pər SENT-əm.

per contra
pehr KAWN-trah
on the contrary

This expression is used today most often to mean "on the opposite side of the argument."

per diem
pehr DEE-em
daily

Literally "by the day." The English pronunciation of *per diem* is pər DEE-əm.

per fas et nefas
pehr fahs et NEH-fahs
justly or unjustly

Literally "through right and wrong." "This is what I plan to do, *per fas et nefas*."

periculum in mora
peh-REE-kuu-luum ihn MAW-rah
danger in delay

A good expression to use when counseling against inaction.

per impossibile
pehr ihm-paws-SEE-bih-leh
as is impossible

An elegant way to qualify a proposition that cannot now or ever be true: "Assume, *per impossible,* that you were born in Shakespeare's time."

per incuriam
pehr ihn-KOO-ree-ahm
through carelessness

per interim
pehr IHN-teh-rihm
meanwhile

The English noun *interim* (IN-tə-rəm) is visible here.

per Iovem (or **Jovem**)
pehr YOH-wehm
by Jupiter

Also rendered in English by the phrase "by Jove," Jove being another name for Jupiter.

per mensem
pehr MEN-sehm
monthly

per minas
pehr MIH-nahs
by threats

permitte divis cetera
pehr-MIHT-teh DEE-wees KAY-teh-rah
leave the rest to the gods

Horace gives us this line in the *Odes*, suggesting that there is just so much we can do to order our lives, make our plans, and the like. "When you have done all you can in the interest of prudence, *permitte divis cetera* and take the plunge."

per se
pehr say
intrinsically

Literally "by or in itself." The English pronunciation of *per se* is pər say.

persona grata
pehr-SOH-nah GRAH-tah
an acceptable person

While this term can be taken to mean "a welcome guest" or "a favorite person," it is most generally used to describe a diplomatic representative who is acceptable to the government to which he or she is accredited. When a diplomat is no longer *persona grata*, he or she becomes **persona non** (nohn) **grata**.

persta atque obdura
PEHR-stah AHT-kweh awb-DOO-rah
be steadfast and endure

pessimum genus inimicorum laudantes
PEHS-sih-muum GEH-nuus ihn-ihm-ih-KOH-ruum
low-DAHN-tays
flatterers are the worst type of enemies

petitio principii
peh-TEE-tee-oh prihn-KIH-pee-ee
begging the question

The logical fallacy, literally "begging of the principle," of taking for granted that which remains to be proved. For example, stating as a matter of proof that parallel lines will never meet because they are parallel assumes as fact the very thought one is supposed to prove.

pictor ignotus
PIH-ktawr ih-GNOH-tuus
painter unknown

A way of indicating an anonymous work of art.

pinxit
PIN-ksiht
he or she painted it

This word, preceded by the name of the artist, is found on many old paintings.

placet
PLAH-keht
it pleases

Used as an affirmative vote or an expression of assent. (See NON PLACET.)

plaudite, cives
PLOW-dih-teh KEE-ways
let's hear it for the cast

Literally "applaud, citizens," *plaudite, cives* was the call addressed to an audience at the end of a Roman play.

plures crapula quam gladius
PLOO-rays KRAH-puu-lah kwahm GLAH-dee-uus
more people die partying than fighting wars

The Romans knew the toll taken by overindulgence: This grim expression translates literally as "drunkenness (kills) more than the sword."

poeta nascitur, non fit
paw-AY-tah NAH-skih-tuur nohn fiht
a poet is born, not made

See ORATOR FIT, POETA NASCITUR for yet another reminder for unpublished poets.

pollice verso
PAWL-lih-keh WEHR-soh
thumbs down

When a gladiator in a Roman amphitheater had an opponent at his mercy, he customarily looked toward the spectators for guidance on whether to administer the *coup de grâce*. If the spectators turned their thumbs toward their chests—*pollice verso*, literally "with thumb turned"—they were making clear that they wanted to see the opponent killed. If they wanted the opponent to live, they kept their thumbs in their fists—**pollice compresso** (kawm-PRES-soh), literally "with thumb folded." Our modern phrases of approval and disapproval, "thumbs up" and "thumbs down," do not ordinarily apply to situations of life and death, but they may derive from the Roman practice.

posse comitatus
PAWS-seh kaw-mih-TAH-tuus
a posse

Western fans will be pleased to know that a *posse comitatus*, literally "the power of a county," is the full phrase from which derives the word "posse" (pronounced PAHS-ee in English). Members of any self-respecting posse—in reality, too often a group of vigilantes—are enlisted on the spot by a sheriff just after the local bank has been robbed or some other outrage has been committed. Fortunately, everyone in a Hollywood Western has a horse to ride on and a rifle to fire at the bad guys, who are heading for the hills and soon will be ensconced behind boulders that will prove no more than a temporary barrier against the bullets of the posse's guns.

possunt quia posse videntur
PAWS-suunt KWEE-ah PAWS-seh wih-DEN-tuur
they can do it because they think they can do it

The power of positive thinking, as expressed by Virgil in the *Aeneid*, with the literal meaning "they can because they seem to be able to." The appearance of power bestows power.

post equitem sedet atra cura
pawst EH-kwih-tem SEH-det AH-trah KOO-rah
behind the horseman sits black care

One of the less appealing thoughts from Horace's *Odes*. The implication is that no one is free of anxiety.

post festum venisti
pawst FEH-stuum way-NIH-stee
sorry, too late!

Literally "you have arrived after the feast." This expression can be invoked whenever the overly cautious have let opportunity slip through their fingers. (See CARPE DIEM.)

post hoc, ergo propter hoc
pawst hawk EHR-goh PRAW-ptehr hawk
after this, therefore because of this

The logical fallacy that because one event follows another, the former must have caused the latter. For example, ingestion of a large quantity of vitamin C upon the first sign of a cold may well be followed by complete remission of cold symptoms, yet the true explanation of the phenomenon could lie elsewhere: a mistaken diagnosis, removal of an offending allergen, an improvement in astrological signs—heaven knows what. But until the jury returns on this one, perhaps it's better to take the megadose and risk the consequences of *post hoc, ergo propter hoc*.

post meridiem
pawst meh-REE-dee-em
after noon

The phrase we all know in its abbreviated form, **P.M.** (See ANTE MERIDIEM.)

post mortem
pawst MAWR-tehm
an autopsy

Literally "after death." The English noun "postmortem" is pronounced pohst-MAWRT-əm.

post nubila Phoebus
pawst NOO-bih-lah POY-buus
every cloud has a silver lining

Literally "after clouds, Phoebus." Phoebus, one of the names for Apollo, god of the sun, was used by poets to mean "the sun."

post partum
pawst PAHR-tuum
after childbirth

The period after delivery of a child. In English, we may hear of "postpartum depression." (See ANTE PARTUM.)

post scriptum
pawst SKRIH-ptuum
written afterward

Better known as **P.S.**

potius mori quam foedari
PAW-tee-uus MAW-ree kwahm foy-DAH-ree
death before dishonor

Literally "rather to die than to be dishonored." Whenever one expresses oneself in this vein, there is a tendency to run wild. Consider New Hampshire's "live free or die" and the once-current "better dead than red."

praemonitus praemunitus
prī-MAW-nih-tuus prī-MOO-nih-tuus
forewarned, forearmed

praestat sero quam nunquam
PRĪ-staht SAY-roh kwahm NUUN-kwahm
better late than never

prima facie
PREE-mah FAH-kee-eh
at first sight

This phrase, which finds frequent use in the law, has an English pronunciation: PRĪ-mə FAY-shə. *Prima facie* can be taken as "at first view or appearance" or "on first consideration." It suggests that thorough investigation has not been conducted, but an inference can be drawn that appears to be valid: "Notes found in the possession of a student sitting for an examination are considered *prima facie* evidence of intent to cheat." In law, therefore, a *prima facie* case is one based on facts legally sufficient to establish the case unless the facts presented are disproved.

primus inter pares
PREE-muus IHN-tehr PAH-rays
the first among equals

This paradoxical phrase finds use in describing the pecking order within a group of males of equal rank. The full professors in a university department are a good example. No individual professor stands above the others in rank, but the professor who is designated chairman may be said while holding that position to be *primus inter pares*. While he may not fire or otherwise affect the careers of the other professors, since they all are of equal rank, for the period of his chairmanship he presides over departmental meetings and has certain prerogatives not enjoyed by the others. There is a corresponding Latin phrase for a woman who is first among equals: **prima** (PREE-mah) **inter pares.**

probitas laudatur et alget
PRAW-bih-tahs low-DAH-tuur et AHL-geht
honesty is praised and is neglected

A cynical observation from Juvenal's *Satires*, sometimes rendered as "virtue is praised and then left to freeze." The implication is clear: Society may approve goodness of character but won't reward it.

pro bono publico
proh BAW-noh POO-blih-koh
for the public good

The full phrase for the expression **pro bono** (pronounced in English proh BOH-noh), often heard these days. Some attorneys devote a portion of their working time to cases *pro bono publico*, usually called *pro bono* cases, in which they represent the indigent or seek redress for public grievances, and a necessary condition of true *pro bono* work requires forgoing one's customary professional fees. Attorneys who take positions in firms that concentrate exclusively on such cases are said to be *pro bono* attorneys, and they can expect fewer of the legal life's customary rewards for their efforts. Undoubtedly there are countervailing rewards.

profanum vulgus
praw-FAH-nuum WUUL-guus
the common people

Literally "the profane multitude." (See MOBILE VULGUS.)

pro forma
proh FAWR-mah
as a formality

Literally "for form." "They made a *pro forma* appeal for a stay of execution, knowing they had little chance of saving their client's life."

promotor fidei
proh-MOH-tawr fih-DEH-ee
promoter of the faith

See ADVOCATUS DIABOLI.

pro patria
proh PAH-tree-ah
for one's country

Literally "for the country."

proprio motu
PRAW-pree-aw MOH-too
by one's own initiative

Literally "on one's own motion."

proprium humani ingenii est odisse quem laeseris
PRAW-pree-uum huu-MAH-nee ihn-GEN-ee-ee est oh-DIHS-seh kwehm LĪ-seh-rihs
it is human nature to hate a person whom you have injured

An insightful observation from Tacitus, in the *Agricola*.

pro rata
proh RAH-tah
in proportion

The English pronunciation of *pro rata* is proh RAYT-ə.

prosit
PROH-siht
l'chaim

A Latin toast, literally "may it benefit you," but freely trans-
latable as "to you," "your good fortune," "to life"—as rendered
above—and any of the multitude of expressions we use to wish
someone good health when we lift a glass of spirits or, in these
times, a glass of white wine. Perrier water does not qualify.

pro tempore
proh TEM-paw-reh
temporarily

The full phrase for **pro tem**, pronounced in English proh tem.
A chairperson *pro tem* is chairperson *pro tempore*, to serve until
a permanent chairperson is selected.

proxime accessit
PRAW-ksih-may ahk-KEHS-siht
he or she came nearest

See ACCESSIT.

P.S.

See POST SCRIPTUM.

punctatim
puun-KTAH-tihm
point for point

Punica fides
POO-nih-kah FIH-days
treachery

This ironic phrase, which translates literally as "Punic [Carthaginian] faith," reflects the Roman attitude toward their rivals in the Punic Wars. (See DELENDA EST CARTHAGO.)

Q.E.D.

Abbreviation of QUOD ERAT DEMONSTRANDUM.

Q.E.F.

Abbreviation of QUOD ERAT FACIENDUM.

qua
kwah
in the capacity of

A form of the pronoun **qui** (kwee), literal meaning "who," and pronounced kway or kwah in English. "He puts his duties *qua* citizen above other loyalties."

quae nocent docent
kwī NAW-kent DAW-kent
things that hurt teach

The rhyming way to indicate the educational validity of the curriculum offered by the College of Hard Knocks.

quaerenda pecunia primum est, virtus post nummos
kwī-REN-dah peh-KOO-nee-ah PREE-muum est
WIHR-toos pawst NUUM-mohs
let's keep our eye on the bottom line

A practical thought from Horace's *Epistles*, with the literal
meaning "money is the first thing to be sought, good reputation
after wealth."

quaere verum
KWĪ-reh WAY-ruum
seek the truth

qualis artifex pereo
KWAH-lihs AHR-tih-feks PEHR-ay-oh
what an artist dies in me

Suetonius reports that Nero—he who is said to have fiddled
while Rome burned—spoke these words shortly before committing suicide. While Nero is known to have loved music, there is
no indication that he was a man of great talent.

qualis pater talis filius
KWAH-lihs PAH-tehr TAH-lihs FEE-lee-uus
like father, like son

**quando hic sum, non ieiuno (or jejuno) Sabbato;
quando Romae sum, ieiuno (or jejuno) Sabbato**
KWAHN-doh heek suum nohn yay-YOO-noh
SAHB-bah-toh KWAHN-doh ROH-mī suum
yay-YOO-noh SAHB-bah-toh
when in Rome, do as the Romans do

The Latin for this thought is rendered in various ways, but the
thought is always attributed to St. Ambrose. The version sup-

236 quandoque bonus dormitat Homerus

plied above may be translated literally as "when I'm here [in Milan] I do not fast on Saturday; when I'm in Rome I fast on Saturday." No matter how the Latin reads, the advice is the same: Follow local customs.

quandoque bonus dormitat Homerus
kwahn-DOH-kweh BAW-nuus DAWR-mih-taht
haw-MAY-ruus
sometimes even good Homer sleeps

These words from Horace's *Ars Poetica* are generally taken to suggest rather gently that even good writers are not always at their best. You win some, you lose some.

quantum
KWAHN-tuum
as much

This word gives us several useful phrases. **Quantum libet** (LIH-beht), "as much as one pleases." **Quantum meruit** (MEH-roo-iht), "as much as one has deserved." **Quantum placeat** (PLAH-kay-aht), "as much as pleases." **Quantum satis** (SAH-tihs), "as much as is sufficient." **Quantum sufficit** (SUUF-fih-kiht), "as much as suffices." **Quantum valeat** (WAH-lay-aht), "as much as it may be worth." **Quantum vis** (wees), "as much as you wish."

quare impedit?
KWAH-ray IHM-peh-diht
why is he fighting us?

Literally "why does he obstruct?"

quem di diligunt, adolescens moritur
kwem dee DEE-lih-guunt ah-daw-LEH-skens
MAW-rih-tuur
only the good die young

The literal translation of this consoling line is "whom the gods love dies young." *Quem di diligunt, adolescens moritur* is a translation into Latin made by Plautus in the *Bacchides* of a line by Menander, a fourth-century B.C. Greek dramatist.

qui bene amat bene castigat
kwee BEH-neh AH-maht BEH-neh KAH-stih-gaht
he who loves well chastises well

The Latin argument opposing permissiveness in raising children and favoring frankness of expression in dealing with all people one loves or respects.

qui desiderat pacem praeparet bellum
kwee day-SEE-deh-raht PAH-kem prī-PAH-reht BEL-luum
let him who wants peace prepare for war

Vegetius, a Roman military writer, advocating anything but arms control.

quid faciendum?
kwihd fah-kee-EHN-duum
what's to be done?

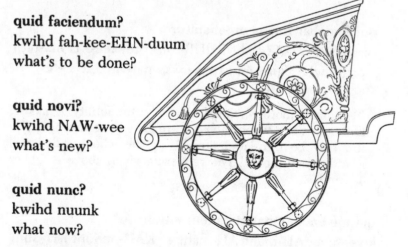

quid novi?
kwihd NAW-wee
what's new?

quid nunc?
kwihd nuunk
what now?

This phrase gives us the English word "quidnunc" (KWID-nunk), "a busybody."

qui docet discit
kwee DAW-keht DIH-skiht
the best way to learn a subject is to teach it

Literal translation, "he who teaches learns." Every experienced teacher knows the truth of this aphorism.

quid pro quo
kwihd proh kwoh
something given in return for something

Literally "something for something." "I will not give up that privilege without a *quid pro quo*." The phrase has been taken into English, with the pronunciation unchanged.

quidquid agas prudenter agas
KWIHD-kwihd AH-gahs proo-DEN-tehr AH-gahs
whatever you do, do with caution

See RESPICE FINEM.

qui fugiebat rursus proeliabitur
kwee fuu-gee-AY-baht RUUR-suus proy-lee-AH-bih-tuur
"for he who fights and runs away may live to fight another day"

Tertullian, quoting a Greek source on the futility of making a last-ditch stand when the odds are heavily against one. The Latin may be translated literally as "he who has fled will do battle once more." The rendering given above is Oliver Goldsmith's.

qui me amat, amat et canem meam
kwee may AH-maht AH-maht et KAH-nehm MAY-ahm
love me, love my dog

The Latin words for telling the world that it will have to take you as you are. The literal translation is "who loves me loves my dog as well."

qui nescit dissimulare nescit vivere
kwee NEH-skiht dihs-sih-muu-LAH-reh NEH-skiht WEE-weh-reh
he who doesn't know how to fib doesn't know how to survive

More formally, "he who does not know how to dissemble does not know how to live." This same Latin line, with the last word replaced by **regnare** (reh-GNAH-reh, "to rule"), may give us some insight into the way nations large and small are governed.

qui scribit bis legit
kwee SKREE-biht bihs LEH-giht
he who writes reads twice

This maxim recognizes the effectiveness of writing out something one wishes to learn thoroughly.

quis custodiet ipsos custodes?
kwihs kuu-STOH-dee-eht IH-psohs kuu-STOH-days
who will guard the guards themselves?

Juvenal, in his *Satires*, poses this vexing question, suitable today for situations in which we have little confidence in the people appointed to positions of trust, for example, those who are duty-bound to watch over public funds. Juvenal may actually have been more concerned with the problem of hiring guards to prevent infidelity among women whose husbands were out of town. The modern challenge more likely is to avoid assignment of a fox to guard the henhouse.

quis fallere possit amantem?
kwihs FAHL-leh-reh PAWS-siht ah-MAHN-tehm
who can deceive a lover?

Virgil, in the *Aeneid*, giving us wisdom about the human condition.

qui tacet consentit
kwee TAH-keht kawn-SEN-tiht
silence implies consent

Literally "he who remains silent consents." This observation may be applied to a range of situations, from silence at an everyday business meeting to silence of an entire people in a country that is pursuing an inhumane policy.

qui timide rogat docet negare
kwee TIH-mih-day RAW-gaht DAW-keht neh-GAH-reh
don't be afraid to ask

Literally "he who asks timidly teaches to refuse." In better translation, "he who asks timidly invites refusal."

qui transtulit sustinet
kwee trahn-STOO-liht SUU-stih-neht
he who transplanted sustains

Motto of Connecticut: God brought us here and still looks after us.

quo animo?
kwoh AH-nih-moh
with what intention?

Even when we report all the words someone has used in telling us something, we may not be conveying a true reflection of what was intended. Facial expression, emphasis, and the like may be as significant as the words themselves in revealing the full story. Thus, we are not surprised when we are asked, "*Quo animo*?"

quod avertat Deus!
kwawd ah-WEHR-taht DAY-uus
God forbid!

Literally "which may God avert."

quod cibus est aliis, aliis est venenum
kwawd KIH-buus est AH-lee-ees AH-lee-ees est weh-NAY-nuum
one man's meat is another man's poison

Literally "what is food to some is poison to others." What you and I find attractive, others may well find abhorrent. (See DE GUSTIBUS NON EST DISPUTANDUM.)

quod cito acquiritur cito perit
kwawd KIH-taw ahk-KWEE-rih-tuur KIH-taw PEHR-iht
easy come, easy go

Literally "that which is quickly acquired quickly vanishes."

quod erat demonstrandum
kwawd EH-raht day-mawn-STRAHN-duum
which was to be demonstrated

The statement, abbreviated **Q.E.D.**, that is appended to a mathematical solution, with the meaning "we have proved the proposition we set out to prove."

quod erat faciendum
kwawd EH-raht fah-kee-EN-duum
which was to be done

The statement, abbreviated **Q.E.F.**, that is appended to a mathematical solution, with the meaning "we have done the work we were required to do."

quod vide
kwawd WIH-deh
which see

See Q.V.

quo iure (or jure)?
kwoh YOO-reh
by what right?

A challenge: "Why have you done this? *Quo iure?*"

quomodo vales?
KWOH-maw-daw WAH-lays
how are you?

A Roman greeting.

quondam
KWAWN-dahm
former

Used in English and pronounced KWAHN-dəm: "my quondam [erstwhile] friend."

quorum
KWOH-ruum
of whom

Given here primarily to show the origin of the English noun *quorum*, "the minimum number of people that must be present at a meeting before its proceedings are to be regarded as valid." In commissions written in Latin appeared the words **quorum vos . . . unum [duos, etc.] esse volumus** (waws . . . OO-nuum ES-seh waw-LUU-muus), "of whom we will that you . . . be one [two, etc.]." The intent was to designate the person (or persons) so addressed as member (or members) of an official body, without whose presence work could not go on. And that's how *quorum* was born.

quos Deus vult perdere prius dementat
kwohs DAY-uus wuult PEHR-deh-reh PREE-uus day-MEN-taht
whom God wishes to destroy, he first makes mad

A Latin rendering of a line from Euripides.

quot homines, tot sententiae
kwawt HAW-mih-nays tawt sehn-TEN-tee-ī
complete lack of agreement

A phrase from Terence's *Phormio*, literally "so many men, so many opinions," leaving one as far from consensus as possible.

quo vadis?
kwoh WAH-dihs
whither goest thou?

The well known question from John.

q.v.

The abbreviation of **quod vide** (kwawd WIH-deh), literally "which see," a scholar's way of providing a cross-reference. For example, "*quondam, q.v.*" indicates to the reader who does not know the meaning of *quondam* that the term is explained elsewhere in the text, in the case of the present book in its alphabetical location.

radit usque ad cutem
RAH-diht UUS-kweh ahd KUU-tehm
he drives a hard bargain

Literally "he shaves all the way to the skin."

radix omnium malorum est cupiditas
RAH-dihks AWM-nee-uum mah-LOH-ruum est
kuu-PIH-dih-tahs
the love of money is the root of all evil

Please notice that this observation from Timothy is not concerned with wealth, but with avarice: Money *per se* is not the root of evil.

rara avis
RAH-rah AH-wihs
a rarity

A prodigy or anything that is quite out of the ordinary may be described as a *rara avis* (English pronunciation RAIR-ə AY-vis), literally "a rare bird." Juvenal used the phrase in his *Satires*: **rara avis in terris nigroque simillima cycno** (ihn TEHR-rees nih-GROH-kweh sih-MIHL-lih-mah KIH-knoh), "a rare bird upon the earth and very much like a black swan." Black swans were unknown to the Romans. They were discovered in modern times.

raram facit misturam cum sapientia forma

RAH-rahm FAH-kiht mih-STOO-rahm kuum
sah-pee-EN-tee-ah FAWR-mah

beauty and brains don't mix

We have Petronius's *Satyricon* to blame for this canard, literally "beauty and wisdom are rarely found together." The myth of "beautiful but dumb" is destroyed by university teachers each time they look up from their notes. What they see is a lecture hall filled with intelligent and attractive students. What the students see may be another matter.

re

ray

concerning or regarding

rebus sic stantibus

RAY-buus seek STAHN-tih-buus

as matters stand

A phrase, literally "things staying as they are," that lawyers use as one criterion for determining that an obligation or a contract remains in force.

recte et suaviter

REH-ktay et SWAH-wih-tehr

justly and mildly

recto

REH-ktoh

right

Pronounced in English REK-toh. This term is used to denote a right-hand page of a book, the full Latin phrase be-

ing **recto folio** (FAW-lee-oh), "the page being straight." See
VERSO.

reddite quae sunt Caesaris Caesari, et quae sunt Dei Deo
REHD-dih-teh kwī suunt KĪ-sah-rihs KĪ-sah-ree et kwī
suunt DAY-ee DAY-oh
render unto Caesar the things that are Caesar's, and
unto God the things that are God's

Matthew recounting Christ's response to the Pharisees, who
asked whether they should pay tribute to the Romans.

redime te captum quam queas minimo
REH-dih-meh tay KAH-ptuum kwahm KWAY-ahs
MIH-nih-moh
only name, rank, and serial number

The Latin prescription for soldierly behavior following cap-
ture by enemy troops, literally "when taken prisoner, pay as
little as you can to buy your freedom." In ancient times, the
enemy wanted money, not information, but the principle was
the same: Give the enemy as little help as possible.

redivivus
reh-dih-WEE-wuus
brought back to life

In English pronounced red-ə-VEE-vəs. This word gives us an
opportunity to call "a second Beethoven" a Beethoven *redivi-
vus*—and probably be wrong in both languages.

redolet lucernam
REH-daw-leht luu-KEHR-nahm
it's labored

This destructive phrase may be used by critics to convey the literal thought "it smells of the lamp," suggesting that a composer or writer stayed up nights—that is, worked too hard—to create the work. The implication is that genius doesn't sweat in creating a masterpiece—do you believe it? When critics have exhausted the possibilities of this phrase, they can always describe a work of art as "careless." (See OLET LUCERNAM.)

reductio ad absurdum
reh-DUU-ktee-oh ahd ahb-SUUR-duum
reduction to absurdity

In English pronounced ri-DUK-tee-oh ad əb-SURD-əm. Disproof of a principle or proposition by showing that it leads to an absurdity when followed to its logical conclusion.

regina
reh-GEE-nah
queen

rem acu tetigisti
rehm AH-koo teh-tih-GIH-stee
right on!

Where the old-fashioned among us might say, "You've hit the nail right on the head," Romans would have said *rem acu tetigisti*, literally "you've touched the thing with a needle."

remis velisque
RAY-mees weh-LEES-kweh
giving one's best

Literally "with oars and sails," a phrase that reminds us that the airplane is a modern invention. "He took out after them *remis velisque*."

repente dives nemo factus est bonus
reh-PEN-teh DIH-wehs NAY-moh FAH-ktuus est
BAW-nuus
no one who is rich is made suddenly good

Publilius Syrus, as shown in this aphorism, was a keen observer of people and their ways. Of course, Syrus lived before the era of multimillion-dollar contracts for sports heroes, million-dollar payoffs in lotteries, oil wells in one's backyard, etc. The intent of his observation applies even now, however, absent any of the legitimate ways to strike it rich overnight: When someone you know appears suddenly to have made a quantum improvement in his style of living, don't be surprised if the law shows up one day to ask him embarrassing questions.

requiescat in pace
reh-kwee-EH-skaht ihn PAH-keh
may he or she rest in peace

The plural form of this final thought is **requiescant** (reh-kwee-EH-skahnt) **in pace**, "may they rest in peace." The abbreviation for both the singular and the plural is **R.I.P.**

res age, tute eris
rays AH-geh TOO-tay EH-rihs
wash that man right out of your hair

Ovid gives advice to the lovelorn in *Remedia Amoris*, saying literally "be busy and you will be safe." Who needs Ann Landers?

res angusta domi
rays ahn-GUU-stah DAW-mee
Daddy has lost his job

This sad statement, literally "straitened circumstances at home," is useful in itself, but one may also find it instructive to recall a line from Juvenal's *Satires* in which the words appear: **Haud facile emergunt quorum virtutibus opstat** (howd FAH-kih-leh ay-MEHR-guunt KWOH-ruum wihr-TOO-tih-buus AWP-staht) **res angusta domi,** "by no means is it easy for those to rise from obscurity whose noble qualities are hindered by straitened circumstances at home." Juvenal, in expressing concern for the unfortunate among us, was far ahead of many hard-nosed people in positions of power today, who insist that the poor have only themselves to blame.

res in cardine est
rays ihn KAHR-dih-neh est
the next twenty-four hours will tell the story

Literally "the matter is on a door hinge," or as we are apt to say more conventionally, "we are facing a crisis."

res inter alios
rays IN-tehr AH-lee-ohs
it's no concern of ours

Literally "a matter between other people."

res ipsa loquitur
rays IH-psah LAW-kwih-tuur
the facts speak for themselves

Literally "the thing itself speaks." A complainant in an automobile accident case who appears in court swathed in bandages and escorted by nurses should not have to go to great lengths to establish that he has been injured: *res ipsa loquitur*.

respice, adspice, prospice
REH-spih-keh AHD-spih-keh PRAW-spih-keh
look to the past, the present, the future

Motto of the City College of New York, literally "examine the past, examine the present, examine the future."

respice finem
REH-spih-keh FEE-nehm
look before you leap

Literally "examine the end." The full proverb, **quidquid agas prudenter agas et** (KWIHD-kwihd AH-gahs proo-DEN-tehr AH-gahs et) **respice finem**, may be translated as "whatever you do, do with caution, and look to the end."

respondeat superior
reh-SPAWN-day-aht suu-PEHR-ee-awr
the buck stops here

The tradition of accountability, literally "let the superior answer," more freely "a supervisor must take responsibility for the quality of a subordinate's work."

res publica
rays POO-blih-kah
the commonwealth

Literally "the affairs of the people." What the Romans meant when they said *res publica*—it is the origin of the English word "republic"—was "the state" (in the sense of "the body politic"), "the republic," or, as given above, "the commonwealth." However interpreted, by *res publica*, the Romans meant their own commonwealth. *Res publica* was also written as a single word, **respublica**.

resurgam
reh-SUUR-gahm
I shall rise again

retro Satana!
REH-troh sah-TAH-nah
get thee behind me, Satan!

The abbreviated form of VADE RETRO ME, SATANA. (See also
APAGE SATANAS.)

rex non potest peccare
reks nohn PAW-test pehk-KAH-reh
the king can do no wrong

rex regum
reks REH-guum
king of kings

R.I.P.

See REQUIESCAT IN PACE.

ruat caelum
ROO-aht KĪ-luum
come what may

Literally "though the heavens fall." (See FIAT IUSTITIA RUAT
CAELUM.)

rus in urbe
roos ihn UUR-beh
country in city

The phrase is used most often to describe a city building, garden, or view that suggests the countryside. "How can they leave their *rus in urbe* for a loft in SoHo with a view of Canal Street?" *Rus in urbe* is also used, but less often, to denote the creating of an illusion of countryside in a city setting. "In her designs for urban buildings, she specializes in *rus in urbe*."

sal Atticum
sahl AHT-tih-kuum
wit

This phrase from Pliny's *Historia Naturalis*, and often given in English as "Attic wit," is literally "Attic salt," reflecting the refined elegance, the taste—no pun is intended—of the ancient Athenian (Attic) intelligentsia. The wit denoted is often taken as "acerbity" or "intellectual wit." Byron, in his *English Bards and Scotch Reviewers*, referred to a taste for punning as "Attic salt."

salus mundi
SAH-loos MUUN-dee
the welfare of the world

salus populi suprema lex esto
SAH-loos PAW-puu-lee suu-PRAY-mah leks EH-stoh
let the welfare of the people be the supreme law

Motto of Missouri. Cicero, in *De Legibus*, had it this way: **Salus populi suprema est lex**, "the welfare of the people is the supreme law."

salus ubi multi consiliarii
SAH-loos UU-bih MUUL-tee kawn-sih-lee-AH-ree-ee
where there are many advisers there is safety

An excellent reminder for politicians whose words and actions hold hostage the future of the world. (See SALUS MUNDI.)

salve!
SAHL-weh
hail!

A Roman greeting.

sanctum sanctorum
SAHN-ktuum sahn-KTOH-ruum
a place of inviolable privacy

Sanctum in English is a noun meaning "a retreat or a private room" and pronounced SANK-təm. In Latin, *sanctum* is a neuter adjective meaning "sacred." Combining the Latin *sanctum* with *sanctorum* gives us a phrase that can be translated literally as "holy of holies," useful in denoting a place in a house of worship proscribed for all but the high priests, or a room in a home that is off limits to everyone but the master or mistress —either one, not both—of the establishment.

sapiens nihil affirmat quod non probat
SAH-pee-ehns NIH-hihl ahf-FIHR-maht kwawd nohn PRAW-baht
don't swear to anything you don't know firsthand

Excellent advice, translated literally as "a wise man states as true nothing he does not prove."

Sartor Resartus
SAHR-tawr reh-SAHR-tuus
The Tailor Reclothed

Title of a book by Thomas Carlyle that examines life under the guise of expounding a philosophy of clothing. Not to be confused with *Dress for Success* or others of that ilk.

satis
SAH-tihs
enough

Satis gives us several interesting phrases. **Satis superque** (suu-PEHR-kweh), "enough and to spare." **Satis verborum** (wehr-BAWR-uum), "enough of words"; by extension: "let's have some action." The most satisfying is **satis eloquentiae, sapientiae parum** (eh-law-KWEN-tee-ī sah-pee-EN-tee-ī PAH-ruum), "enough eloquence, too little wisdom." Ah, the joys of Latin.

Saturnalia
sah-tuur-NAH-lee-ah
a real wingding

We know the English word "saturnalia," pronounced sat-ər-NAYL-yə, as "unrestrained revelry," but the Latin original is worth reviewing. The *Saturnalia* was the week-long Roman festival said to have begun in mid-December—sometimes given as the seventeenth of the month, sometimes as the nineteenth. The nature of the festival is not in dispute: public spectacles and banquets, freedom from restraint, general merrymaking, debauchery, and exchanges of presents. Indeed, during *Saturnalia* masters waited on slaves, courts and schools were closed, and sentencing of criminals was suspended. Who could ask for anything more? And all this in honor of Saturn, in Latin **Saturnus** (sah-TUUR-nuus), the god of planting and harvest, among other things.

scientia est potentia

skee-EN-tee-ah est paw-TEN-tee-ah

knowledge is power

An appropriate maxim for illicit wiretappers and those who record their telephone conversations without informing the people they speak with that they are doing so.

scilicet

SKEE-lih-keht

namely

Used in English in place of "to wit" and pronounced SIL-ǝ-set. *Scilicet* is the Latin abbreviation of **scire licet** (SKEE-reh LIH-keht), "it is permitted to know."

scripsit

SKRIH-psiht

he or she wrote it

With the author's name given first, a way to sign a literary work.

sculpsit

SKUUL-psiht

he or she carved (or cut) it

With the artisan's name given first, a way to sign a carving, engraving, etc.

scuto bonae voluntatis tuae coronasti nos

SKOO-toh BAW-nī waw-luun-TAH-tihs TOO-ī kaw-roh-NAH-stee nohs

with the shield of thy good favor, thou hast encompassed us

Motto on the Great Seal of Maryland.

semel insanivimus omnes
SEH-mehl ihn-sah-NEE-wih-muus AWM-nays
we have all been mad once

A good point to keep in mind when dealing with someone who has committed an antisocial act or made an egregious error. No one goes through life without slipping now and then.

semper fidelis
SEM-pehr fih-DAY-lihs
always faithful

Motto of the United States Marine Corps.

semper idem
SEM-pehr IH-dehm
always the same thing

A descriptive phrase suitable for characterizing something whose appearance does not change. *Semper idem*, the identical Latin phrase, but pronounced SEM-pehr EE-dehm, means "always the same person."

semper paratus
SEM-pehr pah-RAH-tuus
always ready

Motto of the United States Coast Guard.

Senatus Populusque Romanus
seh-NAH-tuus paw-puu-LUUS-kweh roh-MAH-nuus
the Roman Senate and People

Abbreviated **S.P.Q.R.** and, for the Romans, emblematic of their constitution.

senex bis puer
SEH-neks bihs POO-ehr
second childhood

This disagreeable Latin phrase, evocative of Shakespeare's characterization of the final stage of man—he called it "second childishness"—literally translates as "an old man is twice a boy."

seniores priores
seh-nee-OH-rays pree-OH-rays
elders first

A civilized precept.

seq.

Abbreviation of **sequens** (SEH-kwens) and **sequentes** (seh-KWEN-tays), respectively the singular and plural forms meaning "the following," and of **sequitur** (see the next entry). The plural of *seq.* is sometimes written as *seqq.*

sequitur
SEH-kwih-tuur
it follows

This word can be used to mean "it follows logically" (see NON SEQUITUR) or to mean "the following remark."

seriatim
seh-ree-AH-tihm
in series

A scholar's term, used to indicate that a publication is part of a series.

sero venientibus ossa
SAY-roh weh-nee-EN-tih-buus AWS-sah

sorry, too late

The Latin version of "the early bird catches the worm." Literally "for latecomers, the bones." (See POST FESTUM VENISTI.)

sesquipedalia verba
seh-skwih-peh-DAH-lee-ah WEHR-bah

oppressively long words

The English word "sesquipedalian" (ses-kwi-pi-DAY-li-ən) is an adjective carrying the meanings "having many syllables" and "tending to use long words." The Latin phrase, from Horace's *Ars Poetica*, literally means "words a foot and a half long." If Horace was referring to metrical feet, the phrase would describe words having at least four or five syllables, but he could also have had linear measure in mind, in which event the length of such words would boggle the mind. In either case, the meaning is clear, and Horace has given us an excellent way to characterize writers whose vocabularies are so pretentious that their readers must go repeatedly to an unabridged dictionary in order to understand what they are reading. *Sesquipedalia verba* may also be used to characterize the writing of such authors. John Simon, are you listening?

sic
seek

thus

This common word is used by writers and editors to indicate an apparent misspelling or a doubtful word or phrase in a source being quoted. "This dessiccant [*sic*] is useless." "The meeting was the most fortuitous [*sic*] I ever attended." Insertion of *sic* in these examples absolves the quoter of misspelling the word "desiccant" and misusing the word "fortuitous," and lays the blame—if blame it is—on the source quoted.

sic itur ad astra
seek IH-tuur ahd AH-strah
this is the path to immortality

Literally "thus one goes to the stars."

sic semper tyrannis
seek SEM-pehr tih-RAH-nees
thus ever to tyrants

Motto of Virginia, and said to be the words shouted by John Wilkes Booth after assassinating Abraham Lincoln. Booth is also said to have added, "The South is avenged."

sic transit gloria mundi
seek TRAHN-siht GLOH-ree-ah MUUN-dee
so passes away the glory of the world

Thomas à Kempis, in *De Imitatione Christi*, commenting on the transitory nature of human vanities. The Latin phrase is used at the coronation of a pope: A rope bundle is burned during the ceremony and, as the flame dies, the words "**Pater sancte** (PAH-tehr SAHN-kteh, "holy father") **sic transit gloria mundi**" are intoned.

sicut patribus, sit Deus nobis
SEE-kuut PAH-trih-buus siht DAY-uus NOH-bees
as with our fathers, may God be with us

Motto of Boston.

si dis placet
see dees PLAH-keht
if it pleases the gods

The equivalent of "God willing." (See DEO VOLENTE.)

si fecisti nega!
see fay-KIH-stee NEH-gah
stonewall!

Literally "if you did it, deny it."

si finis bonus est, totum bonum erit
see FEE-nihs BAW-nuus est TOH-tuum BAW-nuum
EH-riht
"all's well that ends well"

Literally "if the end is good, everything will be good."
Shakespeare couldn't have said it better.

sigillum
sih-GIHL-luum
a seal

Seen on the seals of states, cities, universities, etc.

silent leges enim inter arma
SIH-lent LAY-gays EH-nihm IHN-tehr AHR-mah
laws don't count in wartime

The principle used to justify imposition of martial law. This
maxim, found in Cicero's *Pro Milone*, translates literally as "for
laws are silent in the midst of war."

similia similibus curantur
sih-MIH-lee-ah sih-MIH-lih-buus koo-RAHN-tuur
fight fire with fire

Literally "like things are cured by likes," more freely "similar
ailments are treated successfully by similar remedies." This is
the doctrine of homeopathy, which advocates treatment of a
disease by giving the sick person small amounts of substances

that would produce symptoms of the same disease if they were given to a healthy person. It is also the basis for the putative hair-of-the-dog cure of a hangover, in which the afflicted person is encouraged to imbibe small amounts of the same substance that caused the unfortunate condition in the first place. (See CONTRARIA CONTRARIIS CURANTUR.)

sine die
SIH-neh DEE-ay
until an unspecified date

When a meeting adjourns *sine die*, literally "without a day," don't hold your breath until it reconvenes. For example, when a national convention of one of the major political parties in the United States adjourns *sine die* (pronounced sī-ni-DĪ in English), you can bet you'll have to wait four years for that party's next national convention. For this reason, it is only at the end of the final day of such a convention that the chairman declares the convention adjourned *sine die*.

sine dubio
SIH-neh DUU-bee-oh
without doubt

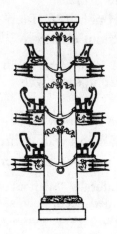

sine invidia
SIH-neh ihn-WIH-dee-ah
without envy

sine ira
SIH-neh EE-rah
without anger

sine loco et anno
SIH-neh LAW-koh et AHN-noh
without place and date

A bibliographer's term. A book that does not provide information concerning its place and date of publication is said to have been published *sine loco et anno*. Modern books normally supply such information.

sine mora
SIH-neh MAW-rah
without delay

sine praeiudicio (or **praejudicio**)
SIH-neh prī-yoo-DIH-kee-oh
without prejudice

sine prole
SIH-neh PROH-leh
without children

A legal term, often translated as "without issue," encountered in some wills.

sine qua non
SIH-neh kwah nohn
an indispensable condition

Literally "without which not." Anything that may be described accurately as *sine qua non* is absolutely necessary. "Warm outer clothing is a *sine qua non* at the North Pole."

si post fata venit gloria non propero

see pawst FAH-tah WEH-niht GLOH-ree-ah nohn
PRAW-peh-roh

if one must die to be recognized, I can wait

One of Martial's epigrams, literally "if glory comes after
death, I'm not in a hurry." For a writer, this means "better
unread than dead."

si quaeris peninsulam amoenam circumspice

see KWĪ-rihs peh-NIHN-suu-lahm ah-MOY-nahm
kihr-kuum-SPIH-keh

if you seek a lovely peninsula, look about you

Motto of Michigan.

si sic omnes

see seek AWM-nays

why couldn't it last forever?

A wistful expression, literally "if everything had been thus."

siste viator

SIH-steh wee-AH-tawr

stop, traveler

A favorite inscription on Roman tombstones.

sit non doctissima coniux (or **conjux**)

siht nohn daw-KTIHS-sih-mah KAWN-yuuks

a Roman formula for a happy marriage

One of Martial's epigrams, literally "may my wife not be very
learned," revealing more than we would like to know about one
Roman's attitude toward women.

sit tibi terra levis
siht TIH-bih TEHR-rah LEH-wihs
may the earth be light upon you

An ancient Roman tombstone inscription.

si vis me flere dolendum est primum ipsi tibi
see wees may FLAY-reh daw-LEN-duum est PREE-muum IH-psee TIH-bih
if you wish me to weep, you yourself must first feel grief

Method acting? Horace, in *Ars Poetica*, explaining to the writer that emotion must be felt in order to be conveyed successfully in words.

si vis pacem para bellum
see wees PAH-kehm PAH-rah BEL-luum
if you want peace, prepare for war

A traditional justification for an arms buildup, from Vegetius, a Roman military writer, in his *Epitoma Rei Militaris*. Stand by for further developments.

socius criminis
SAW-kee-uus KREE-mih-nihs
a partner in crime

soli Deo gloria
SOH-lee DAY-oh GLOH-ree-ah
glory to God alone

sol lucet omnibus
sohl LOO-keht AWM-nih-buus
the sun shines for everyone

spectatum veniunt, veniunt spectentur ut ipsae
speh-KTAH-tuum WEH-nee-uunt WEH-nee-uunt
speh-KTEN-tuur uut IH-psī
they wish as much to be seen as to see

An observation by Ovid, in *Ars Amatoria*, literally "they come to see, they come that they themselves be seen," making it clear that the beautiful people have not changed much in two millennia.

spolia opima
SPAW-lee-ah AW-pee-mah
how sweet it is!

This phrase, literally "the choicest spoils," was used by Livy to denote the booty personally taken by a victorious general who has slain the commanding general of an enemy army.

sponte sua
SPAWN-teh SOO-ah
of one's own accord

Usually given as **sua sponte**.

S.P.Q.R.

Abbreviation of SENATUS POPULUSQUE ROMANUS, "the Roman Senate and People." *S.P.Q.R.* is often seen in depictions of Roman military standards.

stans pede in uno
stahns PEH-deh ihn OO-noh
effortlessly

Horace used this expression, literally "standing on one foot," in his *Satires*. Some of us use the equivalent expression in English: "I can do that standing on one foot." Now we can do it *stans pede in uno*.

status
STAH-tuus
condition or state

This Latin word, which can also be translated as "status" (in English, STAY-təs), is used commonly in a handful of Latin expressions: **statu quo** (STAH-too-kwoh), "as things were before"; **status quo**, "the state in which anything is (or was)"; **status quo ante bellum** (AHN-teh BEL-luum), "the condition (or military boundaries) that existed before the war"; and **status quo ante**, an abbreviated version of the previous phrase, with the same meanings. "Even though the couple had reunited, both husband and wife knew that too many recriminations had been exchanged, too much bitterness remained. They would never return to *status quo ante*."

stet
steht
let it stand

An editor or proofreader's mark, pronounced stet in English, canceling a deletion or other change previously made in a manuscript or proof. *Stet* also appears in various Latin expressions, including two of quite different intent. **Stet fortuna domus!** (fawr-TOO-nah DAW-muus) means "may the good fortune of the house endure!" **Stet pro ratione voluntas** (proh rah-tee-OH-neh waw-LUUN-tahs) means "let my will stand as a reason," giving a person in command a way of dismissing any arguments advanced to question his judgment; in English, "end of discussion, we'll do it my way."

stillicidi casus lapidem cavat
stihl-LIH-kih-dih KAH-suus LAH-pih-dehm KAH-waht
slow and steady does it

A Roman proverb, literally "dripping moisture hollows out a stone."

stultorum calami carbones moenia chartae
stuul-TOH-ruum KAH-lah-mee kahr-BOH-nays MOY-nee-ah KAHR-tī
no graffiti, please

The Romans, in this saying, literally "chalk is the pen of fools, walls (their) paper," reveal that the graffiti artist is far from a modern phenomenon. Archaeologists have found graffiti on walls of buildings in many ancient Roman cities, including Pompeii, and the nature of the literary, artistic, political, and cultural content revealed in these ancient graffiti does not vary substantially from what can be seen today in many American cities. O TEMPORA! O MORES!

sua cuique voluptas
SOO-ah KWEE-kweh waw-LUU-ptahs
to each his own

Literally "everyone has his own pleasures." A related expression is **sua cuique sunt vitia** (suunt WIH-tee-ah), "everyone has his own vices."

sua sponte
SOO-ah SPAWN-teh
of one's own accord

Sometimes given as **sponte sua**.

suaviter in modo, fortiter in re
SWAH-wih-tehr ihn MAW-daw FAWR-tih-tehr ihn ray
he does what has to be done, but with the necessary compassion

In our everyday lives, we must inevitably do things we would prefer not to do. It is then that we are called on to be *suaviter in modo, fortiter in re*, literally "gentle in manner, resolute in deed," or to behave *suaviter in modo, fortiter in re*, literally "gently in manner, resolutely in deed." Thus, *suaviter in modo, fortiter in re* describes the model parent, executive, personnel manager, *et al*.

sub iudice (or judice)
suub YOO-dih-keh
before the courts

This legal phrase, literally "under consideration," is used so often that it has an English spelling, *sub judice*, and an English pronunciation, sub JOOD-ə-see. When a matter is before the courts, that is, still under litigation, the case generally is not discussed publicly by those directly involved. The intent is to avoid prejudicing the legal process. (See ADHUC SUB IUDICE LIS EST.)

sub poena
suub POY-nah
under penalty

Add "of a fine" or "of imprisonment" or what you will after this phrase, and the result is threatening. The derivation of the English noun "subpoena" (sə-PEE-nə), "a writ commanding a person to appear in a law court," reflects the opening words of such documents: *Sub poena* . . ., "under penalty . . . ," which go on to specify that the person summoned will be punished if the writ is not obeyed.

sub quocunque titulo
suub kwoh-KUUN-kweh TIH-tuu-loh
under whatever title

sub rosa
suub RAW-sah
in strict confidence or secretly

In this age of covert operations, *sub rosa* is understood all too well and said all too often in English, with the pronunciation sub ROHZ-ə. The phrase is of interest primarily because it has the literal meaning "under the rose." The rose is a symbol of secrecy, perhaps deriving from a story involving Cupid, the Roman god of love, who is said to have given a rose to Harpocrates, the god of silence, as a bribe for not revealing the amorous activities of Venus, the goddess of sensual love, well known for practicing what she preached. Roman dining room ceilings were decorated with roses to remind guests not to make public things that might be said **sub vino** (suub WEE-noh, "under the influence of wine"). And the American press frequently reports that Presidents walk with important visitors in the White House rose garden in order to gain privacy for discussion of matters of state. The power of the rose?

sub verbo
suub WEHR-boh
under the word

A scholar's term, abbreviated s.v., for example, "*s.v. sine prole*," used for making a cross-reference to an entry in a dictionary, encyclopedia, index, or other portion of a text.

sufficit
SUUF-fih-kiht
it is sufficient

sui generis
SOO-ee GEH-neh-rihs
one of a kind

This phrase, literally "of its (or his or her or their) own kind," is pronounced SOO-ee JEN-ə-rəs in English. One should take some care in applying *sui generis*, lest the phrase lose its value. Properly used, *sui generis* requires that the person, place, or thing be of an entirely distinctive character. Jimmy Durante comes to mind, perhaps the Grand Canyon, maybe Bach's Mass in B Minor—do you see how difficult it is to qualify?

summa cum laude
SUUM-mah kuum LOW-deh
with highest praise

See CUM LAUDE.

summa sedes non capit duos
SUUM-mah SAY-days nohn KAH-piht DOO-ohs
there's only room for one at the top

Literally "the highest seat does not hold two." And that's the story in all corporations.

summum bonum
SUUM-muum BAW-nuum
the highest good

summum ius (or jus) summa iniuria (or injuria)
SUUM-muum yoos SUUM-mah ihn-YOO-ree-ah
extreme law, extreme injustice

Lawmakers and judges beware: Strict enforcement of a law sometimes results in great injustice.

summum nec metuas diem nec optes
SUUM-muum nek MEH-too-ahs DEE-ehm nek
AW-ptays
neither fear nor wish for your last day

One of Martial's epigrams.

sumptus censum ne superet
SUUM-ptuus KEN-suum neh SUU-pehr-eht
live within your means

One of Martial's epigrams, literally "let not your spending exceed your income." Good advice for all but modern governments. It is worthwhile to reflect on the word *censum* in this epigram. The Roman **census** (KEN-suus), conducted every five years, registered all citizens in classes according to their property holdings. So *census* came to mean "wealth" and "property," and a poor Roman could be called **homo sine censu** (HAW-moh SIH-neh KEN-soo), literally "a man without property."

suo iure (or **jure**)
SOO-oh YOO-reh
in one's own right or in its own right

suo motu
SOO-oh MOH-too
spontaneously

Literally "by one's own motion" or "by its own motion."

suo tempore
SOO-oh TEM-paw-reh
at one's own time or at its own time

supra
SUU-prah
above

A scholar's word, used to make reference to an earlier portion of a text, usually in the phrase **vide** (WIH-deh) **supra**, "see above."

supremum vale
suu-PRAY-muum WAH-lay
farewell for the last time

Before death, that is.

sursum corda
SUUR-suum KAWR-dah
lift up your hearts

Heard in the mass.

sutor, ne supra crepidam
SOO-tawr nay SUU-prah KREH-pih-dahm
cobbler, stick to your last

See NE SUPRA CREPIDAM SUTOR IUDICARET.

suum cuique pulchrum
SOO-uum KWEE-kweh PUUL-kruum
love is blind

Literally "to everyone, his own is beautiful." Alone, *suum cuique* may be rendered as "to each his own."

s.v.

Abbreviation of **sub verbo**, "under the word." A lexicographer or encyclopedist's phrase, informing readers that the entry for a specified word or topic, for example, "*s.v. quorum*," contains information germane to the subject under discussion to which reference is made.

tabula rasa
TAH-buu-lah RAH-sah
a clean slate

This phrase, literally "a scraped writing tablet," is used most often to denote a mind devoid of preconceptions. Thus, a person who has practiced hunt-and-peck typewriting for most of his adult life must become a *tabula rasa* before he can learn to use the touch system, and a newborn child is presumed to be a *tabula rasa*.

tacent, satis laudant
TAH-kent SAH-tihs LOW-dahnt
silence is praise enough

A line from Terence's *Eunuchus*, literally "they are silent, they praise enough," recognizing that rapt attention in an audience can be more flattering than applause.

tacet
TAH-keht
be silent

A musical notation, literally "it is silent," directing a singer or instrumentalist to maintain silence during the portion of a score so marked.

taedium vitae
TĪ-dee-uum WEE-tī
ennui or Weltschmerz

Literally "weariness of life."

tam facti quam animi
tahm FAH-ktee kwahm AH-nih-mee
as much in deed as in intention

tamquam alter idem
TAHM-kwahm AHL-tehr EE-dem
as if a second self

See ALTER IDEM.

tangere ulcus
TAHN-geh-reh UUL-kuus
to touch a sore

This expression is used with the meaning of "to hit the nail on the head" and with the meaning of "to touch a sore spot."

tarde venientibus ossa
TAHR-day weh-nee-EN-tih-buus AWS-sah
for latecomers, the bones

See SERO VENIENTIBUS OSSA.

telum imbelle sine ictu
TAY-luum ihm-BEL-leh SIH-neh IH-ktoo
an ineffectual argument

In Virgil's *Aeneid*, aged Priam throws a *telum imbelle sine ictu*, literally " a feeble weapon without a thrust," giving us a metaphor for an argument that falls short of the mark or misses it altogether.

tempora mutantur nos et mutamur in illis

TEM-paw-rah moo-TAHN-tuur nohs eht
moo-TAH-muur ihn IHL-lees

times change and we change with them

   Attributed to John Owen, died 1622, a Welshman known for his Latin epigrams.

tempori parendum

TEM-paw-ree pah-REN-duum

one must keep abreast of the times

   An essential thought—literally "one must yield to time"—for anyone who wishes to remain in the swim. A related expression is **temporibus inserviendum** (tehm-PAW-rih-buus ihn-sehr-wee-EN-duum), literally "one must pay attention to the times."

temporis ars medicina fere est

TEM-paw-rihs ahrs meh-dih-KEE-nah FEH-ray est

time is a great healer

   This phrase, literally "time usually is the best means of healing," may have application in the field of medicine, but it appears in Ovid's *Remedia Amoris*, which is concerned with the amatory rather than the medical arts.

tempus abire tibi est

TEM-puus ahb-EE-reh TIH-bee est

make way for someone else

   Horace, in his *Epistles*, giving all of us excellent advice: When we have ceased being productive, it is time to make room for those who are. Horace put it this way: "You have played enough, eaten and drunk enough." Now *tempus abire tibi est*, literally "it is time for you to go away." Senior faculty, super-annuated executives, old soldiers and politicians, hearken unto Horace.

tempus edax rerum
TEM-puus EH-dahks RAY-ruum
time, the devourer of all things

Ovid, in *Metamorphoses*, calling our attention to the irreversible results—both good and bad—of the passage of time.

tempus fugit
TEM-puus FUU-giht
time flies

Who doesn't know this? Pronounced TEM-pəs FYOO-jət in English.

tempus ludendi
TEM-puus loo-DEN-dee
a time for playing

Workaholics, take heed. All work and no play . . .

tempus omnia revelat
TEM-puus AWM-nee-ah reh-WAY-laht
time reveals all things

So wait.

tenax propositi
TEH-nahks proh-PAW-sih-tee
resolute

Literally "tenacious of purpose."

tenere lupum auribus
teh-NAY-reh LUU-puum OW-rih-buus
to take the bull by the horns

This phrase, literally "to hold a wolf by the ears," implies fearlessness in confronting a dangerous situation or boldness in dealing with a difficulty.

te nosce
tay NAWS-keh
know thyself

A Latin translation of a precept incised in the stone of the temple of the oracle at Delphi, reflecting the oracle's interest in individual morality.

teres atque rotundus
TEH-rehs AHT-kweh raw-TUUN-duus
well-rounded

Horace's phrase, in the *Satires*, literally "polished and round," describing the Stoics' conception of a wise man as one who rolls smoothly through life. The full phrase is **totus** (TOH-tuus) **teres atque rotundus**, "complete, polished, and round."

terra es, terram ibis
TEHR-rah es TEHR-rahm EE-bihs
"dust thou art, to dust thou shalt return"

This entry comprises a well-known line from Genesis as rendered in Latin in the Vulgate and in English in the King James Version. The edition of the Bible known as the Vulgate, from the Latin **editio vulgata** (ay-DIH-tee-oh wuul-GAH-tah), "the common edition," first appeared in print in 1456, after translation more than a thousand years earlier by St. Jerome. The King James Version, also known as the King James Bible (1611), was produced at the direction of King James I (1566–1625) by a

team of scholars who worked for several years, relying on existing English translations. The line *terra es, terram ibis* is the one
in which God explains the consequences of Adam's disobedi-
ence. In one stanza of "A Psalm of Life," Longfellow incorpo-
rated the King James translation of this melancholy line:

> Life is real! Life is earnest!
> And the grave is not its goal;
> Dust thou art, to dust returnest,
> Was not spoken of the soul.

(See MEMENTO, HOMO, QUIA PULVIS ES ET IN PULVEREM REV-
ERTIS.)

terra firma
TEHR-rah FIHR-mah
dry land

This well-known phrase, in English pronounced TER-rə
FIR-mə, literally means "solid land." It is used to differentiate
land from sea.

terra incognita
TEHR-rah ihn-KAW-gnih-tah
unknown territory

This phrase is used to designate a subject or place about
which nothing or next to nothing is known. "Modern phy-
sics, by its nature, continually concerns itself with *terra incog-
nita*."

testis unus, testis nullus
TEH-stihs OO-nuus TEH-stihs NUUL-luus
one witness, no witness

A legal maxim indicating that unsupported testimony is no
better than complete absence of testimony, and suggesting to

all of us that we not give full credence to a story we hear from one source only.

timeo Danaos et dona ferentes
TIH-may-oh DAH-nah-ohs et DOH-nah feh-REN-tays
when an enemy appears friendly, watch out

This advice, literally "I fear the Greeks [ancient name Danai], even when bearing gifts," comes from Virgil's *Aeneid* and is addressed to the men of Troy. The Trojans were told by one of their priests to mistrust the huge wooden horse—the fabled Trojan horse—left behind by the departing soldiers of Greece, ostensibly as an offering to the gods to secure safe passage for Ulysses during his return to Greece. Ignoring the advice, the Trojans did not look the gift horse in the mouth, but dragged it inside their city, with predictable results. Recall that it contained a contingent of Greek soldiers sufficiently numerous to open the city gates and admit enough additional troops to destroy Troy. The irony is that Troy, not Greece, is stigmatized in the naming of the wooden horse: To this day, "a Trojan horse" is a thing or person that subverts from within. The Greeks come in for their share of opprobrium in the expression "Greek gifts," today scarcely cited, except as *timeo Danaos et dona ferentes* and its translation.

timeo hominem unius libri
TIH-meh-oh HAW-mih-nehm OO-nee-uus LIH-bree
I fear the man of one book

An observation attributed to Aquinas, with two possible interpretations. The older, more customary interpretation has it that a person steeped in a single source is a formidable opponent in debate. In a more recent interpretation, *timeo hominem unius libri* expresses fear in confronting a man for whom the knowledge, opinions, and dogma of a single book are sufficient and who recognizes no truths but the literal statements of his own book.

toga
TAW-gah
a toga

The *toga* (English pronunciation TOH-gə) is well known as the standard Roman outer garment. It was a white woolen upper garment worn in public by men in times of peace as a sign of their status as citizens. Freedmen and freedwomen also wore the *toga*, but women of higher status wore the **stola** (STAW-lah), a long outer garment. The adjective **togata** (taw-GAH-tah) was applied to women of doubtful reputation, an indication that the practice of judging a book by its cover, or a person by the way he or she dresses, did not originate in modern times.

totidem verbis
TAW-tih-dem WEHR-bees
in so many words

totis viribus
TOH-tees WEE-rih-buus
with all one's powers

toto caelo
TOH-toh KĪ-loh
diametrically opposite

We say the views of two people or two governments are "worlds apart," but the Romans said they were separated *toto caelo*, literally "by the entire heavens."

totus teres atque rotundus
TOH-tuus TEH-rehs AHT-kweh raw-TUUN-duus
well-rounded

See TERES ATQUE ROTUNDUS.

tu ne cede malis sed contra audentior ito
too nay KAY-deh MAH-lees sed KAWN-trah
ow-DEN-tee-awr EE-toh
yield not to misfortunes, but advance all the more
boldly against them

Advice for all of us, from Virgil's *Aeneid*.

tu quoque
too KWAW-kweh
you too

A retort to an accusation: You are guilty of the very misdeeds
or mistakes you attribute to me; it takes one to know one.

ubi bene ibi patria
UU-bee BEH-neh IH-bee PAH-tree-ah
I owe my allegiance to the country in which I prosper

A patriotic Roman sentiment, also expressed as **ubi libertas**
(LEE-behr-tahs, "liberty") **ibi patria**, "where there is freedom,
there is my fatherland."

ubi mel ibi apes
UU-bee mel IH-bee AH-pays
honey attracts bees

This saying from Plautus, literally "where there is honey,
there will be bees," reminds us that there is a surefire way to
attract followers.

ubi solitudinem faciunt pacem appellant
UU-bee soh-lih-TOO-dih-nehm FAH-kee-uunt
PAH-kehm AHP-pel-lahnt
they create desolation and call it peace

A more literal translation of this line from Tacitus's *Agricola* is "where they create a desert, they call it peace." Tacitus was quoting the leader of the Britons, who had made the mistake of coming out second best in a war against the invading armies of the Romans. While the Romans customarily treated conquered peoples with respect, their destruction of Carthage and sack of Corinth were notable exceptions.

ultima forsan
UUL-tih-mah FAWR-sahn
it's later than you think

These words, literally "perhaps the last," are sometimes inscribed on the face of a clock, to convey the thought that the moment of death—indeed, the moment of eternal judgment—may be at hand. The prudent person treats every hour as though it were his last.

ultima ratio
UUL-tih-mah RAH-tee-oh
the final argument

This phrase has literal applications, for example, "We find many reasons for denying your loan application, but your four bankruptcies are the *ultima ratio*." Louis XIV of France, recognizing that force is the final argument, directed that his cannons carry the legend **ultima ratio regum** (RAY-guum, "of kings"). As a result, *ultima ratio regum* signifies "war."

ultima Thule
UUL-tih-mah TOO-lay
the end of the world

Ancient mariners believed that the northern end of the world was an island called Thule, which stood six days' sail from Britain. The precise location of Thule is not known today, but *ultima Thule*, mentioned in Virgil's *Georgics*, survives as a useful expression for describing any place whose appearance gives one the feeling of standing at the end of the world.

ultimum vale
UUL-tih-muum WAH-lay
farewell for the last time

See SUPREMUM VALE.

ultra vires
UUL-trah WEE-rays
beyond legal authority

A court or other agency of government that exceeds its legal authority in a particular matter is said to be acting *ultra vires* (pronounced UL-trə VĪ-reez in English), literally "beyond the powers."

una salus victis nullam sperare salutem
OO-nah SAH-luus WIH-ktees NUUL-lahm
spay-RAH-reh sah-LOO-tehm
knowing there is no hope can give one the courage to fight and win

Virgil, in the *Aeneid*, gives us this insight, which translates more literally as "the one safety for the vanquished is to abandon hope for safety." Thus, when we know we are doomed, we take risks we would dismiss as imprudent if we thought we still had a chance. This is the stuff that brings dazed prizefighters back to their feet at a count of nine.

una voce
OO-nah WAW-keh
unanimously

Literally "with one voice."

unguibus et rostro
UUN-gwih-buus et RAW-stroh
with all one's might

When the Romans fought *unguibus et rostro*, they fought "with claws and beak." After all, they used the eagle as their device on banners etc. We moderns sometimes are said to fight "tooth and nail," which implies that we bite and scratch, and some of us have been known to claw our way to the top. Civilization marches on.

unus vir nullus vir
OO-nuus wihr NUUL-luus wihr
two heads are better than one

This Roman proverb translates literally as "one man, no man" giving the sense shown above. But it also can be taken in a second sense: Before machines came along, many heavy tasks were beyond the strength of a person working alone, so *unus vir nullus vir*, "one man, no man."

urbi et orbi
UUR-bee et AWR-bee
to the city and the world

In papal blessings and documents addressed *urbi et orbi*, the city is Rome, the world the rest of humanity.

urbs in horto
uurbs ihn HAWR-toh
a city in a garden

Motto of Chicago.

usque ad aras
UUS-kweh ahd AH-rahs
even to the altars

See AMICUS USQUE AD ARAS.

usque ad nauseam
UUS-kweh ahd NOW-say-ahm
even to the point of (inducing) nausea

See AD NAUSEAM.

usus promptos facit
UU-suus PRAWM-ptohs FAH-kiht
practice makes perfect

Literally "use makes men ready." A related proverb is **usus te plura docebit** (tay PLOO-rah DAW-kay-biht), "experience will teach you many things." And then there is **usus est optimum magister** (est AW-ptih-muum mah-GIH-stehr), "experience is the best teacher."

utcumque placuerit Deo
UUT-kuum-kweh plah-KOO-eh-riht DAY-oh
howsoever it shall please God

ut fata trahunt
uut FAH-tah TRAH-huunt
at the mercy of destiny

Literally "as the fates drag." This expression recognizes that we have limited control over our lives. "We have done all we can; from here on, it's *ut fata trahunt*."

ut infra
uut IHN-frah
as cited below

A scholar's phrase, literally "as below." See UT SUPRA and VIDE.

uti non abuti
UU-tee nohn ahb-OO-tee
treat with respect

Literally "to use, not abuse."

uti possidetis
UU-tee paws-sih-DAY-tihs
we stole it fair and square

The principle, literally "as you possess," that one is entitled to keep what one has acquired. It is applied most often during diplomatic negotiations prior to a peace treaty. According to *uti possidetis*, the territory a country has won during a war may be retained by that country from then on. The principle works well because strong countries usually win wars and can continue to work their will. It does not work well when a comparatively weak nation happens to win a war against an even weaker adversary. At that point, the great powers usually team up to arrange for return of conquered territory to the defeated nation. So *uti possidetis*, "as you possess," depends on who the "you" is.

ut supra
uut SUU-prah
as cited above

A scholar's phrase, literally "as above." See UT INFRA and
VIDE.

vade in pace
WAH-deh ihn PAH-keh
go in peace

A Roman way to say goodbye.

vade mecum
WAH-deh MAY-kuum
go with me

A *vade mecum*, in English pronounced VAY-dee MEE-kəm,
is usually a small manual or reference book that is regularly
carried in one's pocket—today, a *vade mecum* as often as not
travels in a handbag or in the ubiquitous attaché case—because
it contains information that is frequently consulted. A *vade
mecum* may also be something other than a small book: a pocket
calculator, a portable dictating machine, even a personal computer.

vade retro me, Satana
WAH-deh REH-troh may sah-TAH-nah
get thee behind me, Satan

The well-known phrase in Mark, in which Jesus rebukes
Peter, concluding "for thou mindest not the things of God, but
the things of men." (See APAGE SATANAS.)

vae soli
wī SOH-lee
woe to the solitary men

  Bachelors, take heed.

vae victis
wī WIH-ktees
it's tough to be a loser

  The words, literally "woe to the vanquished," attributed by Livy to Brennus, a chief of the Gauls arranging terms of peace with the Romans in 390 B.C. According to Livy, when the Romans complained that the Gauls were using excessive weights in measuring the amount of gold the Romans were to pay, Brennus threw his sword onto the weights, exclaiming, "*Vae victis.*" Brennus was telling the Romans that he, not they, had the upper hand.

vale
WAH-lay
farewell

  See AVE ATQUE VALE.

valeat quantum valere potest
WAH-lay-aht KWAHN-tuum wah-LAY-reh PAW-test
take it for what it's worth

  Literally "let it stand for what it is worth." Appropriate when passing information of doubtful authenticity.

valete ac plaudite
wah-LAY-teh ahk plow-DEE-teh
let's hear it for the cast

The words, literally "farewell and applaud," said at the end
of a Roman play. Remember that theaters were not equipped
with curtains in those days. (See PLAUDITE, CIVES.)

vanitas vanitatum, omnis vanitas
WAH-nih-tahs wah-nih-TAH-tuum AWM-nihs
WAH-nih-tahs
everything man does is in vain

This phrase from Ecclesiastes is often given the literal translation "vanity of vanities, all is vanity," leading to a misunder-
standing of what is intended. When it is understood that *vanitas*
means "emptiness" or "fruitlessness," the true intention of Ecclesiastes is perceived.

varia lectio
WAH-ree-ah LEH-ktee-oh
a variant reading

A scholar's phrase. The plural is **variae lectiones** (WAH-ree-ī
leh-ktee-OH-nays).

variorum
wah-ree-OH-ruum
of various persons

The English word "variorum," pronounced va-ree-OH-rəm
and also given as "variorum edition," is a shortened form of the
Latin **cum notis** (kuum NAW-tees) **variorum,** "with the notes of
various persons." "Variorum" has two applications in English.
It is used to designate an edition or a text containing the notes
of various scholars, and to designate an edition supplying variant readings of a text. The full Latin phrase for a variorum or
a variorum edition is **editio** (ay-DIH-tee-oh) **cum notis variorum.**
Variorums generally supply both comments by various scholars
and variant readings of a text.

varium et mutabile semper femina

WAH-ree-uum et moo-TAH-bih-leh SEM-pehr
FAY-mih-nah

la donna è mobile

This is the argument, literally "woman is ever fickle and changeable," advanced to Aeneas as a sound reason for leaving Dido, and thanks to Virgil—and to Giuseppe Verdi's *Rigoletto* —it has been parroted ever since, perhaps primarily by men. Let the record—according to Virgil at least—show that lovelorn Dido committed suicide by fire after Aeneas departed. So who was fickle? On the other hand, if the story can be believed, it does appear that old flames die.

vel caeco appareat

wel KĪ-koh ahp-PAH-ray-aht

it's obvious

Literally "it would be apparent even to a blind man."

velis et remis

WAY-lees et RAY-mees

an all-out effort

Literally "with sails and oars," also given as **remis velisque** (way-LEES-kweh). What would the Romans have said if they had invented the jet airplane?

veni, vidi, vici

WAY-nee WEE-dee WEE-kee

I came, I saw, I conquered

The best-known Latin sentence of them all, freely rendered as "a piece of cake," reported by Plutarch to have been uttered by Julius Caesar by way of reporting his victory in 47 B.C. over Pharnaces, king of Pontus.

verbatim et litteratim
wehr-BAH-tihm et liht-teh-RAH-tihm
accurately rendered

Literally "word for word and letter for letter." To this phrase is sometimes appended **et punctatim** (et puun-KTAH-tihm), "and point for point."

verba volant, scripta manent
WEHR-bah WAW-lahnt SKREE-ptah MAH-nent
get it down on paper

Literally "spoken words fly away, written words remain."

verbum sat sapienti
WEHR-buum saht sah-pee-EN-tee
a word to the wise

Literally "a word is enough for a wise man."

veritas
WAY-rih-tahs
truth

Motto of Harvard.

veritas odium parit
WAY-rih-tahs AW-dee-uum PAH-riht
truth breeds hatred

Terence, in *Andria*, telling us it is not always wise to be frank with one's friends.

veritas simplex oratio est
WAY-rih-tahs SIHM-pleks aw-RAH-tee-oh est
the language of truth is simple

By contrast, with apologies to Sir Walter Scott: "Oh, what a tangled web we weave, When first we practice to deceive!"

veritas vos liberabit
WAY-rih-tahs wohs lee-beh-RAH-biht
the truth shall make you free

Motto of The Johns Hopkins University.

verso
WEHR-soh
left

This term (pronounced VUR-soh in English) is used to indicate a left-hand page of a book, the full Latin phrase being **verso folio** (FAW-lee-oh, in English FOH-lee-oh), literally "the page being turned." (See RECTO.)

versus
WEHR-suus
against

In English pronounced VUR-səs.

via
WEE-ah
a way

This word gives us several interesting combinations. **Via Appia** (AHP-pee-ah), "the Appian Way," leads from Rome to Brindisi (ancient name **Brundisium**, bruun-DIH-see-uum). **Via**

Dolorosa (daw-law-ROH-sah), "the road of sadness," is the road Jesus followed on the way to his crucifixion. **Via media** (MEH-dee-ah), "the middle way," is the moderate course so frequently recommended in Latin proverbs. Another bit of Roman advice is **via trita** (TREE-tah), **via tuta** (TOO-tah), which translates as "the beaten path is the safe path." *Via* has also given us an English preposition, pronounced VEE-ə or VĪ-ə, meaning "by way of" or "through."

vice versa
WIH-keh WEHR-sah
conversely

A phrase we all know in English. The Latin words translate literally as "the change being turned."

victis honor
WIH-ktees HAW-nawr
let's hear it for the losers

Literally "honor to the vanquished."

vide
WIH-day
see

Vide gives us several useful expressions. **Vide et crede** (et KRAY-deh), "see and believe." **Vide infra** (IHN-frah), "see below," used by scholars to refer a reader to something that follows in a text. **Vide supra** (SUU-prah), "see above," a scholar's way of referring a reader to something that appears earlier in a text.

videlicet
wih-DAY-lih-keht
namely

Commonly abbreviated viz., which is expressed orally as "namely," not as "viz." *Videlicet*, literally "it is permitted to see," is also translated as "to wit."

video meliora proboque, deteriora sequor
WIH-day-oh meh-lee-OH-rah praw-BOH-kweh
day-teh-ree-OH-rah SEH-kwawr
even though I know better, I keep on doing the wrong thing

A line from Ovid's *Metamorphoses*, literally "I see the better way and approve it, but I follow the worse way," confirming what we know too well about recidivism.

vi et armis
wee et AHR-mees
by force of arms

vigilate et orate
wih-gih-LAH-teh et aw-RAH-teh
watch and pray

About all one can do in the nuclear age.

vincam aut moriar
WIHN-kahm owt MAW-ree-ahr
I will conquer or die

vincit qui patitur
WIHN-kiht kwee PAH-tih-tuur
patience wins out

Literally "he prevails who is patient."

vincit qui se vincit
WIHN-kiht kwee say WIHN-kiht
first we must learn to overcome our own bad habits

This advice, literally "he conquers who conquers himself," and perhaps appropriate for display in a psychotherapist's office, recognizes that most of us have traits or habits that are less than desirable. By changing our ways, we make it possible to win out in larger arenas. *Vincit qui se vincit* is an adaptation of one of Syrus's maxims, **bis** (bihs) **vincit qui se vincit in victoria** (ihn wih-KTOH-ree-ah), which has a narrower meaning, but one worth learning because it calls attention to the human tendency to gloat: "he conquers twice who conquers himself in victory."

vincit veritas
WIHN-kiht WAY-rih-tahs
truth wins out

Even though it may take a long time. This sanguine thought may also be expressed as **vincit omnia** (AWM-nee-ah) **veritas**, "truth conquers all things."

vinculum matrimonii
WIHN-kuu-luum mah-trih-MOH-nee-ee
the bond of matrimony

Vinculum may also be translated as "noose" or "chain."

virginibus puerisque canto
wihr-GIH-nih-buus poo-ehr-EES-kweh KAHN-toh
I chant to maidens and to boys

A line in Horace's *Odes*.

viribus totis
WEE-rih-buus TOH-tees
with all one's strength

viribus unitis
WEE-rih-buus oo-NEE-tees
with forces united

viri infelicis procul amici
WIH-ree ihn-FAY-lih-kihs PRAW-kuul ah-MEE-kee
success has many friends

Those who achieve eminence or wealth find suddenly that they are surrounded by friends, but when their fortunes have changed find just as suddenly that they are alone. *Viri infelicis procul amici*, literally "friends stay far away from an unfortunate man," affirms that fair-weather friends are friends we can rely on as long as we don't have to. (See FELICITAS HABET MULTOS AMICOS.)

vir sapit qui pauca loquitur
wihr SAH-piht kwee POW-kah LAW-kwih-tuur
know when to hold your tongue

Literally "that man is wise who talks little." (See CAVE QUID DICIS, QUANDO, ET CUI for another way of giving this same advice.)

virtus post nummos
WIHR-toos pawst NUUM-mohs
keep your eye on the bottom line

This cynical advice—one man's cynicism is another man's wisdom—freely adapted from one of Horace's *Epistles*, translates literally as "virtue after wealth." The full thought is **quaerenda pecunia primum est** (kwī-REN-dah peh-KOO-nee-ah PRIHM-uum est) **virtus post nummos**, which may be translated as "money is to be sought after first of all, virtue after wealth."

virtus probata florescit
WIHR-toos praw-BAH-tah floh-REH-skiht
grace under pressure

A maxim, literally "manly excellence flourishes in trial," suggesting that we learn our true character only when we put ourselves to the test and come out on top.

virtute et armis
wihr-TOO-teh et AHR-mees
by courage and arms

Motto of Mississippi.

virtutis fortuna comes
wihr-TOO-tihs fawr-TOO-nah KAW-mehs
good luck is the companion of courage

The suggestion is that good things don't just happen; we must prepare ourselves to grasp opportunity when it comes our way.

vis consili expers mole ruit sua

wees kawn-SIH-lee EK-spehrs MOH-leh ROO-iht
SOO-ah

discretion is the better part of valor

An observation from one of Horace's *Odes*, literally "force without good sense falls by its own weight."

vis inertiae

wees ihn-EHR-tee-ī

the power of inactivity

It is to *vis inertiae* that we ascribe the willingness of many people to put up with their troubles rather than change their lives and risk encountering new and possibly more vexing troubles. With *inertiae* translated as "of inertia," *vis inertiae* explains why a plan set in motion is difficult to stop, and vice versa.

vita brevis, ars longa

WEE-tah BREH-wihs ahrs LAWN-gah

life is short, art is long

See ARS LONGA, VITA BREVIS.

vitam impendere vero

WEE-tahm ihm-PEN-deh-reh WAY-roh

to devote one's life to the truth

A noble resolve from Juvenal's *Satires*.

vitam regit fortuna non sapientia

WEE-tahm REH-giht fawr-TOO-nah nohn
sah-pee-EN-tee-ah

it's mostly a matter of luck

Literally "chance, not wisdom, governs human life."

vita non est vivere sed valere vita est

WEE-tah nohn est WEE-weh-reh sed wah-LAY-reh
WEE-tah est

life is more than merely staying alive

One of Martial's epigrams, literally "life is not to live, but life is to be strong, vigorous." Food for thought for all of us.

vivamus, mea Lesbia, atque amemus

wee-WAH-muus MAY-ah LEH-sbee-ah AHT-kweh
ah-MAY-muus

let's live it up

Advice from Catullus, in one of his poems, literally "Lesbia mine, let's live and love." (See CARPE DIEM.)

vivat

WEE-waht

long live . . .

Vivat regina (ray-GEE-nah), "long live the queen." **Vivat rex** (reks), "long live the king."

viva voce

WEE-wah WAW-keh

orally

A *viva voce* (English pronunciation vī-və VOH-see), also a "viva voce examination," is an oral examination. To respond *viva voce* is to respond orally, rather than in writing. The Latin phrase literally means "with the living voice."

vive hodie
WEE-weh HAW-dee-ay
live today

From one of Martial's epigrams, telling us in full that it is not wise to say I'll live tomorrow; tomorrow is for tomorrow's living. *Vive hodie*. (See CARPE DIEM for a fuller explanation.)

vivere parvo
WEE-weh-reh PAHR-woh
to live on little

Little income, that is.

vive ut vivas
WEE-weh uut WEE-wahs
live that you may live

Sound advice on how to conduct one's life, albeit contrary to that given in CARPE DIEM.

vive, vale
WEE-weh WAH-lay
farewell

Literally "live, be well," also given as **vive valeque** (wah-LAY-kweh), "live and be well."

vixere fortes ante Agamemnona
wee-KSAY-reh FAWR-tays AHN-teh
ah-gah-MEM-naw-nah
we don't have a monopoly on all that is good

This line from Horace's *Odes* tells us literally that "brave men lived before Agamemnon." The words that follow this line translate as "all unwept and unknown, lost in the distant night, since they lack a divine poet." Thus, Horace tells us that great acts of heroism, kindness, and the like have often been performed by unsung heroes—unsung in the sense that no record was made of their exploits—yet even though we know nothing of those acts, we must not assume they never happened. The public relations industry flourishes because it understands that perception of events may count for more than the events themselves.

vixit
WEE-ksiht
he or she has lived

A word found on tombstones, usually **vixit . . . annos** (AHN-nohs), "he or she lived (a certain number of) years."

viz.

Abbreviation of VIDELICET.

volens et potens
WAW-lens et PAW-tens
willing and able

volente Deo
waw-LEN-teh DAY-oh
God willing

See DEO VOLENTE.

volenti non fit iniuria (or injuria)
waw-LEN-tee nohn fiht ihn-YOO-ree-ah
to a willing person no wrong is done

The legal maxim we all know, for example, in the phrase "consenting adults."

volo, non valeo
WAW-loh nohn WAH-lay-oh
I am willing, but unable

voluptates commendat rarior usus
waw-luu-PTAH-tays kawm-MEN-daht RAH-ree-awr
OO-suus
all pleasure's no pleasure

Juvenal, in his *Satires*, counseling moderation in living the good life, literally "rare indulgence increases pleasures."

vox clamantis in deserto
wawks klah-MAHN-tihs ihn deh-SEHR-toh
the voice of one crying in the wilderness

Familiar words from various books of the New Testament, in Matthew continuing "prepare you the way of the Lord; make his paths straight." The motto of Dartmouth College, with apologies to the New Testament, is **vox clamans** (KLAH-mahns) **in deserto**, usually translated as "a voice crying in the wilderness."

vox et praeterea nihil
wawks et prī-TEH-ray-ah NIH-hihl
empty words

Plutarch's phrase, used to denote an empty threat. Plutarch tells a story of a man who plucks the feathers from a nightingale. Finding that its body sans plumage is pathetically small, he remarks, "*Vox et praeterea nihil*," literally "a voice and nothing more."

vox populi vox Dei
wawks PAW-puu-lee wawks DAY-ee
the voice of the people is the voice of God

Political leaders take heed, the wishes of the people are irresistible.

vulneratus non victus
wuul-neh-RAH-tuus nohn WIH-ktuus
bloodied but unbowed

Literally "wounded but not conquered."

vultus est index animi
WUUL-tuus est IHN-deks AH-nih-mee
the face is the mirror of the soul

Literally "the expression on one's face is a sign of the soul."

English Index

A

about, 80

about tastes there is no disputing, 97

above, 272

absolute divorce, 65

absolutely necessary, 262

absurd etymology, 175

acceptable person, 224

accommodation, 187

accomplice, 216

according to custom, 124

according to what is just and good, 120

accurately rendered, 291

acerbity, 252

acme, 193

actions speak louder than words, 128

admire nothing, 195

after childbirth, 229

after clouds, Phoebus, 229

after death, 228

after making the necessary changes, 189

after noon, 228

after this, therefore because of this, 228

again and again, 119

against, 292

against the best interests of society, 87

against the man, 22

agree, 84

agreement, 84

agreement of all, 85

agreement of rash men, 85

alas, the fleeting years glide by, 115

alliance between two states, 76

all or nothing, 63

all-out effort, 290

all people of that type, 143

all pleasure's no pleasure, 302

all's well that ends well, 260

all that glitters is not gold, 202

all that sort, 148

all that work and nothing to show for it, 217

all the more, 34

all things change, and we change with them, 211

all things yield to money, 220

all this sort, 143

all to one, 28

also known as, 37

altar, 41

altogether, 163

always faithful, 256

always ready, 256

always the same person, 256

always the same thing, 256

among other persons, 161

among other things, 161

and all that sort, 119

and even of several other things, 102

and everything of the kind, 119

and forever, brother, hail and farewell, 64

and other men, 118

and other people, 118

and others, 118

and other things, 118

and other women, 118

and so of similar people or things, 119

and so on, 118

and the rest, 119

and wife, 120

anew, 98

anger is brief madness, 166

annotations, 29

annually, 221

another day wasted, 106

another I, 39

because of death, 188
bed, 42
before a judge who does not have
  jurisdiction, 88
before a judge who has jurisdiction,
  88
before childbirth, 48
before Christ, 48
before death, 48
before noon, 48
before the courts, 268
before the war, 47
before us, 88
begging of the principle, 225
begging the question, 225
behind closed doors, 146
behind the horseman sits black care,
  227
behold the man, 113
behold the sign, 114
be increased in merit, 176
being unwilling, willing, 197
believe one who has experience,
  125
the belly is the teacher of art and
  bestower of genius, 176
below, 153
beneath one's dignity, 153
be prepared for hard times, 200
be silent, 273
be steadfast and endure, 224
best friend, 133
the best way to learn a subject is to
  teach it, 236
better late than never, 230
between a rock and a hard place,
  34
between cups, 162
between equals, 161
between living persons, 162
between ourselves, 161
between the devil and the deep
  blue sea, 34
between themselves, 162
between us, 161
beware, consuls, that the republic is
  not harmed, 77
beware of the dog, 78
beware that first misstep, 128
beware what you say, when, and to
  whom, 78
beyond legal authority, 283

beyond the powers, 283
bier, 42
the Big Apple, 74
bird, 70
a bird in the hand is worth two in
  the bush, 26
birds, 70
birds of a feather, 115, 216
blackguards both, 52
black pebble, 194
blameless of life, 160
blessed are the peacemakers, 66
blessed are the poor in spirit, 66
blessed are those who possess, 67
Blessed Mary, 66
blessed person, 67
Blessed Virgin, 66
Blessed Virgin Mary, 66
blockhead, 81
blood from a stone, 11, 124
bloodied but unbowed, 303
A Boastful Soldier, 185
body of law, 90
body of the crime, 89
body politic, 250
boldness, 277
bond, 65
bond of matrimony, 65
book, 81
book learning, 110
books dated prior to A.D. 1500, 12
born with a silver spoon in his
  mouth, 35
bosom pal, 39, 133
the boundaries that existed before
  the war, 266
brave men lived before
  Agamemnon, 300
bravo, 176
bread and circus games, 215
break out the champagne, 205
brief written comments, 29
British peace, 219
brought back to life, 246
the buck stops here, 250
burden of proof, 212
burden of proving, 212
by courage and arms, 297
by doing nothing, men learn to act
  wickedly, 194
by equally valid reasoning, 216
by faith and confidence, 132

easily first, 128
easy come, easy go, 241
eat, drink, and be merry, 75
edition with notes of various
   persons, 114
effortlessly, 265
eggs today are better than chicken
   tomorrow, 26
either Caesar or nobody, 63
either emperor of Rome or nothing,
   63
either learn or leave, 63
either to conquer or to die, 64
elders first, 257
elementary school, 177
Emperor by the Grace of God,
   97
emptiness, 289
empty threat, 70
empty words, 302
the end crowns the work, 134
the end hangs from the beginning,
   190
the end justifies the means, 123
endlessly, 23
endlessly displeasing, 25
end of discussion, we'll do it my
   way, 266
the end of the world, 283
enemy of the human race, 146
enjoy, enjoy, 75
enjoy today, trusting little in
   tomorrow, 75
enjoy yourself, it's later than you
   think, 75
ennui, 274
enough, 254
enough and to spare, 254
enough eloquence, too little
   wisdom, 254
enough of words, 254
entirely, 162
entire people, 26
envy is blind, 72
equitably, 120
error, 117
erstwhile, 242
even a god finds it hard to love and
   be wise at the same time, 41
even good writers are not always at
   their best, 236
even more certain, 34

even though I know better, I keep
   on doing the wrong thing, 294
even to the altars, 285
even to the point of inducing
   nausea, 285
everlasting, 33
ever upward, 121
every cloud has a silver lining, 229
every day is not a holiday, 201
every day we die a little, 190
every effect must have a cause, 124
every madman thinks everybody
   else is mad, 159
everyone has his own pleasures, 267
everyone has his own vices, 267
everything in threes is perfect, 211
everything man does is in vain, 289
everything unknown is thought
   magnificent, 210
everything unknown is thought to
   be more difficult than it really is,
   210
evidence that a crime has been
   committed, 89
examine the end, 250
examine the past, examine the
   present, examine the future, 250
the exception establishes the rule,
   121
existing, 152
experience is the best teacher, 285
experience will teach you many
   things, 285
the expression on one's face is a sign
   of the soul, 303
expurgated, 283
extemporaneously, 23, 126
extreme law, extreme injustice, 270
an eye for an eye, 171

F
the face is the mirror of the soul,
   303
the facts speak for themselves, 249
the fact that I wish it is reason
   enough for doing it, 144
faithful Achates, 133
fall, 75
falling, 75
fall of the city of Troy, 76
familial strife, 76
farewell, 288, 300

guardian of morals, 94
guardians of the household, 107
guardian spirit of a place, 138

H

hail, 64, 253
hail and farewell, 64
hail, Caesar, those who are about to
die salute you, 64
hail, Caesar, we who are about to
die salute you, 64
hail Mary, 65
"Hail, Queen of Heaven," 65
hair of the dog, 261
hallucination, 32
Hannibal is at the gates, 141
haphazardly, 197
happy is he who owes nothing, 131
hatred, 208
having book learning, 110
having served his time, 116
head of a household, 218
head of the world, 74
hear the other side, 60
heart of hearts, 221
the heavens bespeak the glory of
God, 72
he came near, 17
he came nearest, 233
he carved it, 255
he conquers twice who conquers
himself in victory, 295
he conquers who conquers himself,
295
he died, 206
he died without issue, 206
he doesn't know beans about
anything, 191
he does what has to be done, but
with the necessary compassion,
267
he drew this, 99
he drives a hard bargain, 244
he flourished, 134
he gives twice who quickly gives, 68
He has favored our undertaking, 47
he has gained every point who has
combined the useful with the
agreeable, 211
he has lived, 301
he has not even thumbed through
Aesop, 191

he himself said so, 160
he is his father's son, 218
he is sick, 32
he leaves the stage, 123
he lived . . . years, 301
he lives twice who lives well, 69
hell calls hell, 17
he made it, 130
hence those tears, 142
he painted it, 225
he prevails who is patient, 295
here and everywhere, 141
here and now, 141
here and there, 217
here begins, 152
here lies, 142
he shaves all the way to the skin,
244
he speaks, 174
he struck, 122
he touched nothing he did not
adorn, 204
he who asks timidly invites refusal,
240
he who asks timidly teaches to
refuse, 240
he who does not know how to
dissemble does not know how to
live, 239
he who doesn't know how to fib
doesn't know how to survive, 239
he who fights and runs away may
live to fight another day, 238
he who has fled will do battle once
more, 238
he who has given will give, 95
he who has lived in obscurity has
lived well, 67
he who loves well chastises well,
237
he who remains silent consents, 240
he who teaches learns, 238
he who transplanted sustains, 240
he who writes reads twice, 239
he would have been considered
capable of governing if he had
never governed, 86
he wrote it, 255
hidden danger, 44
higher, 121
highest attainable point, 193
the highest good, 270

L

laborer, 58

la donna è mobile, 290

Lamb of God, 34

the language of truth is simple, 292

lapse of memory, 169

last utterance, 203

laughter succeeds where lecturing won't, 75

the law does not concern itself with trifles, 100

the law is hard, but it is the law, 113

law is the art of the good and the just, 166

the law of retaliation, 171

the law of the land, 170

the law of the place, 170

laws are silent in the midst of war, 260

laws don't count in wartime, 260

a lawsuit before the judge, 172

l'chaim, 233

league, 76

a learned man always has wealth within himself, 144

learned with a book, 110

leave no stone unturned, 210

leave the rest to the gods, 224

leaving without announcement, 158

the left, 292

left-hand page, 292

legal holidays, 192

legal separation, 41

leisure with dignity, 214

the leopard cannot change its spots, 190

Lesbia mine, let's live and love, 299

let arms yield to the gown, 78

let him either drink or depart, 63

let him go forth, 122

let him live, 226

let him who wants peace prepare for war, 237

let ill will be absent, 14

let it stand, 266

let it stand for what it is worth, 286

let justice be done though the heavens fall, 132

let my will stand as a reason, 266

let not your spending exceed your income, 271

let's get on with it, 188

let's get this show on the road, 188

let's have some action, 254

let's hear it for the cast, 226

let's hear it for the losers, 293

let's keep our eyes on the bottom line, 235

let's live it up, 299

let the buyer beware, 77

let them hate, provided they fear, 208

let there be light, 132

let the seller beware, 77

let the superior answer, 250

let the welfare of the people be the supreme law, 252

let us therefore rejoice, 137

liars should have good memories, 184

the license of poets, 171

life is more than just being alive, 198

life is more than merely staying alive, 299

life is not a bowl of cherries, 148

life is not being alive but being well, 198

life is not to live, but life is to be strong, vigorous, 299

life is short, art is long, 298

lift up your hearts, 272

light and truth, 175

like father, like son, 235

like persons most readily crowd together, 216

like things are cured by likes, 260

List of Prohibited Books, 152

a little originality, please, 69

little things affect little minds, 95

live and be well, 300

live, be well, 300

live that you may live, 300

live today, 300

live within your means, 271

logic, 56

logical fallacy, 201

long live, 299

long live the king, 299

long live the queen, 299

long outer garment, 280

money-mad, 61
money makes the world go round, 220
money talks, 61
monthly, 223
morals, 94
more durable than bronze, 33
the more humane letters, 172
more people die partying than fighting wars, 226
most authoritative passage, 173
most frequently cited passage, 173
mountaineers are always freemen, 187
mountains will be in labor, and an absurd mouse will be born, 217
the movable public, 187
move every stone, 210
much in little, 189
mud, 134
mutual admiration society, 59
mutual hatred among theologians, 208
"My soul doth magnify the Lord," 177
my turn today, yours tomorrow, 144
my works shall live forever, 200

N
the name having been changed, 190
namely, 255, 294
name, rank, and serial number, 246
nature makes no leaps, 191
nay, 200
necessary condition, 76
necessity is the mother of invention, 176, 219
neither fear nor wish for your last day, 271
never, 20
never-ending work conquers all things, 160
never judge a book by its cover, 136
never say die, 195
never unprepared, 206
new man, 203
a new order of the ages is created, 203
nip it in the bud, 207
nitpicking, 71
no accounting for tastes, 97
no bad man is happy, 193

no contract, 203
no desire exists for a thing unknown, 149
no further may you go, 193
no graffiti, please, 267
no man is a hero to his valet, 178
no offense, 14
no offense intended, 14
no one can become expert in all things, 199
no one contradicting, 192
no one dissenting, 192
no one ever became extremely wicked suddenly, 193
no one is free who is a slave to his body, 192
no one provokes me with impunity, 193
no one's son, 204
no one who is rich is made suddenly good, 248
noose, 65
no reliance can be placed on appearance, 136
northern lights, 62
no stranger to misfortune myself, I learn to relieve the sufferings of others, 198
not a day without a line, 204
note from the doctor, 32
notes, 29
not everyone is permitted to go to Corinth, 199
note well, 202
not for you, not for me, but for us, 109
nothing comes from nothing, 100, 124
nothing hinders it from being published, 195
nothing in excess, 193
nothing in poverty so ill is borne, 196
nothing is to be despaired of, 195
nothing new under the sun, 196
nothing stands in its way, 195
nothing travels faster than scandal, 129
nothing unless good, 196
nothing ventured, nothing gained, 60
nothing without divine will, 196
not more beyond, 190

not new things but in a new way, 199
not of sound mind, 198
not twice for the same thing, 197
not unequal to most, 191
notwithstanding, 199
nourishing mother, 39
now and forever, 119
no way!, 200
now for then, 205
now I have written so much for Christ, give me a drink, 206
now it's time to drink, 205
now or never, 205
nude pact, 203
number one, 128
nursling, 40

O

occasion, 76
O come, all ye faithful, 21
of a different kind, 37
of all the things one can know, 102
of another's law, 37
of blessed memory, 66
of evils, the least, 185
of good and bad, 96
of his age, 33
of his own kind, 270
of its own motion, 103
of one's own accord, 126, 265, 267
of one's own will, 19
of sound mind, 82
of the dead, say nothing but good, 100
of the same flour, 115
of two evils, the lesser is always to be chosen, 96
of various persons, 289
of whom, 243
oh, blessed beyond all bliss, the farmers, 208
oh, if everything were thus, 214
oh, the times! Oh, the habits!, 214
O Lamb of God, 34
an old man is twice a boy, 257
omen, 70
omen of a better time, 62
on a living organism, 159
on each hundred, 222
one fool rubs the other's back, 59

one holding the place, 173
one is entitled to keep what one has acquired, 286
one man, no man, 284
one man's meat is another man's poison, 241
one misstep leads to another, 17
one must keep abreast of the times, 271
one must pay attention to the times, 271
one must yield to time, 271
one of a kind, 270
one out of many, 117
the one safety for the vanquished is to abandon hope for safety, 283
one's crowning achievement, 178
one witness, no witness, 278
on first consideration, 230
on his own authority, 19
only the good die young, 236
on one's own motion, 232
on the alert, 55
on the contrary, 114, 222
On the Nature of Things, 104
on the opposite side of the argument, 222
on the threshold, 154
on the way, 163
on the whole, 163
open sea, 181
opportunity, 76
opportunity for repentance, 174
opposites are cured by opposites, 87
oppressively long words, 258
optical illusion, 96
orally, 299
an orator is made, a poet is born, 214
origin, 12
origin of evil, 214
other things being equal, 80
otherwise called, 37
our country's in danger, 141
our father, 218
our sea, 181
out of pure, simple impulse, 123
out of the depths of despair, 103
out of the frying pan into the fire, 151
over drinks, 162

times change and we change with
  them, 275
time, the devourer of all things,
  276
time usually is the best means of
  healing, 275
tit for tat, 216
to absurdity, 19
to accept a favor is to sell one's
  freedom, 68
to a fingernail, 27
toastmaster, 51
to a willing person no wrong is
  done, 301
to be made certain, 79
to be rather than seem, 118
today to me, tomorrow to you,
  144
to each his own, 267, 272
to err is human, 117, 146
to everyone, his own is beautiful,
  272
toga, 280
to God, the best, the greatest, 102
to holy places through narrow
  spaces, 20
to honors through difficulties, 20
to infinity, 23
to life, 233
to live on little, 300
to live twice is to make useful profit
  from one's past, 143
too much freedom debases us, 210
to one's taste, 22
tooth and nail, 284
to please the common people, 20
to seasickness, 25
to taste, 22
to the ancestors, 25
to the city and the world, 284
to the clergy, 21
to the fathers, 25
to the highest authority, 24
to the intelligent, few words, 161
to the last jot, 24
to the letter, 24
to the Lord, best and greatest,
  110
to the Lord God, supreme ruler of
  the world, 110
to the matter at hand, 27
to the memory of, 155

to the people, 26
to the place, 24
to the point of causing nausea, 25
to the same degree, 21
to the stars through difficulties, 20
to the thing, 27
to the thresholds of the Apostles,
  24
to the word, 29
touch a sore, 274
touch a sore spot, 274
touch me not, 197
to use, not abuse, 286
to what damage, 26
to which, 26
to whom, 26
to whom for a benefit?, 91
to wit, 294
to you, 233
treachery, 234
treat with respect, 286
treaty, 76
tree trunk, 81
trembling delirium, 99
trip oneself up, 58
Troy has been, 137
Troy has had it, 136
Troy is no more, 137
true art conceals the means by
  which it has been achieved, 56
trust me, 125
truth, 291
truth breeds hatred, 291
truth conquers all things, 295
the truth shall make you free, 292
truth wins out, 295
twenty-four hours will tell the story,
  249
two heads are better than one, 284
a two-legged animal without
  feathers, 44
two of a kind, 52
two persons having like tastes, 52

U

unacceptable person, 224
unanimity of the nations, 85
unanimously, 28, 192, 284
under adjudication, 23
under consideration, 268
under control of a guardian, 37
under favorable signs, 70

About the Author

Eugene Ehrlich is series coeditor of *Contemporary Studies in Literature*, as well as principal editor of the *Oxford American Dictionary*, *The Volume Library*, and the *NBC Handbook of Pronunciation*.

Among his many other books are *The Oxford Illustrated Literary Guide to the United States*, *English Grammar*, *Basic Grammar for Clear Writing*, *Writing and Researching*, and *A Concise Index to English*.